To Nina, Jet and Harry
all the love, all the knowledge

"Profound Ananda, is this Dependent Origination, and profound does it appear. It is through not understanding, not penetrating this Code, that this world resembles a tangled ball of thread, a bird's nest, a thicket of sedge or of reed, and that mankind fails to escape from the lower states of existence, from the course of lamentation and loss, and suffers from the round of rebirth."

DIGHA NIKAYA, Sutta 15

"Whoso understands Dependent Origination, understands the Code, and whoso understands the Code, understands Dependent Origination."

MAJJHIMA NIKAYA, Sutta 28

Yoga
beyond the thinking mind

Simon G. Mundy

Foreword by Ramiro Calle

Publishing Details:

Title: YOGA BEYOND THE THINKING MIND
Author: Mundy, Simon Godfrey
Publisher: Simon Godfrey Mundy

ISBN: 978-84-09-52056-5 (Paperback)
ISBN: 978-84-09-53816-4 (ePub)

Except for the 3 hathayoga illustrations, all other images including the cover painting are the physical and/or intellectual copyright of the author.

NEBOT·TORRELLA: Graphic design. Illustration & Digital photo retouching.

Design layout interior and cover: Pickawoowoo Publishing Group
Editing: Eddie Albrecht, Pickawoowoo Publishing Group

Spanish title: **'Yoga, más allá de la mente pensante'**
Published by Editorial Kairos, Barcelona, first edition autumn 2023

editorial **K**airós

"The omnipresence of Code – its everywhereness – has not been spotted by sciences, therefore its central importance has been missed. Psychology hardly mentions the code and coding."

"If enough people get hold of a few simple assumptions not yet connected in sciences, psychemechanics will emerge as a 'new science' where the code – so far playing no role in mechanics – will play a top role."

Dr N. Dimovic

* * *

"Your manuscript, poem and article on paticcasamuppada is in safe keeping here at the Vihara – they are a valuable contribution to the knowledge – if one reads this book one can learn different aspects of human nature and activities, as well as the Tibetan Buddhism. Yours in the Dhamma."

Ven. Dr H. Saddhatissa
Author of "The Buddha's Way". President of British Mahabodhi Society
Letter (extract) 11th November 1982

* * *

"Dear Mr Mundy,
Thank you for your most thoughtful letter. It must be interesting to pursue such studies abroad though perhaps more difficult unless you read other languages easily.
I am not answering the questions you asked because they are unanswerable.
Cordially."

Frank Herbert
Author of Dune
Letter October 27. 1975

* * *

"Yoga and understanding has been a dilemma for the time since Patanjali. You rewrote it to modern times. That's a great endeavour!"

Wim Hof

Contents

Foreword

BY RAMIRO CALLE

Yoga Beyond the Thinking Mind presents a new perspective on the relationship between mind and body based on the yogas of Mahavir and Buddha. I completely agree with the author that without both their immense contributions, yoga – in the form and content compiled by Patanjali in his Yogasutra centuries later – is simply inconceivable. The author's insistence on the colossal role played in the establishment of yoga by both Mahavir and Gautama Buddha is emphatic and necessary. This book's fresh perspective into the most ancient and authentic yoga centuries before Patanjali is most illuminating and contains no less than 5 re-interpretations of key terms that enable a better understanding of yoga's original purpose.

Neither Mahavir nor Gautama Buddha claimed their teachings were original or their own, but emphasized that – by retracing the noble perennial path – they rediscovered the paths of Tirthankaras and Buddhas of former times. Their explicit recognition of the vast anti-quity of these lofty teachings and practices—going back to far earlier ages and time cycles—clashes head-on with the modern linear notion of constant improvement and progress. From this first reflection of the Buddha after enlightenment one can only guess at the extent of decline over the millennia:

"This truth I have attained to is profound, difficult to see and difficult to comprehend, peaceful and sublime, unapproachable by mere reaso-ning, subtle, to be grasped by the wise. But this generation delights in identification, revels in identification, loves identification.

"It is difficult for such a generation to recognize the truth of the conditional origination (of suffering). And difficult to realize this truth, namely – the stilling of all codes (sankhara), the renunciation of identification, the destruction of compulsiveness – detachment, cessation and Nibbana."

Majjhima Nikaya 26

It is said the Buddha hesitated for weeks to teach because he realized that human beings of his time were 'attached to worldly pleasures' and 'fond of superficial distractions'.

Of special note is the research work of Dimovic, whom I never met in person, but whose insistence on *connectoring properly* is indispensable for untangling the conceptual mess the human being is in, and will be of enormous value and usefulness to any seeker of truth throughout his or her life. The author likens Dimovic's 'proper connectoring' to the Buddha's key teaching of *satipatthana*. Equally insightful is Dimovic's discovery of the *psychemechanics of the code* in the interplay between mind and body.

On the long march to self-realization we are fortunate to meet with people who become loyal and inspiring friends in the Quest, with whom we can share our knowledge, inner experiences, spiritual aspirations and methods for enlightening the mind and awakening intuition. One such person, with whom I have had a close friendship for many years, is Simon Mundy, whom, for his admirable discipline and conquest of not a few achievements on the inner journey, I have featured in many of my lectures, classes, seminars and various books, "A Spiritual Autobiography", "My Life's Journey" and others.

Simon Mundy has a colossal knowledge of the various Eastern techniques of self-enquiry, but most especially of Buddhism and genuine Yoga. He is not only a great scholar of these subjects, but also a tireless practitioner of yogic methods such as satipatthana, vipassana, tai-chi, chi kung and others. It is not surprising that the great Theravada Buddhist scholar and writer Amadeo Solé Leris, said to me shortly after introducing them: "Simon is an *ariya*!". He is, and I also realized this the first time he came to my yoga and meditation classes at Shadak in 1971. I would say we recognized each other rather than met each other, as from the very first moment we were very much in synchronicity as we sifted through the "perennial philosophy".

In our youth we both travelled frequently to India and other Asian countries. With great enthusiasm we would get together on returning from our journeys and stay up until the early hours of the morning sharing experiences and insights. Simon was an advanced student, so to speak, of Swami Chaitanyananda, whom I met on various occasions and interviewed twice—these interviews appear in my book "Conversations with Yogis". More than three decades ago, we published two books together and a number of other works.

Simon practiced with several other mentors, both Hindu and Buddhist, including Buddhadhasa Bhikkhu and SN Goenka; and from a western background, with John Coleman among others. The conversations we have had over the years about wisdom from the East are countless. His insights on these subjects are not the usual or common ones. He goes much further—with great respect but with a necessary boldness.

I encourage the reader of this work – whether or not a specialist in the subject – to set aside preconceptions and get hold of the valuable and sometimes striking angles the author reveals. Herein are useful and modern tools for untangling the ever-increasing complexity of modern life. The reader can be assured this is not just another book on yoga.

Nowadays at a time when society has largely turned its back on the teachings of the great enlightened ones such as the Buddha (which I emphasize in my book "The Smile of the Buddha") – it is more necessary and timely than ever to reconnect with these authentic teachings to understand their origins and sources, avoiding misrepresentation and keeping true to them. That is why I have always greatly appreciated and valued the author's inquiring and honest spirit, and why I consider works such as the present one to be necessary, as it stands out among so many books whose pages contribute little or nothing, and often disorient rather than orient.

Yoga Beyond the Thinking Mind is a deep read, because it aims at the essentials, and does not get lost in concessions. It is to be read and re-read: such is its greatness.

Ramiro Calle bio: Netflix documentary 'Sadhaka, the Path of Yoga'; a leading authority on yoga in the Spanish-speaking world; tireless promoter of yoga and related systems of self-enquiry for over 50 years; founder-director in 1971 of Madrid's first and largest yoga centre; author of over 100 books; countless radio and TV programmes; YouTube podcasts; Facebook and Instagram.

Preface

In the simplest sense yoga is about reconnecting our thinking mind with our heart, where the true Nature of Reality resides and is experienced. By 'heart' is meant the 'heart-mind'.

By thinking about Reality, we lose touch with Reality – that's the paradox!

The more we think about Reality, the more we get out of touch with Reality.The assumption underlying ancient paths of yoga is that *Maya* veils the true Reality. And that *outside the veil of the thinking mind of the human being everything in Nature is perfect*. Loss of harmony at every level occurs when the thinking mind confuses the **abs**tract with the Real.

The more we think about things, instead of feeling them, the more we end up living mostly inside our mental cinema under *its* 'rules' ignoring Nature's laws!

This applies both individually and collectively.

Vi-yoga – the opposite of yoga – points to exactly that. Put another way, we live using feeble light reflected in the moon of our thinking mind, oblivious to the sun's radiance reflected in our heart-mind. The light of the thinking mind is but the reflection of a reflection in a corridor of mirrors.

> "The moon can often be seen in the daytime sky—what light does it add at that time?"
>
> Ramana Maharshi

Thus the word *yoga* from Sanskrit (from the root *yuj*) signifies joining together, reconnecting to the Real Nature. And the path to *yoga*, called *yoga sadhana*, is the way to do this.

In the technical sense, the two specific things to be reconnected, reconciled and merged are what is known in yoga as the 'sun-breath' and the 'moon-breath'. Yoga is the actual physiological joining and merging of these two breaths.

The wise of ancient times knew that disharmony and asymmetry between the 'sun-energies' and 'moon-energies' within the human being – between feeling and thinking – prevent the joining and merging of the two breaths.

Seeing what was happening and how—*the extent to which imagination, pretence and make believe replace the True, the Authentic and the Real,* they devised strategies to return to being fully in touch with Reality – with Nature – which is human being's nature too. This they called *yoga.*

Vi-yoga means separation – losing touch with the Real. Yoga means abiding in full acknowledgement of the Real with full awareness of indivisibility.

So yoga is in fact the natural state. And the 'e-motion' spontaneously present in this supremely natural state was recognized thousands of years ago as *satchitananda!*

Existence—Awareness—*Joie de vie!*

Hard to find a better translation for *ananda* than the French '*joie-de-vie*'.

All thinking is abstraction: a departure from the Real

Abstraction always involves the thinking mind making **equations of identity** between two things which are not the same, but pretending that they are the same when they are not. This mental trick involves imagination, pretence, make-believe, intention and agreement. All thinking is based on this. And the resultant equations of identity (let's call them **ab**'s) become all our concepts, all our images and all our codes (languages), *none of which are the reality they stand-in for but are mere representations of Reality.*

A simulacrum—pretence—make believe.

As a result belief, hope and doubt replace certainty. And guessing and theorizing about the Nature of Reality replaces direct knowledge and insight.

Thinking too has its place in Reality – in the scheme things – but our mental cinema has proliferated to such an extent that it has usurped its place and function in the natural order of things, and to a large extent superimposed an Artificial World onto the Real World, obscuring it.

Without thinking I could not write this book. And without thinking you could not read these words nor appreciate the feeling and intention they carry. Yet we must not lose sight of the fact that whatever descriptions using words, images and concepts are able to convey, all of it amounts only to a **map**, however good. However good the map is, it is no substitute for direct experience and insight.

Alfred Korzybski famously exclaimed: "the map is not the territory!"

Korzybski was not the only one to spot that the map in our thinking minds is an **ab**straction and not the territory of the Real World. Bishop Berkeley, and other philosophers long before him, including those of ancient Greece and ancient India, were on to a 3-fold and 4-fold tiering of Reality. The Buddha too had pointed out this distinction in his teaching on *patisambhida*:

"Compare a teaching to a raft – its purpose is for crossing over from one bank of the river to the other side – not for the purpose of latching onto. Understanding (this), you should let go even of correct teachings, how much more so incorrect teachings!"

Majjhima Nikaya 22

In *Yoga Beyond the Thinking Mind*, a 4-fold conjoint Nature of Reality is explored from the perspective of Mahavir, of Gautama Buddha and of *Samkhya* and Patanjali, as well as from a modern viewpoint using scientific method and modern language.

The assumption underlying chapters 1-12 is that *life-force intelligence* (*vijnana* in Sanskrit; *viññāṇa* in Pali) is guiding the entirety of Nature, including us, whether we realize this or not. But inside our body the life-force intelligence has become severely compromised, conditioned and interfered with by the thinking mind's own codes/coding (*sankhara* in Pali; *saṃskara* in Sanskrit). These codes are embedded in our brain and nervous system in the circuitry known to yoga as the *nadi* network.

And so what has to be done—*and there is so little time!*—is to erase these 'tapes', deblock the subtle plumbing (*nadis*), feel the true power of the life force, appreciate its wisdom and intelligence, acknowledge it, embrace it, join it, become one with it and flow with it.

Each of us can check all this out for ourselves in our own mindbody. *And to do that, we do not need to follow anybody!*

What has to be done is to drop all pretence, become totally honest and recognize what is Real and of real value. Whatever is not Okay, stop pretending it is Okay. By continuing to go along with pretence, by acquiescing, we are doing a disservice to ourselves, a disservice to others and a disservice to Nature.

Nature is the Supreme Teacher! By remembering to pay careful attention to her signs, signals and symptoms, any healthy human being can recognize for herself or himself what needs to be done in order to do away with all pretence, put his or her 'house' in order, re-establish harmony, follow the Natural Order of Things, put an end to confusion, delusion and disappointment and achieve rel-ease from all dis-ease.

Ehi Passiko!

***

Introduction

"Aneka jati samsaram, Sandhavissam anibbisam;
Gaha karakam gavesanto, Dukkha jati punappunam.
Gaha karaka ditthosi, Puna geham na kahasi;
Sabba te phasuka bhagga, Gaha kutam visankhitam;
***Visankhara gatam cittam,** Tanhanam khaya majjhaga."*

First words spoken by Siddhartha Gautama after freeing the mind from
all codes:

"Life after life I have sought the creator of this house,
in ceaseless search
taking on again and again new birth, new suffering
but Now I see you O builder—no more shall
you build my house!
broken are the beams, shattered is the ridge pole,
gone to the codeless is mind – compulsion rooted out
from the body!"

Imagination is at the core of the creation of code and coding.

Pretence and make-believe are present to a greater or lesser extent in
every single code. Code is the master tool of imagination and coding
its favourite pastime. And in the Natural World there are fundamentally
two types of code/coding going on and interacting:

- code created by Nature's Mind
- code created by the thinking mind of humans

Code is present everywhere at every level of life regardless of whether the human being is aware of this or not.

Life as a whole, with each of its myriad parts participating – gigantic, our-size and minute – is an evolving orchestration of disturbances, oscillations, vibrations, ebbs and flows of energy, each moment bringing in the new, discarding the old, renewing the melody, keeping the dance of Life ever fresh, ever vigorous, ever alive.

Change and renewal are the appearance and characteristic of Life, of Existence, while underneath, in essence, it remains the same. And in the composition and structuring of this ongoing evolving symphony of Life, Nature's coding plays an essential, everpresent, invisible role.

Waves of life energy continuously form new patterns and arrangements, trembling with momentary intensity, in fleeting presence; waves interacting, colliding, diffracting, transforming into countless shapes, shades and sounds, ever arising and subsiding in a Sea which always – all ways – remains Ocean.

Oscillation and renewal happen very fast or very slow depending on the type of lifeform, its cycles, the conditions and prevailing circumstances.

The human lifeform is doing exactly that with every single inbreath and outbreath, with every cycle of respiration, with every pulsation of the heart.

In order to stay anchored in the Real, we need to recognize and remember this as often as possible and not overlook it. Yet the human being's thinking mind has forgotten this essence of Eternal Life, and programmed itself since millennia into a state of *vi-yoga*. So thorough has human forgetfulness become established that *even the name of the central channel visible beneath the entrance to the two nostrils* has been forgotten! Even for most yoga practitioners this key part of human anatomy – so visible and utterly familiar – is ignored, nameless and forgotten! And what is ignored does not exist for the thinking mind. It becomes part of what can be called *"the escaped"* or *"the missing"*.

Vi-yoga is the opposite of *yoga*. It is a state of imaginary separateness, a division caused by the thinking mind's perception and belief in a separate *self* somehow existing and operating independently from the rest of Nature.

> Whenever the thinking mind imposes its mental cinema onto the Real Nature of Reality – what the ancients called Maya – we think, speak and behave as if we believe this imaginary entity or persona is our real reality. But in origin it is a pretence, a make-believe, a sham.

As a direct result of an imagined, pretended separate identity somehow independent of Nature, the human imagination has in compensation conjured up all sorts of fantastic belief, hope and doubt systems. Not knowing its true nature, the human thinking mind goes on concocting and fabricating ever more complex equations and solutions to the unsatisfactory and angst-filled problem of separation.

> This separation – this separate independent existence of 'self' – is *purely conceptual* and has no basis in Reality whatsoever.

> This is the true meaning of the Buddha's key statement

> '*sabbe dhamma anatta*'   'all mental constructs are not-self'

Yet the habit of ingrained belief in a separate self, built up, reinforced and perpetuated over generations and generations and generations, has become a formidable conditioning that causes countless human activities to revolve around it. Fortunately not all of them.

Animals, especially those in the wild – away from human interference – seem not to have any such sense of separate identity. They seem to live their lives intensely in the present moment of existence, each behaving according to the code/coding of its own unique nature.

Vi-yoga's deeply rooted belief in separate selfhood is the root-cause of negative emotions such as fear, hate and greed. Hate and greed are two sides of the same coin: symptoms of *adharma* leading to all sorts of negative consequences while the even deeper sentiment of fear is directly related to belief in separateness.

For millennia the human being has mistakenly tried to find solutions outside in the external world by *forcing* things to behave in a way to fit the image of how things *should* be. By doing so we have created endless unnecessary complications and fomented ignorance by missing the opportunity to see and discover what Nature is, what Nature is doing and what Life's purpose is.

Fear, greed, hate and delusion all feed upon each other perpetuating fundamental misinterpretations which cultivate and maintain a vicious circle/vicious cycle of misbehaviour, mischief, misuse and abuse of Nature. Abuse of Life.

Although its expressions and manifestations keep on changing over time inasmuch as the thinking mind tries first this way, then that way, then another way, and then yet another and another way to lift the stuck needle of the mental record onto a new groove, all such misdirected efforts turn out to be futile.

Trying to solve an internal problem of mindbody by rearranging things in the outside world is tantamount to trying to pull oneself off the ground by tugging on one's shoelaces—however great the effort, it simply does not work because it goes against the laws of physics, the law of Nature.

For millennia – for as long as human memory reaches backwards in Time – the consequences of *viyoga* have been causing immense disharmony and harm both to human beings internally to themselves, externally to others in interaction with each other, and to the animal, insect and plant kingdoms, as well as most other parts of the Natural World in contact with humans.

As tools and technology have developed, bringing increased tinkering and tankering, meddling and interference, so too has the scale of havoc and damage increased exponentially. And as I write—still hard at it with tremendous zeal, hope and expectation of **sati**sfaction at some imaginary future point in Time!

> Cleverer and cleverer becomes the human thinking mind, but with no satisfaction in sight.
>
> "Seeking **sati**sfaction in the world, monks, I pursued my way. That **sati**sfaction in the world I found. In so far as **sati**sfaction exists in the

world, I have well perceived it by wisdom. Seeking for misery in the world, monks, I pursued my way. That misery in the world I found. In so far as misery exists in the world, I have well perceived it by wisdom. Seeking for the escape from the world, monks, I pursued my way. That escape from the world I found. In so far as an escape from the world exists, I have well perceived it by wisdom"

Anguttara Nikaya 111, 101

"If there were no **sati**sfaction to be found in the world, beings would not become attached to the world ... If there were no misery to be found in the world, beings would not be repelled by the world ... If there were no escape from the world, beings could not escape from it."

Anguttara Nikaya 111, 102

Here Gautama Buddha clearly states that satisfaction exists in the world. And there are plenty of other passages in the texts where the Buddha refers to positive aspects of life such as friendship, loving kindness and the beauty of Nature.

Therefore to understand *sabbe sankhara dukkha* **as** '*all conditioned things* **are unsatisfactory' cannot be correct.**

* * *

About the author's experience

Dear Reader,
This safari on the fundamentals of yoga – a yoga outside the thinking mind – begins in 1971. Encouraged by my good friend and first yoga teacher Ramiro Calle, I now relate what must be told with as much enthusiasm and conviction as I can deliver.

The time for pretence is over. The age of authenticity is at hand.

It is time to fully value the Real, fully appreciate the genuine, the authentic, the true and to relegate all that is artificial, phoney, false and make-believe to its rightful place. I sincerely wish what is written here can bring about a fresh approach to the practice of yoga, and encourage meditators and students from every system of self-enquiry to take a new look at the life-affirming aspect of the ancient teachings of immortal yoga. I am convinced it can also provide useful clues for open-minded scientists to advance in their research and deblock current *impasses* in physics, physiology, medicine and psychology.

What must be said, will be said here, and afterwards you dear Reader will be the judge of its usefulness and value.

* * *

1970 ended a disappointing and painful relationship with a remarkable woman – one of those impossible-love situations the details of which are not important. What is important is that the disappointment and despair brought upon myself by myself attempting to make a success out of an unworkable situation, drove me in early 1971 to the gates of Shadak Yoga Centre in Madrid. There, under the enthusiastic guidance of Ramiro Calle, I plunged wholeheartedly into the study of classical yoga including the yoga of the Buddha and Taoism, therein to seek answers to life's manifold insatisfactions and conflicts.

During the first year and a half of practice I read most of the leading authors of the time as well as embarking on a detailed study of the *Sutta Pitaka* and *Visuddhimagga* of *Theravada* Buddhism.

In the summer of 1972 I made a maiden trip to India with my brother Carlos, and in Delhi we met Swami Chaitanyanda Saraswati, resident sadhu and secretary of the *Bharat Sadhu Samaj*, an organization supervising the principal orders of sadhus throughout India.

Chaitanyanda was a charismatic don-Juan-like character, *siddha yogi par excellence*, erudite *advaita* vedantin, and despite his fair girth, Swamiji was also an agile accomplished hatha yogi able to leap backwards from a floor mat into padmasana in mid-air and land on a string bed there to sleep the whole night supine in *padmasana*.

He was also able to easily perform that most horrendous-to-westerners of hatha yoga asanas – *purna gorakshasana* – the double ankle backwards twist from *badakonasana* folding the ankles completely backwards underneath his pelvis.

Purna gorakshasana

I never found out what the purpose of this extreme asana is other than to put aspiring western hatha yogis firmly in our place convincing us that such body-twisting feats lie beyond reach.

The other asana that does the job almost as well is the full spinal twist – *purna matsyendrasana*. I have only seen Indian yogis perform this asana with relative ease.

Purna matsyendrasana

Curiously my other brother Ivan is the only westerner I ever met who could easily get into full lotus *padmasana* without using his hands. He could fold his legs and feet into full lotus as easily and perfectly as a person can fold their arms and hands across the chest! For most of us *padmasana* remained a challenge and for years a constant threat to knee joints and ligaments!

Chaitanyanda had a contagious sense of humour. He laughed a lot and loudly, talked little but loved to sing the *Sivaslokas* of Shankaracharya. I still have recordings on cassette somewhere.

Swamiji and I struck up an instant bond which was to last till his passing away in 1986 of kidney failure after attempting to transmute a poison into nectar. He never let on exactly what he was up to but he said it had to do with perfecting a *siddhi*.

With a twinkle in his eye and a broad smile, he admitted to a remnant of craziness leftover from arduous *sadhana* and *tapas*. Swamiji believed in pushing the limits 'to keep on learning through testing boundaries': a true experimenter in the laboratory of his own mind-body!

Over the course of follow up visits to India, Swamiji imparted *kriya yoga* – a form of sustained *pranayama* – allegedly passed down orally from Shankaracharya (adi-Shankara 8th Century). He claimed not only Shankara but many other *siddhas* down the centuries had successfully used this same kriya to deblock the subtle nadi network – which I dubbed *the plumbing* – the purpose of which is to effect a deep deblocking operation on the mindbody.

Ancient texts tend to use terms like "purify" ..."impurities" ... "defilements" ... "cankers" "biases" ... and centuries-later Tantric texts would put the entire process into alchemical language. What they are all talking about is cleaning out the subtle plumbing from obstructions and blockages—namely accumulated coding.

> "Unless you suffer this 'death' of the thinking mind, you cannot rise above death, conquer misery and anguish, attain samadhi and realize that Almighty in you!"
>
> Swami Chaitanyanda Sarawati 1976

Thanks to Chaitanyananda's unique relationship to sadhus throughout India through the *Bharat Sadhu Samaj*, he was able to introduce me to a number of renowned *jivanmuktas*, both male and female, considered to have attained realization, in other words to have successfully carried out this de-blocking of the subtle plumbing.

This was remarkable luck for me and a great privilege! The most memorable of these encounters were with:

- Ananda Mayi Ma, Hardwar
- Kashmir baba
- Amarnath cave base-camp
- Vishwanath Yatee, Hardwar

Ananda Mayi Ma

Swamiji explained the legendary Ananda Mayi Ma lived permanently in such an exalted state of non-separateness that it was almost impossible to have a normal conversation with her. Moreover whatever she sang or said was only in her native Bengali.

I met Ananda Mayi in Hardwar one afternoon seated beside the river Ganges, and following the custom of respect I presented her with a garland of flowers – I think they were marigolds – which smilingly she promptly gave back to me placing the garland over my head instead of hers.

We sat in silence for a while before Swamiji and I bade her farewell with upraised hands. Through her I felt a connection to Sri Yukteswar whom Paramahansa Yogananda had written about in *Autobiography of a Yogi*.

The over-riding impression I received from her was one of utter detachment and disinterest in the physical body and body-related life.

Kashmir baba

On another of the visits to India, we travelled together to Kashmir. Some way outside Srinagar Swami took me one day to a remote hut to meet a yogi who had lost both hands and both feet from frostbite practicing *tapas* in the Himalayan ice and snow. His disciples had to carry him around like a piece of live furniture, feed him, bathe him, clothe him and attend to all needs. This in itself was striking but what was especially remarkable and stayed with me was the *ananda—the joy of life* emanating from what was left of his person. He too spoke no English and while Swami and he conversed, he smiled radiating happiness, eyes shining with a golden light as if from an internal source unrelated to reflected ambient light. This baba whose name I do not recall and maybe never properly knew, was another living example of complete detachment from the physical material body.

Amarnath cave base-camp

On that same trip to Kashmir Swami took me one day to a gathering of *sadhus* – perhaps numbering eighty or more – assembled in preparation for pilgrimage (yatra) to the Siva Lingam Cave at Amarnath where a natural *lingam* of ice waxes and wanes with each moon cycle reaching maximum size during the summer full moon.

To be inside this gathering of sadhus – even for just some hours – made me acutely aware of a collective state of energy and emotion on a whole other level of vibration from anything I had ever experienced before. Any gathering of sadhus is bound to be a motley crowd but I remember in particular several impressive sadhus whose demeanor and mere force of eye contact called conventional thinking and lifestyle into question. To be in among these sadhus was to palpably feel they were on a totally different wavelength to modern, comfort-obsessed, mollycoddled consumer society people. When one of such sadhus looks you in the eye, the one standing naked is you, not they!

Vishvanath Yatee

Perhaps the most impressive encounter at that time was a meeting with a 106 years old hatha yogi clad just in a white loin cloth, seated on a floor mat in half lotus position (*siddha asana*). Vishvanath Yatee had the look and bearing of an ancient lion king, huge and magnificent. His skin was wrinkled, very wrinkled, yet shone with resplendent health and vigour. He too spoke no English. Through the interpretation of Swamiji I asked if it was possible to take some fotos, to which Swami after asking baba replied "Yes! but he says the fotos might not come out!".

And so it was. Alas, every foto taken turned out overexposed, blank!

Jiddu Krishnamurti

Although not chronologically belonging to this list or time, here seems a good place to share with you a most impactful encounter with Jiddu Krishnamurti at his house in Madras (later renamed Chennai) in December 1985. Krishnamurti a few days before had taken a fall and suspended his programme of open talks to large gatherings.

A fellow meditator and yoga practitioner from Madrid Juan Vicente and I had just arrived in Chennai from Igatpuri after completing 3 consecutive *vipassana* courses during a month-long stay at Dhammagiri with SN Goenka.

As luck would have it, at our hotel we ran into Damaso Escauriaza – a long-time 'friend' of Krishnamurti – who told us Krishnamurti was to give a silent *satsang* to a few friends at his house the next day, suggesting we join.

The next day we duly joined a group of eight to ten people in the garden standing close beside the veranda to his house. Everyone was silent.

Krishnamurti came out of the house onto the veranda, silently greeted every person in turn, gazing at length in full eye contact with each one of us. When it came to my turn to gaze into each other's eyes I felt unequivocally that Krishnamurti was myself and that I was Krishnamurti: no barrier, no separation of any kind whatsoever existed between us – what JK knew I knew, and what I felt and knew, he knew and felt – and in that timeless moment of wordless exchange I perceived in Krishnamurti the essence of us all as woman, man and child—all in a single Human Being.

It was a lance to the heart! I never before or since had such an intense encounter of non-verbal synchronicity with another human being, and I have had the immense good fortune to meet a number of truly great ones.

A short time later Krishnamurti returned to Ojai, California where he was diagnosed with untreatable pancreatic cancer, whereupon he left the clinic to spend his last days at home. It is said his mind was clear until the very last moment, and that his last advice was:

"Remain absolutely aware with no effort at all!"

***

In 1976 aided by crowd-funding – the crowd being myself! – Swamiji purchased a mountain retreat property in Mussoorie earmarked for the 'Chaitanya Yoga Vedanta Research Centre'.

There under his supervision I made an initial 7 day retreat doing the 24/7 kriya which triggered what was to come ...

Continuing to practice on returning to Madrid I began to feel sensations of acceleration throughout the framework of the body. This was unpleasant, and whenever the bouts occurred, Swamiji had instructed "just stay still, stay calm and watch it pass over" which it did.

Ramiro was having similarly unpleasant sensations from time to time as a result of his own yoga *sadhana*. Together we found out such sensations of dissolution and acceleration are described in Burmese vipassana meditation manuals as *bhanga* and *bhaya* and are a prelude to insight knowledge.

We named these unwelcome disturbances of brain and nervous system *"the visits of Kali"* — the goddess Kali being She who destroys even the ignorance of Lord Siva's thinking mind, let alone the mental cinema of us mere mortals!

I remember one particularly severe 'Kali visit' after a hard game of squash at the local club. At the time I competed in tournaments, even winning a few cups at club level. I had to stop in the middle of changing out of squash gear, stand stock still in the locker room, and wait in a 'neutral' passive state of mind for the unpleasant sensations of dissolution to pass over. I found it helpful recalling a passage from Frank Herbert's Dune:

> "Fear is the mind-killer. It is the little death which brings total oblite-ration. I will face my fear. I will permit it to rise up and pass over me. When the fear has gone past, I will turn to see the fear's path. Where the fear has gone, there will be nothing. Only I will remain"
>
> Litany of Fear | Dune

By autumn 1977 I made arrangements to take a sabbatical 9 months, and much to my father's disapproval, embarked with yoga mat and flamenco guitar on a round-the-world trip starting in Rio de Janeiro ... Santiago de Chile .... Easter Island... French Polynesia... Fiji ... Australia staying a month with cousins in Sydney ... Indonesia... Malaysia visiting old school friends Bill and Pete ... Thailand stopping for several weeks ...

In Thailand in early 1978 I made an informal 2-week *satipatthana* forest retreat at Suanmok, Surathani under Buddhadhasa Bhikkhu's twinkling watchful eye.

Achan Buddhadhasa dubbed me *"the hatha yogi!"* which was not entirely accurate because at the time my primary focus was studying the Buddha's 8-fold path. Still, the name stuck and while at Suanmok, I became "the hatha yogi"! ....

Buddhadhasa made two noteworthy contributions during those memorable 14 days at Suanmok. The first was to provide written in his own hand the Pali rendering of the first two verses of the Dhammapada (below), considered to be among the few reliable recordings of exact sentences spoken by Siddhartha Gautama later to become world-renowned and venerated universally as the Buddha:

"Mano-pubbangama dhamma,
mano-settha, mano-mayā.
Manasa ce padutthena
bhasati va karoti va,
tato nam dukkhamanveti
cakkam'va vahato padam.

Mano-pubbangama dhamma,
mano-settha, mano-mayā.
Manasa ce pasannena
bhasati va karoti va,
tato nam sukhamanveti
chaya'va anapayini."

Dhammapada, 1 1 and 2.

"Mind precedes all mental constructs,
mind is their leader and they are mind-made,
think and speak with an impure heart and misery follows as surely
as the cartwheel the ox's hoof

Mind precedes all mental constructs,
mind is their leader and they are mind-made,
think and speak with a pure heart and happiness follows
like a shadow which never departs."

I mention this here because many years later it became part of the key to unlocking the puzzle surrounding the precise meanings and relationships between Awareness, Consciousness, Mind, Thought, Imagination and Code all of which are discussed in Chapter 1 Language.

The second contribution was his frequent exhortation "Die well from the first day!"

At the time I did not quite understand why he kept repeating this as a form of greeting but some months later it became clear.

For those of you who have never heard of Buddhadhasa he was renowned throughout Thailand as an original thinker and reviver of forest meditation practice as originally encouraged by the Buddha.

***

From Thailand to India ... where Swamiji again urged continuity of practice without worrying about increasingly frequent sensations of acceleration throughout the body.

He reassured that – unpleasant as they are – it is perfectly normal when *kundalini* is aroused and awakens to cause seismic shifts in awareness of realities.

> "Just continue to practice, keep calm and watch what unfolds. There is nothing to fear except fear itself."
>
> Chaitanyananda

Easier said than done!

This reminds me of a humorous moment when Swamiji discussed the financial appetite of the 'Chaitanya Vedanta Research Centre' and shed comforting words:

"Acha Simon, don't worry about money! Look!—you and I are like one person—this means my money is your money, and your money is my money!"

And I replied, "Yes, Swamiji ... that's great, but ... hang on a moment ... *you don't have any*!!"

"Don't worry about details!" came the siddha's reply!

Easier said than done!

After India came Egypt to meet up with Ingeborg Zänder, dear friend, eminent astrologer and hermeticist and together we stood dwarfed at the base of the Great Pyramid. Inside it was equally imposing. Impressive place, powerful ancient energies.

Somehow Ingeborg had managed to bamboozle and charm Zahi Hawass, then Minister of Antiquities, into allowing her to spend one full night completely alone inside the innermost chamber! This was no longer permitted at the time because a number of former brave night-time solo visitors had become unhinged but Ingeborg was persuasive, and obtained authorization to spend the full night alone!

Together with an Afghan friend Waji, we stood in awe watching her enter alone and be swallowed up into the black vastness of the Great Pyramid of Giza in the dark of night armed with bedroll, mineral water, two flashlights, a box of matches and some candles. Next morning a somewhat paler version of Ingeborg emerged to report every single one of her light sources had failed halfway through the night!

Here in the presence of the Great Pyramid *kali* sensations again mani-fested intensely. But the bout passed over as it had always done before.

From Egypt westwards to Greece there to relax under flowering lemon trees in Corinth before returning by end may 1978 to the fishing village of Cadaqués, Catalonia, where I had rented a small house for the summer.

Here in Cadaqués – the home of Salvador Dalí – was to take place the climax of 7 years of yoga sadhana.

It was during a swim on 21ˢᵗ June at the 'flat rocks' that I dived down for a shell and felt a sharp stab of pain upwards into the right sinus. Thinking little of it, I returned to the house after sunbathing but later that evening a pain developed over and behind the right eye. That night I bore with it but sleep was fitful and impaired.

The next morning, I decided to use the presence of pain as medi-tation object and face the sensation in order to come to terms with the pain. *dukkha!*

Thus began a confrontation which was to last another 5 days and 5 nights during which I did take an aspirin twice but with no noticeable relief. In fact the pain slowly and steadily increased, and periods of rest through sleep became increasingly hard to come by.

By the 27ᵗʰ June I became worried, imagining I had something other than a headache, maybe something serious. I became sufficiently con-cerned to seek out the village doctor. I remember the visit well because in the waiting room I had another *kali* visitation with intense fear that perhaps my health was in jeopardy ...

However, the good doctor Vergara on hearing about the dive tapped the right-side sinus causing a flare of agony, and declared "right-sided sinusitis!", which would clear up in a matter of days under the right antibiotic treatment.

Hearing his words, the severe pain remained unchanged but the added imaginary anxiety and fear evaporated into thin air. Right there and then that provided quite an insight into how imagination colours perception of reality!

Shankara's snake in the rope!

I duly purchased the prescribed antibiotics on my way uphill back to the house confident that in a few days the pain would subside as the sinusitis cleared up.

Nevertheless, the same severe pain I had before visiting the good doctor remained acutely present but now there was no fear. And in the absence of fear – with renewed determination – I returned to my meditation seat, and continued steadfastly observing the pain.

I sat most of the rest of that day and night, and throughout the next morning, with mind and attention in relentless confrontation with the painful sensation.

Until the afternoon of the 28th June the stalemate between the *immovable object* and the *irresistible force* persisted.

One of the two had to give way! There was no alternative. Co-existence of the two was unsustainable. Something had to give way and go: either the insufferable pain or the "I" observing it had to go.

In a nutshell: either the participating part of mind had to go or the observing part of mind had to go! Thus was the master-code put under stress! *Could that be the 'untraceable step' that Patanjali refers to in his Yogasutra?!*

I remember even thinking this thought at the instant something – a quantum shift in awareness – happened!

Suddenly, awareness had no object of perception describable in terms of senses, yet awareness was fully present. It was as if awareness had been engrossed watching the Cinema of Life, and then that film had come to an abrupt end, like an old cinema reel suddenly running out and ending, spinning disconnected from any content, leaving the viewer facing a blank screen—except this screen was not blank either ... it had no characteristic to it at all, not even light or darkness.

Exactly how long this full awareness of suspension of sensory perception lasted, is hard to say because at the time the thinking evaluating mind was entirely absent. It could have been an instant or several minutes before awareness of body, senses and surroundings returned as abruptly as they had become absent. Upon the return of awareness of body, senses and surroundings, what was immediately evident as '*changed*' was the acute pain was no longer felt as 'painful' but only as an '*intense sensation*' with no sense whatsoever of affliction or discomfort.

I rose from the sitting position and noted down in my diary that 'finally the pain has gone' although the sensation remained but absolutely untroublesome.

It was beginning to be dark by then. I decided to take a walk downtown – the first in 5 or 6 days – to stroll around and savour the feeling of relief and release.

At this point I had no sense yet that anything fundamental had shifted except that awareness was only of sensations and senses but without any sense of anybody being affected or involved.

I walked downhill to the waterfront to the Meliton Café and ran into to Carlos Lozano, an art gallery owner. We sat outdoors on the waterfront and chatted for maybe an hour over a cup of tea before I made my way back home uphill through winding streets.

As I walked back uphill I began to realize that in addition to a noticeable feeling of mental and bodily lightness and ease, vision was subtly different – the motion of walking seemed to cause a shimmering of light in the dimly lit street. The shimmering was somewhat like the shimmering when a glass of water is jogged on a table or the rippling from a pebble thrown into a still pond in moonlight. At first, I thought something was wrong with the street lights causing the flickering and shimmering, so I stopped on a street corner – I still sometimes stop there to this day 44 years later! – to look up at a street lamp which I thought was shorting.

But the light from the street lamp held steady—it was something else that was flickering.

Mind!

And then I realized that I was no longer looking through the normal two eyes but as if through some inner point above and behind them. I then also noticed that the shimmering disturbance of light came not from the movement of walking but from the movement of thought—each time a thought or an emotion arose, a ripple effect spread outwards instantly like sheet lightening in a field of Consciousness. This was the first time I directly perceived what I later realized is the Ether. Many years afterwards I also realized exactly what elusive Consciousness is. Ether and Consciousness are discussed together in chapter 12.

***

From that evening of the 28th June 1978 throughout the following twelve days and twelve nights until the night of the 9th June, Mind and Awareness remained uninterruptedly in what later by cross-checking in yoga texts I recognized as *sahaja samadhi*: a state of mind in which there is no sense whatsoever of body-connected "I"—just continuous recognition and acknowledgement of the totality of Nature as being of a single essence.

The physical body along with the rest of the body's surroundings encompassed all directions with *no difference in essence between any object seen, yet differences of character and appearance were readily apparent.*

Another way of putting it is to say whereas the normal two eyes together with the ordinary thinking mind/brain see, perceive and differentiate into 'this' or 'that' by making connections and meanings based upon *differences*, this extra-ordinary vision now present and functioning was seeing everything as in essence the same – made of the same stuff regardless of outer appearances and characteristics.

It was like having a prism or a diamond inside the forehead which, instead of refracting light into different shades and colours, did exactly the opposite integrating everything into a single translucent crystalline Consciousness. Put simply: whereas the two eyes together with the thinking mind/brain differentiate '10 thousand things', the diamond eye integrates them all into undifferentiated sameness. The same occurred for the sense of hearing as for sight, and markedly so for thinking, thoughts and language.

During those 12 days and 12 nights the ordinary thinking mind and its identification with the physical body were entirely absent. Awareness remained steady in this vastly expanded Mind of Nature yet from time to time there still arose disturbances from thoughts and emotions triggered from the storehouse of memories.

Perceiving this, arose the realization that at the level of bodily coding, what at the time I named the "tapes" (inherited/acquired programming embedded in the brain and nervous system) *had to be rubbed out* (erased) because these *tapes* compromise, obstruct and hamper the life-force intelligence from realizing its full potential. Each and every embedded "tape" of coding impedes the free-flow of life-force intelligence through some part of the body and this restriction in flow of life force is paralleled by a limitation/shut down in a corresponding part of the brain and nervous system preventing awakening to full appreciation of what Life and Nature really is.

Understanding, recognition, acknowledgement and insight flowed effortlessly from whatever attention focused on during those 12 days and 12 nights.

Here below are a few insights from that unforgettable parenthesis in the normal course of embodied life. Other insights form parts of chapters 1-12.

***

- I do not recall a single moment of sleep during those 12 nights. "Long indeed are the nights for he who stays awake!" The conclusion I later came to on re-linking up with mindbody is that us humans need to switch off the thinking mind once in every cycle of 24 hours to rest for a few hours in order to remain 'sane' because the work of maintaining a body-senses-identified personality pretending to be a separate part of existence is exhausting. Animals sleep to recover from energy expenditure of day-to-day survival, from protecting themselves, and the ceaseless search for food. With humans it is more the exhaustion from maintaining the charade of the internal cinema with its endless inside-outside mental tennis.

- Though fully aware of body and ongoing bodily activities such as speaking, moving about, eating, attending the calls of nature and so forth, the importance of the body in relation to the awakened Mind of Nature I compared at the time to a single hair of the little finger to the body as a whole. A tiny existing part, yes, but hardly of any significance ... whether that tiny hair stays on or drops off makes no difference to the body as a whole. Death is of the thinking mind only. In Reality all is Life only.

- I remember thinking that even to lose the sight of the two normal eyes would in no way affect the light and sight of this vastly expanded Awareness and Mind, any more than the presence or absence of the moon's orb adds or subtracts to the light of the midday sun on a cloudless day.

- It was as if there had been a 180 degree turning around in the seat of Awareness – in the heartcentre – the thinking mind with its internal cinema, self-and-body identification having become disconnected, and the unconscious Core Mind of Nature having awakened and taken over.

- Eating hardly – drinking water only – lost 7 kilos. I remembered in former times humans could live on very little solid food—water essential yes, air and light both essential, but *prana* is the main energy source along with impressions.

- Humans come from the sea, and remain mostly seawater—precisely 72%. Number 72 crops up everywhere. We need far less solid food than we think.

- There are indeed beginnings and endings to individual things. Individual things both large and small have beginnings at different times and endings at different times. They do not all start at the same time, and do not all end at one and the same time. Once this is seen and accepted, the Cosmos is understood as having no beginning and no ending. Just like breathing in and breathing out, it has phases of expansion, phases of contraction, and pauses in-between. But It is eternal as are its laws.

- The Mind's eye saw births and deaths of galaxies and a black hole at the centre of every galaxy, this hole acting as gateway of passage between galaxies – portals from one galaxy to another, interdimensional exchange ways structured like moebius. At that time in 1978 only a handful of theoretical physicists had begun to guess the existence of black holes. To my knowledge there was nothing reported in mainstream press about black holes till years afterwards. At the micro scale I saw this paralleled by a black hole in the heartcentre of every human being. Through this atomic scale black hole enters the spirit spark atom with life-force intelligence at birth and through it, departs at death. Even today the possible existence of such a micro black hole has never even been mentioned in science.

- The mind's eye saw numbers as fundamental to the structure of the Cosmos. Try as it did, the Mind's Eye was unable to go behind num¬bers to see what they are, what their origin is. But it saw 12 numbers as truly fundamental numbers from which all others arise. Of these 12, **1 0** ∞ are the three **ab**solute numbers and 1- 9 are the 9 **ordinary** numbers. Fixation on one or other of the 3 absolute numbers leads humans to see the divine in terms of either 1 or 0 or ∞.

- One afternoon I visited a good friend of my mother's Jackie Bisbe. A large inner patio divided two sections of her spacious townhouse in Palafrugell. To one side of the centre of the patio was a tree under which Jackie's husband Ernesto kept a large mastiff-like dog on a long chain attached to a kennel. As we walked across the patio Jackie cautioned not to pass too near the dog saying it was dangerous, and only her husband was able to go near it. However in that state of absence of body-related "I" with which to feel fear – ignoring her advice – I approached the dog feeling nothing but loving kindness and empathy. The dog took one look at me, growled and suddenly leapt at me, its maw reaching to about shoulder height. My body reacted without any tension just calmly raising the left hand and fore-arm in cover while awareness watched its jaws close around my left wrist and then – as if jolted by an invisible energy barrier – the dog rebounded backwards and fell crumpled in a heap at my feet. Awareness noted its saliva on my wrist but its jaws had been unable to close. A most curious thing immediately noticeable was the dog had a full erection as it shakily rose to its feet and slunk backwards sheepishly towards its kennel. Its erection persisted as I continued to stand there contemplating what had just occurred. At that moment I recalled that a subtle force field – metaphorically described in ancient texts as 'serpent power' – is said to protect those in *brahma vihara*. This event showed me that what was occurring those 12 days and nights was a genuine energy phenomenon—something real, tangible and no figment of imagination. All of us have access to far more love and power than we know.

***

The afternoon of the 9th July I finally lay down on a bed, closed the normal eyes and white light manifested everywhere extending and filling all space endlessly in every direction.

I remember the white light had the feel of an actual substance to it: not emanating from any particular source point nor traveling anywhere. It just existed, suspended, abiding as itself, being there, everywhere, timelessly, utterly restful, blissful and nourishing. At that time there was no intellectual acknowledgement of this as a characteristic of pertaining to either Ether or Consciousness.

After abiding as white light within the white light for seemingly an Age, the thought arose *"Not much is happening here!"* and that taking birth in differentiations of this form or that form provides a welcome contrast to undifferentiated white light even considering the price to pay from sufferings arising from identifying with name and form and forgetfulness of the Real.

So—*is alternation/oscillation to and fro between the two, from individual to universal, the ebb and flow of life?* Like waves and ocean? Like seed and tree? is this how experience is structured and how it evolves Mind qualitatively? Yes.

Yet this alternation between undifferentiated bliss of white light and myriad forms of individual existence is tiring – so tiresome repeated again and again and again – endlessly repetitive, and not wholly **satis**-factory either.

What then? Is there something else?

At this point *something third* beckoned at the edge of awareness—an emerald radiance from afar began to be perceptible just at the boundary of Awareness ...

But I sensed it was *not the Time* ... that *whatever I am needed more Time* before going in that direction ... and, upon that thought, abruptly, the white light began to be sucked into a black hole, a **pandora**'s box of unknowable chaotic properties—awareness spiralled like water down a sink's plughole ... disappearing into engulfing blackness.

Approaching the entry point of the black void – the cosmic **drain** – the last thing I remembered as the vestiges of rational thinking mind were annihilated, was the single thought *"Thy will be done!"*

***

Next morning at dawn 10th July 1978, I awoke again with a thinking mind, again with senses functioning, again with normal bodily and sensory perception. The "I" had been born again into a 28 year old body!! With a clean slate!

Thus began this, the third stage of my life. A life of continuing research and further exploration to see how to make something universally useful out of what had been experienced and seen.

It took about 7 years to regain a certain emotional maturity and mental equilibrium. The thinking mind had no major problems adapting since it perfectly well remembered the life of the previous 28 years in all its details, in addition to remembering those of the parenthesis of 12 days and 12 nights immersed in Nature's Mind.

I realized work still had to be done, and effort made, to rub out ancestral tapes and conditioning... blockages, habit patterns, knots, traumas, blind spots.

Although flashes of insight arose from time to time for about a year during which sexual energy remained in the heart-centre and higher mind – dormant in the lower body – the more I re-engaged with ordinary life and habits, the more normal and mundane became the awareness.

***

I did not return to Asia until the following year but occasionally spoke to Swamiji on the phone, who suggested repeating the *kriya* retreat again but this time for 40 days 24/7 to clear out remaining blockages in the "plumbing".

So I made arrangements to do this same *kriya* in silence in a suitable secluded place, and by the end of the 40 days, *pingala nadi* (sun channel) had become unblocked and has remained free ever since. This means the thinking intellectual part of brain and nervous system had become cleared of obstructions. But blockages persisted in *ida nadi* (moon channel) – the one related to emotional energies throughout brain and nervous system. Emotionally there were still ancestral *tapes* – dissonances – to be resolved.

Over the coming years I continued yoga practice by myself building up to sittings of 3 hours duration once a day. To sit still for 2 hours 45 minutes became quite comfortable but the last quarter of an hour provided major challenges for reasons to be explained in chapters 5, Asana, and chapter 9, Nadis.

From 1984 to 1994 I sat 14 10-day vipassana courses, many of them including 2 *satipatthana* courses with SN Goenka, who wrote me a letter in 1991 in reply to a question on the best method of practice. (see appendix)

Four of the courses were in Italy with John Coleman, another renowned vipassana teacher in the same tradition of U Ba Khin. Both SN Goenka and John Coleman were genuine teachers who imparted their knowledge and practice free of charge on the basis of *dana*.

All of these retreats provided valuable insights and further layers of coding were peeled off but *ida-nadi* remained un-fully opened. Some blockage persisted.

However the more I practiced the vipassana system of yoga – *anapanasati* and *satipatthana* as taught at that time – the more convinced I became that the benefits were coming mainly from the austerity (tapas) of patiently sitting 11 hours a day in silence rather than from 'mindfulness of breathing' or 'mindfulness of sensations' or from the contemplation of 'impermanence and unsatisfactoriness of formations' or 'voidness of self'.

By 1994 I had become convinced that the pessimistic Buddhist fixation on impermanence and suffering did not fit nor resonate with what I had directly known and seen in the summer of 1978 (16 years earlier). Neither could I identify with either side of the obsessive debate still going strong over 'self' (*atman*) and 'not-self' (*anatman*).

That meant there had to be something fundamental *missing* – or amiss – in the interpretation of specific keywords and phrases describing the essentials of Buddha Gautama's teaching.

Also, how could ancient Pali texts be disrespectful of Mahavir – a veritable giant of a contemporary teacher – and misrepresent Mahavir's teachings which are so close in spirit to the Buddha's?

What has come through to us down the corridors of time cannot be fully correct. There are just too many inconsistencies.

***

By 1994, I was married with two small children needing loads of attention, and I was busy coming to terms with living and functioning in a world where Nature and the Natural Order is becoming ever more unbalanced and disturbed by the ongoing ravages of an industrial technological consumer society out of control.

Since June 1978 it has taken 44 years of Safari on the Fundamentals of Life to come to the realization that the *thinking mind* of the human being is the artificer of all human-made problems, and that stopping it is how Patanjali precisely defines *yoga*.

The human being over the last several millennia has come to believe that the tool of the thinking mind – which has usurped its place in the hierarchy of mindbody – is the be-all and end-all of existence. And as a result is firmly entrenched and stuck in *vi-yoga*.

Yoga beyond the thinking mind puts the spotlight on key pieces of missing understanding relating not just to Yoga but to Life itself and our place and function in Life. After all, Life and Yoga are not separate.

What was seen and understood during those twelve timeless days and nights beyond the Code, could lead to a timely **Mid-Course Correction** if enough people get hold of a few simple assumptions not yet connected in sciences.

It is Time to set forth the Path to the Codeless – to uncover and recover our immortal Nature – and experience that outside the thinking mind everything in Nature is perfect!

Disc.over

1. Language | Code

The thinking mind is an aggregate of codes, images and concepts.
If their meanings are unclear, the mind is unclear.

In this chapter we confront the colossal problem of language in order to appreciate the extent to which language conditions us at every level the entire time we are awake. Only deep sleep, or *samadhi*, provides provisional release and relief.

Because this has been going on for so long, for many generations in such a repetitive way, almost none of us notices what language/code is doing to us.

We take for granted that it has always been like that and we retain no conscious recollection of any transition from a time when it was not so.

The human species is very likely far, far older than modern science is guessing. Paleo-anthropology, which studies evolution of the human species, and archaeology its traces, both keep on revising their guesses of Time, Time-lines and relationships but fail to consider the cyclical, spiral pattern of how everything in Nature evolves.

Life on planet Earth in its many different forms and myriad expressions – including human – has arisen, endured for a span of time and then succumbed multiple times in its outer forms to destruction:

- through disturbances of the great EARTH element (earthquakes, seismic shifts)
- through disturbances of the great WATER element (floods, inundations; incessant rain)
- through disturbances of temperature: FIRE (sun flares; extremes of heat and drought) and COLD (climate switching from temperate to cold; Ice ages)
- through AIR disturbances (changes in composition, in pressure, extreme winds)

There are some studies (mostly non-mainstream) documenting traces of the first two kinds of destruction (Earth, Water) but hardly a mention of the second two (Fire, Air), these being too far back in Time and less susceptible to leaving the same kinds of traces.

Evolution is unlikely to be in straight lines with Cartesian beginnings and endings. It is far more likely to follow a cyclical, spiral pathway, whose passage through Time ascends and descends as it evolves qualitatively, its contents arising from seed-like residues – imprints from previous creations.

In fact, the whole notion of straight-line evolution – of beginnings and endings – is fundamentally flawed and more a question of language generating incorrect notions than reflecting Reality as it changed into new arrangements.

In Reality there seem to be no beginnings which cannot equally well be described as endings of something else previous. Likewise, there are no endings which are not beginnings of something else to follow. Change and transformation are the essence of Life, and the ancient Indian view of evolution in wave-like spirals of continuously changing outward appearances and characteristics seems to be the more accurate notion.

In fact, almost all the world's old mythologies have a view of repeating Ages of vast Time spans. Even Science has to recognize that for there to have been a big bang, there must have been in existence something beforehand – at least two prior 'things' that collide in a medium. So, the big bang cannot be an absolute beginning, only a beginning in name only – a point on a spiral.

Search for an absolute beginning is merely a game of mental tennis to entertain the thinking mind and distract it from the far more important task of understanding itself and its own repetitive mechanisms which keep the human being trapped in unrealistic beliefs, hopes and doubts – trapped in 'not-seeing' (avijja).

Yoga provides method and insight into far more important aspects of Real things that are going on right now.

***

Language | Code has been conditioning us since long before the beginning of recorded history. And the conditioning weighing upon us is steadily increasing in proportion to added complexities of technology, new tools and new forms of communication and interaction.

Because of over-familiarity – *language being taken for granted* – it is insufficiently recognized how it has bound us in complex layers of coding of our own thinking mind's fabrication – *all of which makes up our elaborate representation of the Real World* – and how this fabrication is the fundamental cause of vi-yoga.

The underlying assumption of *Yoga Beyond the Thinking Mind* is that, *left alone*, Nature is already perfect. Thus, the natural state *is* perfect and can be experienced as such.

> "Outside the thinking mind of the human being everything in Nature is perfect." — assumption

Let us now unsheathe the ancient sword of Wisdom, re-temper its fine steel, sharpen up the blade and systematically slice through the entanglements, confusions and delusion caused by *not seeing* what we are doing with mind-made codes and concepts (*avidya*):

> *What are we doing to ourselves?*
> *What are we doing to others?*
> *What are we doing to Mother Nature?*

None of these are separate.

***

Whenever we use language to communicate it is essential to know as precisely as possible the specific meanings associated with each word. Essential for ourselves, essential for all of us.

> This includes words we use in thinking when we are talking to ourselves.

This may seem obvious yet there are a number of words, such as Mind, Awareness, Consciousness and Thought, which are frequently used in everyday speech that have no commonly accepted definitions.

Moreover, languages can be internal to the body or external to the body, so the word language does not just mean patterns of verbal or written speech. The human being uses both these as well as other kinds of patterns as **code** to represent meanings. It does this both for itself internally and for external use, and for all internal-external dialogue and exchanges.

Whether it be in Sanskrit, Pali or in a Western language there are a number of seriously problematic words frequently used in yoga, and also equally indispensable for making sense in philosophy, psychology and science. Despite the virtues of the scientific method, all too often science is mired in confusion because it gets lost in the labyrinths of its own languages.

These *problem words* are invariably associated with unclear concepts, resulting in not being able to get a clear picture in our heads of what exactly these words are really pointing to. This is putting it mildly.

Clear connections to the Real World of Nature need to be established urgently. Otherwise we will remain stuck, condemned to go on mentally wandering around in vague **ab**stractions, just pretending everything is okay when it is not okay, and continuing to waste valuable time having fun making wrong guesses.

> Yoga is not about distraction, entertainment or guesswork! Quite the opposite. Yoga is about getting Real by putting pretence and delusion to the sword!

The sword of Manjusri! That means 'death' to the internal cinema and an end to identification with endless mental tennis games without which there can be no rising from the ashes of ignorance, disappointment and despair; no awakening from the slumber of forgetfulness nor regaining of Immortal Life and Lost Paradise.

The thinking mind has to drop all pretence, abandon all its make-believe and *non-sense*, and instead live the daily Life of Real Nature which – surprise, surprise – is the nature of every one of us too.

There Is no such thing as 'two Natures'!

***

Problem words in Sanskrit/Pali	Problem words in Western languages
Dharma	Consciousness
Dukkha	Ether
Samskara/Sankhara	Awareness
Sati	Mind
Vijnana/Viññana	Thought

In the appendix section there is a glossary covering a number of important words, but the ones above are so *essential to understanding* that they have to be addressed right away before even beginning to delve deeply into yoga as conceived and practiced by the ancients.

These definitions are to make sure you, dear Reader, and I the author, have the same picture in our heads during the writing and reading of this book. The definitions are proposals for a provisional agreement on meanings, no more than that. I have found them extremely useful. I hope you do too. They represent decades of research and reflection on the fundamentals of Reality.

Language, verbal and written, has become an amazingly useful tool but at the same time narrows, limits and restricts understanding in unforeseen ways. Everything has consequences – there is no such thing as a 'free lunch' in the world of codes.

The consequence of language is that the human organism is seeded/embedded with chains upon chains upon chains of human mind-made connections and codes, our programming. I call these TAPES. They are what is binding us, limiting us, restricting us and what prevents free-dom. This is what is obstructing the *nadis* – either partly or entirely – impeding the free flow of life-force intelligence.

These tapes of codes are a storehouse of fabricated habit-reaction patterns coiled like springs lying outside the field of normal everyday awareness, poised waiting to be triggered. And they are the reason why the human being with very few exceptions – despite the best intentions and all the right sermonizing and exhortation down the corridors of time – has shown itself again and again, both individually and collec-tively, incapable of transforming deviant behaviour into harmonious behaviour in alignment with Nature.

Yet *paradoxically* at the same time this extra-ordinary ability to create new connections – a disproportionately large number of which are **arbi-trary** and random – seems to be the sole chance for freedom from outco-mes predetermined and governed by cause and effect! And this seems to be a unique characteristic of human beings. At least on this planet.

In yoga, what is meant by freedom, by liberation?

In yoga *liberation* means freeing the life force to flow as Nature intends it – unimpeded through every nook and cranny of our extra-ordinary brain, nervous system and physical body which is an aggregate of visi-ble patterns made by invisible pushes (forces acting upon structures). In every case the mechanism of the code is based on an immediate connection between two completely different orders of reality, and this connection triggers meanings. The meanings may be valid knowledge or may not. We will see later that Patanjali enumerates five kinds of knowledge, and there is a whole science of epistemology.

Firstly, the problematic Sanskrit and Pali words.

For each of these ancient venerable words we need translations with clear meanings that make sense and fit the picture. All too often commentators and translators have shoved the fat foot of Cinderella's ugly sister into a finely crafted glass slipper and as a result the entire teaching has been limping painfully along for centuries if not millennia. In no way does the fault lie with the original teacher but with "not-seeing-clearly" followers.

Dharma

The entirety of Chapter 2 is dedicated to this crucially important word and its related concepts. Suffice it to say here that there are more than 20 generally accepted meanings given for this frequently used word so it is no wonder it has been a source of endless confusion and vagueness for centuries, if not millennia.

Samskara | Sankhara

"Profound Ananda, is this Dependent Origination, and profound does it appear. It is through not understanding, not penetrating this Code, that this world resembles a tangled ball of thread, a bird's nest, a thicket of sedge or of reed, and that mankind fails to escape from the lower states of existence, from the course of lamentation and loss, and suffers from the round of rebirth."

Digha Nikaya Sutta 15

For making sense out of the ancient teachings of India, no word or concept is more important to understand thoroughly than Samskara | Sankhara.

Of all words that have driven me crazy over the past 44 years *samskara* (in Sanskrit), *sankhara* (in Pali) without doubt top the list!

Finally, understanding dawned! – **sankhara** means **code**! The interpretation of **SANKHARA** as **CODE** is the absolute key to understanding the depth, genius and precision of Gautama Buddha's unique system of yoga known as *satipatthana* (Chapter 8) and likewise to explaining its synthesis in the formulation of Dependent Origination (*paticcasamuppada,* also Chapter 8).

It enables seeing what Patanjali in his Yogasutra alludes to as the "untraceable step", and why it is an *untraceable step*. It also enables understanding what Shankaracharya's famous three propositions truly point to.

As far as yoga is concerned – be it the Buddha's eightfold path, Patanjali's eightfold system or Shankaracharya's Vedanta – there is no more important word to get clear than this one. Because it is so subtle, so deep, so difficult to apprehend that even with first-hand 'live' instruction its full significance and implications take time to digest.

> "Profound Ananda, is this Dependent Origination, and profound does it appear. It is through not understanding, not penetrating this Code, that this world resembles a tangled ball of thread..."

Sankhara as code is key to understanding the profound meaning of the first two propositions of Dependent Origination:

> "Avijja paccaya sankhara,
> Sankhara paccaya viññanam..."

> "Not seeing conditions code,
> Code conditions life-force intelligence..."

Samskara in Sanskrit – also pronounced *sanskhara*, hence *sankhara* in Pali – is a concept shared by all the major ancient *darshanas* (philosophical viewpoints) of *sanatana dharma*, much later to be called Hinduism including Buddhism and Jainism.

In a nutshell – and without getting lost into details as to why or how they lost track of the precise meaning – the early Buddhists all too soon after the Buddha's passing must have fallen back onto guessing the specific meaning he gave to the word *sankhara*.

The older traditions, including Samkhya and Yoga schools, interpreted *samskara* as *latent tendencies* in the mindbody seeded by past actions causing residual imprints which get stored and accumulate passively until activated.

In contrast, all the various schools of Buddhism – *very likely because during the lifetime and teaching of Siddhartha Gautama he had repeatedly hammered into their heads that sankhara has a specific additional meaning; an active wilful aspect as 'formative' or 'karma formative'* – went so widely off-track that the word *sankhara* started to be used to cover every and any aspect of "formations" or "fabricated things" or "conditioned things" including absolutely anything in the Cosmos capable of arising and ceasing!

Both views are missing the full meaning of *samskara* as **code** but the more ancient view is a lot closer to the mark because it sticks to the framework of the mindbody.

> "Santi satta apparajakkha jatika
> assavanata Dhammassa parihayant.
> Bhavissanti Dhammassa annataro."

> Dutiya Marapasa Sutta, Samyutta Nikaya

> There are beings with only a little dust in their eyes
> who will be lost unless they hear the Teaching.
> Such persons will understand the Code.

Bear in mind that at that time c.2500 years ago there was no concept for code, not even a vague one such as most lay people might have nowadays. The whole business of the code is so fiendishly knotty, so devious and tricky that even in today's modern world, where the concept code has become commonplace and familiar, and where code/coding is used for countless everyday applications, even to control household appliances...even so, the whole of science, philosophy and psychology have not yet spotted the code's omnipresence, its everywhereness.

Because of this gigantic oversight science has omitted making a thorough and precise analysis of the code's construction as well as its operation. Unbelievable but true!

Even the great Korzybski, author of the ground-breaking work *Science and Sanity*, who was onto the importance of the code in the studies of 'General Semantics', missed how it is constructed and how it operates – and therefore failed to see exactly what a code *is* and understand exactly what a code *does*.

> Human beings all too often forget that what something *is* and what something *does* are two completely different aspects.

Once seen that code is the correct meaning of the term *sankhara*, both in its **active** and **passive** aspects, it follows logically that both the Vedic interpretation of *samskara* and at least Buddhadhasa's and Goenka's interpretations fit together and can be reconciled!

The above is confirmed by the Buddha's last words of encouragement (exhortation) to the monks which contain the quintessence of his entire teaching:

> "*Vaya dhamma sankhara appamadena sampadetha!*"

> "Coding is impermanent – steadfastly remove it!"

Paraphrased: mind-made codes can be wiped out as their nature is not something permanent or everlasting. We can free ourselves from them by working them out diligently. This is further confirmed in the formulation of Dependent Origination to be discussed in detail in Chapter 8:

> "Whoso understands Dependent Origination, understands the Code, and whoso understands the Code, understands Dependent Origination."
>
> Majjhima Nikaya Sutta 28

Code & Coding

The role of Code and Coding – its influence, its omnipresence – was discovered by the Buddha, confirmed in the little understood and also incorrectly interpreted teaching of *patisambhida* (conjoint) to be discussed in Chapter 3, Artificial World vs Real World.

For those familiar with Cockney, *'conjoint'* will ring a familiar bell and raise a smile. To explain the role code/coding plays in conditioning, restricting and compromising the life-force intelligence inside the human mindbody is no easy task even now with sophisticated methods of communication, transmission and recording – let alone c.2500 years ago!

At that distant time there was only the language of the day – a variant of vernacular Pali – with which to convey such a profound insight. Hence it is not surprising that once Siddhartha Gautama and his contemporaries had passed away and were no longer present in person to point out its subtleties, subsequent generations rapidly lost track of the precise meaning of *sankhara* and of the proper interpretation of *patisambhida* together with other key terms and concepts such as *sati, dhamma and viññana* redefined in this chapter and Chapter 2.

Adding to inherent limitations of the language, all transmission at that time was oral. Nothing was written down until centuries later, so it is amazing what has reached us 2500 years later, and we have to be most grateful for that.

Even the first three Councils of Elders – gatherings of the most advanced monks assembled for the purpose of clarifying, agreeing and orally recording the teaching's central points and methodology – are a subject of debate amongst scholars. Some have cast doubt that any of the first three councils ever took place.

Even accepting they did take place, it is recorded that at that early stage, disagreements on interpretation – deriving from *misunderstandings on meanings* – broke out causing early schisms in the *sangha* (order of monks). Misunderstanding meanings of key words inevitably leads to misunderstanding the practice and path.

> Even to this day as I write, the omnipresence of the code and coding has not been spotted by sciences. And therefore its key role in the **psychemechanics** of mindbody is entirely missing.

Psychology hardly mentions the code and coding. Korzybski was on the right track and came close but did not spot the construction of the code and missed the connection between the similar and the nonsimilar (below).

Even Jiddu Krishnamurti during decades of efforts at explaining a direct approach to disentangling mental confusion – despite addressing the problem from multiple angles for 70 years – never spotted the role of the code!

The implication of this is that even without full intellectual insight into the code, a human being can complete the mindbody decoding process. But it will take far longer, the path will be less clear, less certain, and afterwards that person will not be able to explain clearly and fully to others how he got to where he got to.

It is revealing that toward the end of his life at the age of 85, J Krishnamurti declared:

"If I knew the Buddha would be speaking here tomorrow morning, nothing in the world could stop me from going to listen to him. And I would follow him to the very end!"

This amazing declaration from such a great teacher, who throughout his entire adult life relentlessly discouraged being a follower, must mean something. At the least it is a major admission of *something missing*.

***

There are of course countless references to the code in biology and neurobiology, in computer programming, in semantics and other areas of research but all fragmentary views. I have not seen anyone anywhere emphasize its omnipresence and everywhereness, nor explain how all the different *fields* of internal and external coding might be connected and interact.

This *missing insight* – both down the centuries and in modern times – is causing all sorts of tremendous issues in communication and understanding to this day, both in communication with ourselves and in communication with others, and in the exchanges between the two – the internal/external interface – that the Buddha so repeatedly hammered into his monks in discourses relating to *sati* and *satipatthana*, his main guide to clear seeing and antidote to not-seeing (ignorance).

Code and coding are in fact everpresent in all aspects of our daily life because whenever we use awareness, observation, thinking, speaking and other forms of language we are using code/coding.

It is present at every level inside the human mindbody and also present outside us in all forms of human behaviour and activity. It is present in all forms of organic life. So it is not confined to human beings. A cat couldn't cross the road without it.

> As a result of its *omnipresence* having so far not been spotted, its wider connections are missing from the understanding of mindbody.

In order to at least gain intellectual insight into the role of the code and coding for yoga purposes, let's together now examine what code *is* and what code *does*, remembering that what something is and what something does is not the same thing.

What Code is

A code is a connection between a similar representation and a non-similar representation with an agreement that one can stand in for the other.

> Not only does the stand-in sooner or later de facto replace the other but the *new connection* becomes a *third thing* taking on an existence of its own and further complicating matters!

The word 'agreement' itself is revealing. In the case of an internal connection becoming a code due to agreement, it implies there are two different parts of our thinking mind, one agreeing with the other. It takes 'two parties' to make any new agreement, isn't that so? And it takes 'two' to modify an old one. As the old saying goes '*It takes two to tangle*'. The sound of one hand clapping is silence.

> Find out for yourself which are the two parts of yourself that are agreeing with each other in order to be able to make any code. Or undo it.

If the agreement is a past agreement, then **habit** comes into it. And habit itself is none other than a past agreement, postponed into the future, used now.

Furthermore – and equally important – the active participation of imagination is required to establish the connections and convert them into *equations of identity*.

It is an agreement to pretend

The agreement to pretend consists in proposing **a** is identical to **b** when a and b are unlike (non-similar to) each other. Therefore, any such agreement to equate/identify a non-similar with a similar involves imagination, agreement, pretence, make believe and volition (the will to do so).

> "...all'inizio di questa costruzione, **a** è considerato come se fosse uguale a **b**...poi il *come se fosse* è dimenticato, eliminato dalla consapevolezza, che diventa un'ecuazione di identità con la sua conseguente inversione nell'ordine naturale delle cose."
>
> Michele Salmeri, Catania 1986

> "...at the beginning of this construction **a** is proposed *as if it were* identical to **b**...later the as if it were part of the proposition is forgotten, eliminated from conscious memory, and thus arises an equation of (**ab**solute) identity with the consequent inversion in the natural order of things."

By *inversion* Dr Salmeri means a "distortion" or "deformation" or "perversion" of factual truth as well as interfering in the natural sequence of cause and effect.

The agreement to pretend gets forgotten. Therefore this is precisely what has to be **remembered** *(sati)* in order to undo the consequences of the knot having been tied and embedded in the first place. Otherwise, each time a code is triggered, artificial feelings relating to **b** are experienced on the framework of the mindbody instead of the natural sensations pertaining to **a**!

> Note that **ab** in Latin and Latin-derived languages carries the clear connotation of "away from", "out of", "departure from".

Code making can be carried out consciously or unconsciously, in other words deliberately or without the slightest clue or idea – without realizing – what we are doing.

> *avijja paccaya sankhara*   not-seeing conditions code

In either scenario, not-seeing *(avijja)* involves not seeing the original causation of perturbation *(dukkha samudaya)*, which is tantamount to not seeing the Real Reality (Dharma) as it is, and, in its place, concocting codes, images and concepts into an artificial reality.

> Us humans are living together in a world of consensual illusion and fantasy, at least partly.

So whenever and wherever any such internal agreement is made inside us in the present, code is created and embedded at least provisionally in the mindbody (brain & nervous system). The human organism is thus seeded (embedded) with chains upon chains upon chains of thinking mind-made connections creating and maintaining all our coding, programming and conditioning.

I call these Tapes. This is what is binding us, limiting us, restricting and preventing freedom. This is the source of our complexes, inhibitions and pavlovian reactions. And it causes mechanical obstructions and restrictions in the natural flow of vital energy throughout the mindbody.

The mechanism of the code in every instance is based on an immediate connection between two different orders of reality, each **ab** connection becoming capable of triggering specific reactions/responses to **arb**itrary meanings, which themselves are a code.

"...the great danger of jumping from one level of coding to another level of coding – which we do all the time in daily life – is because if we don't see what we are doing, and don't decode properly, we are in a mess."

Dimovic 1987

As an example, neither the letters a, p, p, l, e, nor the spoken sound *apple* have anything whatsoever to do with a picture of an apple let alone a real apple. Both the written letters and the sound are non-similar to any apple. A photo or image is at least visually similar to an apple but non-similar in all other aspects. Yet by pretending and agreeing that the one can stand in for the other, the connection to the meaning 'apple' is immediately triggered.

All language is based on this extra-**ordinary** trick.

If we use pictures which are similar to the thing they represent, then this trick is less obvious. We can show a picture of an apple to anyone, even to a child, and providing they have prior experience of apples, they will get the meaning right away without any need for decoding.

In the absence of images, the code becomes *the essential tool* for doing this incredibly useful trick again and again, and in countless different ways on a daily basis. Neither computers nor mathematics could function without it. Neither could our thinking minds.

The code in fact, whether we realize it or not, has become an ubiquitous, omnipresent internal and external *tool*. A tool indispensable for encoding and decoding all exchanges going on at the interface between inside-outside events and between events belonging to different orders of reality.

We have defined what a code is. *But what precisely does it do?*

What a code **does**

A code adds or connects something to something else and causes *that change, that alteration* to make sensations in some way different. *It then uses these differences in sensations as code for meaning.*

But we must remember it is arbitrary. All **a** ≡ **b**s are arbitrary and human mind-made, and we must not lose sight of this fact if we want to avoid entanglements in our thinking mind – and entanglements in our brain and nervous system (mindbody) because such entanglements have specific repercussions on our energy and emotions.

An easy-to-understand trivial example illustrates this:

> Smith is an ardent football fan. Whenever 'his' team wins Smith is elated; whenever it loses, he is deflated. If his team draws he might be either or neither, depending. In all these scenarios the real 22 athletes plus real referee running around a real football field kicking a real ball around have absolutely no connection whatsoever with the different *disturbances* going on inside Smith's mind and nervous system before, during and after each match. Yet dependent on the coding Smith establishes, his mindbody is subjected to all sorts of changing sensations, feelings, emotions – some pleasant, some unpleasant, others neutral – which he would not otherwise have.

Absent identification, no such code gets formed. Absent the code, absent its effects.

sankhara nirodha viññana nirodha

Once it gets embedded...any code from the storehouse in our mindbody is susceptible to activation and getting its specific *meaning* triggered. This mostly happens involuntarily and unconsciously without any effort or intentionality on our part. The triggered meaning can be a feeling, a sensation, an emotion, an image or something at the conceptual level. It can be pleasant, unpleasant or neutral. In every case we tend to react automatically – not to the triggering event itself but to the pre-encoded interpretation (meaning). This is what the Pali word *asava* translated as bias is pointing to.

> The etymology of the Sanskrit word a-sava is non-knowing, the kind of non-knowing specifically caused by not-seeing something correctly or clearly. It has thus come to mean bias because improper knowing inevitably distorts comprehension/understanding.

From scientific experiments it has been shown that Pavlov's dog ends up reacting not to the arrival of food per se but to the bell (non-similar signal) announcing it. The dog has 'learnt' the sound of the bell equates to food.

Chapter 9 looks at how this insight is applied in satipatthana practice by remembering real aspects in every process and filtering out all artificial and false connections, interpretations and expectations.

If we remember to constantly apply this insight, it will speed up erasing phoney connections, free our mind from the bondage of pretence, bring an end to make-believe and fakery, and enable mind to focus on the Reality of Nature. Doing this will gradually rub out the tapes of codes so that vital breath can again flow evenly and properly, enabling us to see, feel and live life *as it is*! *Sati* is!

All codes are therefore tools. Like keys, they are a special kind of tool for locking and unlocking meaning, for storing meaning and for using meaning whenever required.

A same key can lock as well as unlock. The same key performs both operations and functions in forward and reverse order. Once the gateway is closed, if we have lost the key – forgotten how to open the lock – that part of our mind stays hidden from normal awareness! Locked and blocked to conscious access.

External codes in the world such as written language, billboards and signposts are a lot easier to understand than the complex layers of coding present inside the human body.

> "All concepts, all methods, all languages are codes."
> N. Dimovic – Safari on the Fundamentals of Reality 1997

We use codes as tools for meaning. Human beings surround themselves internally and externally with codes and tools. Some of these we can recognize easily, others are not so easy to spot, and some we have not yet even detected. Some of them are very useful, others less useful, most are neutral...but many are dangerous if used incorrectly, such as wrong concepts, wrong images, wrong conclusions.

In regard to codes/coding going on continuously inside our thinking mind, brain and nervous system, our bodymind is a **dynamic** continuum where three types of connections take place:

The first can be likened to a line drawn in water or the sound/vibration of a plucked guitar string – this kind fade away quickly leaving no enduring trace.

The second type are like footsteps in the desert soon blown away by the wind or like a line drawn in sand close to the seaside disappearing within 24 hours when washed away by the tide or other waves. Sleep does this job well.

These two types can be considered provisional or momentary coding, arising and ceasing quite quickly.

The third type is like a sentence carved in wood, stone or metal. Each of these is harder to erase. This type of coding can endure far longer, can even be transmitted from generation to generation, and is created/arises whenever a deep and repetitive impression is recorded/imprinted on structures inside our brain and nervous system. These impressions carry accompanying intense emotions and are the ones that bind us in chains and habit patterns hard to break. Nevertheless, the good news is that these too can be erased if they are confronted, remembered and recognized.

We can train ourselves to become aware of how we use, abuse and misuse codes and images, and how this has led to sacrificing the Real on the altar of the abstract (**ab**stract).

> "...the great danger of jumping from one level of coding to another – which we do all the time in daily life – is because if we don't see what we are doing, and don't decode properly, we are in a mess."

Once we realize this and start spotting the mischief that past and present coding creates, the consequences of which we are experiencing in our body and mind whenever triggered, we can begin the process of remembering to focus on what is really Real, thereby unwinding and unbinding as described in the *Satipatthana sutta* and *Yogasutra*.

Such yoga practice enables us to think more clearly, be more precise, more realistic and improve analysis and synthesis of what is really going on. It helps spot where we are going astray and avoid the trap of confusing one order of reality with another order of reality.

SN Goenka was uncomfortable with the standard interpretations into English of the word *sankhara* as 'conditioned things' or 'formations', and instead used 'reactions' in translation. This shows he was on the right track but his interpretation misses the encoding part of code – its construction – and focuses only on what happens when code gets triggered.

Buddhadhasa Bhikkhu did not speak English but he became famous as an original thinker – a nonconformist – who refused to accept what did not make sense to him in conventional interpretations of the texts and practice.

Most interpretations of **sankhara** go completely away from the Buddha's teaching by insisting that *sankhara* refers to anything and everything constructed or conditioned, and end up associating *sankhara* with the universal impermanence of all formations and conditions. They apply it to every kind of construct in the Cosmos and go completely off-track. This grave error has caused an unwarranted fixation on universal impermanence, and then they go on to somehow link universal impermanence with 'universal suffering'...

This has led countless buddhists to a gloomy and pessimistic outlook on Life. Yet the impermanence or provisionality of things is not in itself the problem. The fact that our sun is non-eternal and will one day pass away when the conditions maintaining it subside, is totally irrelevant to a meditator or yogi.

After all, *change* is the very Nature and Essence of Life. Life without change is inconceivable. How could life be otherwise? We would not even be alive without breathing in and breathing out and constant change.

Life cannot exist without oscillation; without disturbance.

The association of universal *dukkha* (suffering/unsatisfactoriness) with universal impermanence of everything formed in the Cosmos must have arisen as a cover up for the missing insight into the specific yoga path Gautama Buddha actually taught.

The notion of Cosmic and universal impermanence is totally irrelevant to the process of liberation – namely cleaning out the plumbing – and cannot be what the Buddha meant.

All these notions of Cosmic and universal impermanence and Cosmic and universal disturbance are clearly out of context and incorrect because Buddha was teaching solely about dukkha (misery/unsatisfactoriness) and how to put an end to it (*dukkha nirodha*).

Nothing else.

"I teach the origination of dukkha and the cessation of dukkha, nothing more."

Majjhima Nikaya 22.37

Two things and two things only: *samudaya dukkha* and *dukkha nirodha*. This is emphasized in countless discourses again and again.

"I teach the origination of dukkha and the cessation of dukkha, nothing more."

The teaching is solely about **psychemechanics**: about the specific *dukkha* that afflicts the mindbody of human beings, how this *dukkha* is generated and how it can be brought to a complete standstill (*dukkha nirodha*) – literally no more rolling in it.

The Buddha taught psychemechanics not cosmology

Therefore, to translate his three key propositions, the so-called three fundamental characteristics of existence (*trilaksana*) as:

all formations are impermanent	sabbe sankhara anicca
all formations are unsatisfactory	sabbe sankhara dukkha
all things are not-self	sabbe dhamma anatta

is completely wrong, makes no sense and has done untold damage down the ages to the extraordinary legacy of one of the greatest yogis and sages in history, whose heroic quest and effort is to set fellow human beings on the path of right knowledge, on the path to freedom from *dukkha* – whose origin is not-seeing the conditioning role of the code (*avidya paccaya sankhara*) on the life-force intelligence and our understanding of Life.

Thus, the three so-called characteristics of existence are not really such at all. Placed in a context of psychemechanics these three key phrases become crystal clear words of good news, of exhortation, of encouragement connected with the practice and methodology of *sati-patthana*, to wit:

"All codes and coding being mind-made constructs can be erased and wiped out."

How? By **remembering**! By reversing the process, by recovering the memory of the real events leading to the misconnection and erroneous construction of mind-made codes imprinted and embedded in the body.

Sati is remembering the Real in the Real, recovering the Real within each associated memory! Even if the specific details of the past event are not recalled, at least the sensations and associated emotions registe-red in the recording of that event, have to be relived on the framework of the mindbody.

> Relived, processed, digested, let go of, finished with.
> "Done is what had to be done! In such conditions there is no more of this or that: no more compulsive behaviour!"
> Arahant's declaration of victory

Thus the three propositions properly interpreted become:

all codes are non-enduring (provisional)	*sabbe sankhara anicca*
all codes are unsatisfactory	*sabbe sankhara dukkha*
all mental constructs are not-the-thing-itself	*sabbe dhamma anatta*

Chapter 2 explains that in this context here the word *dhamma* means all mental constructs including all ideas, concepts, codes, images – none of which are the 'Real Reality'.

No conceptualization, no idea can be the real Reality of Nature. No conceptualization, no idea can be what you really are, what Life really is.

The other problematic Sanskrit/Pali words

Sati

Therefore, *mindfulness* is an inadequate and misleading translation for *sati* because it leaves out the key aspect of remembering/recollecting/recognizing which is central to *satipatthana*, and at the very heart of all yoga.

The semantic similarity between the ancient Pali language spoken at that time and Sanskrit reinforces this interpretation.

Sati in Pali सति and Sati in Sanskrit: सती as the goddess's name is written the same but with ती in mirror image. (smrti in Sanskrit is स्मृति). Moreover, the word *sati* in Sanskrit – in addition to the goddess's name – also means noble, authentic, true deriving from the Sanskrit word *sat* – truth, existence.

Our true nature and the true Nature of Reality are one and the same – like the drop of salt water and the ocean. All images, all codes, all concepts, all mental constructs whatsoever (*sabbe dhamma*) are only representations of Reality – *Korzybski maps*! – not the territory itself, not the Real Nature. Not the Real Deal.

The meaning of *sabbe dhamma anatta* is exactly that.

Therefore, the translation of *sati* that best fits with satipatthana's specific purpose of decoding is either *remembering* (the Real) or *recollection of* (the Real).

From SN Goenka's letter (in appendix) you can see he chose 'awareness' as translation for the Pali word *sati*, not 'mindfulness'.

In fact, several Western scholars have voiced concerns that *mindfulness* is an incorrect translation for *sati*.

> The concept of *mindfulness* in modern day practice of vipassana causes the meditator to focus on watching the crowd rather than recognizing the individual people. Thus the practice is rendered less precise and may fail to achieve the goal of yoga.
>
> Of course, mindfulness is better than negligence or heedlessness but *you can be mindful till the cows come home – for years on end even – and still not 'get it' because 'getting it' requires actually recognizing and remembering what you are looking at!*

It requires remembering that which has been forgotten or lost.

The proof of this is in Chapter 4, where Siva in the legendary story of Siva and Sati, does not recover Sati, his *lost Shakti*, until he recognizes and remembers her.

Yoga is about remembering the Real. How else can a yogi or yogini obtain release from the bondage and unsatisfactoriness of codes and coding? How else pierce the veils of *Maya* and *Mara?*

Mindfulness though a laudable quality is certainly not enough. Awareness needs to discern between the Real and the phoney; needs to recognize the thief, catch him red-handed and not just watch him mindfully while he engages in robbery after robbery!!

The thinking mind is the thief of *ananda*, and who readily volunteers to be the policeman! It's no use being passively mindful of him as he goes about one job after another. You have to recognize and remember the precise psychemechanics of the thief's behaviour and put an end to the mischief! Only then can we fully breathe in the pure fresh air of *sat chit ananda*.

Vijñāna (Sanskrit) **| viññāṇa** (Pali)
Viññana is another tricky word with a number of distinct meanings depending on context:

> *understanding; awareness; life-force intelligence; consciousness; mind; discernment*

In the context of the vicious circle of Dependent Origination formulated by Gautama Buddha after his realization of the fundamental cause of *dukkha* – namely ignorance of the code; not-seeing the code – the best choice is *life-force intelligence.*

This is discussed in detail in Chapter 8, Satipatthana.

Yet specifically in the context of any of the senses –

- eyes, sight and visible patterns
- ears, hearing and audible patterns
- body, touch and feelable sensations
- tongue, taste and savours
- nose, sniffing and aromas
- mind, thinking and mental constructs

a good general translation for *viññana* is 'awareness' (as defined below in the problematic English words list) since awareness is that part of the thinking mind that watches and gets feedback from what is going on in each of the six sense fields.

Nevertheless, in the formulation of Dependent Origination *viññana* means *life-force intelligence.*

Dukkha

The word *dukkha* has no single English equivalent covering its wide range of connotations. If we want to find the widest universal term then 'disturbance' *or* 'perturbation' or 'disturbing' come close to dukkha's very wide inclusive meaning.

I have chosen un**sati**sfactoriness because of the play on the word **sati**, which is the key to recovering the lost **sati**sfaction of existence.

Sat chit ananda!

***

Problematic words in Western languages

Consciousness
Ether
Awareness
Mind
Thought (thinking, imagining...)

Banished from mainstream scientific understanding since the 1900s, the Ether is now making a 'comeback' – thanks to common sense prevailing!

Consciousness together with **Ether** is discussed in Chapter 12 in relation to Yoga and Samkhya's *Prakriti & Purusha*.

You might be surprised to know there is no consensus among the scientific community – including medicine, psychology and philosophy – on the precise meaning of **Consciousness, Mind, Awareness** and **Thought**, nor the relationship between them. Yet these words are liberally sprinkled around like salt and pepper in everyday conversations as well as used in serious scientific papers and discussions as if everyone knows and understands what they are talking about! But there is still no clear understanding among scientists or philosophers or the yoga community, let alone the general public, on what these most important words are pointing to.

What code *is* and what code *does* has already been explained in detail. Here we apply this explanation by showing the fundamental role of the code in relation to Awareness, Mind, Thought and Imagination, and the connection to each other.

Awareness

The omnipresence of the Code is missing from human perception and understanding because – like the 10th man in the lifeboat – awareness somehow forgets to count itself.

> "The awareness itself is also a code." – Dimovic

The thinking mind makes codes for everything. Why would it not make a code to stand in for itself? It does.

Awareness is the master code – the "I"-code – the one that gets the feedback from all the "non-I" codes.

And this I-code is constructed in exactly the same way as any other code (as explained before) by connecting a similar with a non-similar and agreeing to pretend they are the same, when they are not the same. Thereby creating an equation of identity through *idem*-tification.

Remember every code is a connection of **a** and **b** which arises as something *third* and takes on an **ab** existence of its own, conjured out of thin air like FIAT currency. In the case of awareness, the two non-similar things that are connected together are the participating, sensing part of ourselves and the observing, thinking part of ourselves. Participation gets equated with observation and observation gets equated with participation *as if they were one and the same thing*. But they are not the same. Observation is observation and participation is participation.

> Watching a football game is not the same as playing in a football game!

Among all the multitude of sets of disturbances arising and ceasing inside us, one particular set or group of disturbances is the most repetitive, most similar and the one present – when we are present – in the waking state or in the dreaming state. This most often occurring repetitive similar set of disturbances ends up being recognized by us as standing for ourselves. All less repetitive, non-similar sets of disturbances are recognized as "not-I".

The fact that certain disturbances occur at one and the same time or close by does not mean they are the same. They are not. The connection or nexus of identity is artificial and arises between the observing thinking part of ourselves and the participating sensing feeling part of ourselves. This connection creates the "I-code" which arises as something *third* taking on an imaginary 'life' of its own.

All other oscillations and disturbances are less repetitive ones which come and go depending on circumstances and conditions.

***

The brain and nervous system can be visualized as a tree with many lights on its different parts. Lights of different intensities, sizes, shapes and colours. Some of these lights are "on" all the time we are awake, but all the other lights come on only intermittently, now and then, sporadically. We end up recognizing and associating the ones which are always "on" when we are 'on' (awake) as standing for us. It's as simple as that, and as deeply subtle as that.

Awareness too comes and goes and is dependent on the states of being awake, dreaming or deep sleep. In deep sleep the sense of "I", "me", "myself" and "mine" is gone (absent i.e. not-then-present).

The awareness of our self therefore is a code, a stand-in, not the real "I", not our real Reality. Real Reality continues to be present throughout the three states of waking, dream and deep sleep. The thinking mind is provisionally switched off in deep sleep and is therefore only able to report not noticing anything.

The awareness – the master-code – can also be seen as the connection between the image of oneself (itself a creation of thought in our internal cinema) and the most repetitive sensations of disturbance we experience.

Thus, **awareness itself is a code** – the master-code, the master tool – able to get feedback from all the other codes, likewise concocted from connections between similars and non-similars. In this way our entire internal cinema is built up and acts as a **dynamic** interactive representation of the Real World of Nature.

sabbe dhamma anatta
Awareness is that which is closest to us, gives us our sense of existing and being, and enables us to act and perform as human beings.

> I
> I think
> I think I...lo and behold there are two of us!

Examples abound. The fact that in everyday speech we say
"I think I will do such and such..." or,
"I feel like I should do sports today..." or,
"I enjoyed myself at the conference..."

Countless such daily usages of "I think I..."; "I feel I..."; "I am afraid I..." are revealing and prove the correctness of the above insight that awareness itself is a code. Stop a moment and ask yourself (got it!).

> "Stop a minute! What's going on here?! What are the implications of this ongoing dialogue between a thinking "I" and a participating "I"?!

It shows the Buddha was absolutely correct in stating and emphasizing that every conceptualization of "I" or "self" is not the real self, not-I – not the 'real deal'.

> *sabbe dhamma anatta* – no code, no image, no concept is the Reality of Nature.

That this applies to the entirety of Nature including us will be seen in Chapter 3, Artificial World vs Real World.

Mind

Mind has three aspects, perhaps having correspondences to our different brains though this lies outside the scope of this book. Yoga's primary focus is on integrating.

- Nature's Mind
- Heartmind
- Thinking mind

Mind of Nature or 'deep mind' is that optimizing intelligence operating throughout the mindbody's processes and systems manifesting a homeostasis-maintaining/optimizing tendency at every level. The mind of Nature has embedded the body with its own DNA and RNA coding in such a way as to create/organize/sustain/adjust countless processes automatically and continuously without the thinking mind needing to intervene or pay conscious attention to the myriad details.

Heart-mind is related to awareness and awareness has its seat in the heart-centre. It has its own homeostasis and homeostasis tendency and is concerned above all with feeling and direct sensing in the present moment. Heart-mind reflects the experience of Existence and Continuity. It feels in the now any and all real actions/events perceived going on in the world as well as reactions triggered internally by codes and coding imprinted by the thinking mind.

Thinking mind is a difference hunter and merchant of connections. The thinking mind builds up a dynamic aggregate of codes, images and concepts into a mental representation which, once acquired, acts as a tool for making sense out of the experience of Life. Thinking mind over the course of time creates and builds up an elaborate internal cinema of consensual, representational knowledge which sustains, modifies and refines itself through an endless ongoing game of mental tennis.

Codes, images and concepts get mistaken for the real events they represent and many of their meanings maintain an unclear relationship with the real world of Nature. Thus the mind frequently mistakes the **ab**stract for the Real and gets entangled in a web of confusion.

For hundreds of years, if not thousands of years, Mind | Matter has been thought of as the 'fundamental division of everything'. This main division of everything is also called 'spirit and matter'. Either way, this conceptual division did not satisfy yogis of ancient times who sought to resolve the fundamental cause of vi-yoga – of separation.

Direct insight into the true Nature of Reality whether through *gnana yoga, satipatthana, vedanta* or *samkhya* brings the thinking mind to a standstill, revealing that a more fundamental division of everything is **pushes** and **patterns**. Or if you prefer to use the engineering equivalent – **stresses** and **strains**.

This means that both the **software** aspect of **mind**body and the **hardware** aspect of mind**body** are both mechanical – as mechanical as a computer – and that the 'mirror of Consciousness' is something quite else.

In Newtonian mechanics it is not possible to separate the push from a moving billiard ball carrying the push yet it is clear the push and the carrier of the push are not the same. The guitar string and the vibration of the guitar string are clearly not the same thing yet both acting jointly together are indispensable to creating melody. One thing is the music and another thing the instrument which – whenever 'disturbed' – produces it.

Because we do not perceive energy, forces, vibrations, pushes or stresses unless – and only if – they are directly touching and affecting us, we nevertheless can see their outside effects in the form of changing appearances, patterns, waves, movements, arrangements, strains and shapes (including those of our own bodily structure) and so we fail to understand the interaction of both together as **psychemechanical** in nature.

And instead fancifully ascribe to forces and pushes mysterious non-physical attributes and properties.

But because both the push and the pattern happen so fast, so simultaneously and so close by, the thinking mind which is par excellence *a difference hunter and merchant of connections,* associates them, connects them and agrees to pretend to itself that push and pattern are one and the same thing, when in fact they are *neither one nor the same.*

By creating spurious arbitrary connections of identity between pushes felt and patterns seen, *something third* – the **ab** – arises and takes on a life of its own as a code or as an image (which also ends up behaving as a code). Either way the **ab** is a departure from the Reality of Nature.

Whenever the thinking mind thinks and talks to itself, it is engaged in recognizing and establishing 'differences', and then interpreting these differences to itself, all of which are always code related, therefore purely conceptual, and a departure from similarity or sameness.

As an example. The word '*tree*' exists to point to the concept '*tree*' which englobes the similarities of shape, structure and behaviour of every known kind of tree regardless of differences. There are thousands of types of trees but it is their similarities which the concept '*tree*' latches onto – not their differences.

> With language and thinking structured as it is, it is hard to see how it could be done otherwise. But we must bear in mind that the similarity between images of trees ignores the differences.

So, we have a curious situation here – the thinking mind on the one hand is a *difference hunter* and at the same time a *merchant of connections!*

The thinking mind in fact spends its time and energy dividing and differentiating. At the same time another part of it is engaged in connecting and putting together what it has divided without quite ever being able to achieve this satisfactorily.

This is exhausting work! and a reason why for several hours in every 24-hour cycle the thinking mind has to switch off completely and have a good rest. Otherwise it can become seriously unbalanced.

Thinking/Thought

Thinking is basically talking to oneself making new connections and coding. Guided by an innate tendency to optimize – to seek advantage – thinking's impulse is to seek and secure the best situation in every circumstance. Thought is ever on the lookout for gain of some sort. The advantage may be real or imaginary. And it will involve avoiding, overcoming, maintaining and cultivating. The problem is the thinking mind so often loses the plot because of the many layers of coding. Because coding (*sankhara*) to a certain definite extent deforms the natural order of cause and event.

Imagination

The discussion of imagination and its role as co-creator with the Mind of Nature co-creating an 'artificial' world – which to a certain extent displaces and replaces the Real World of Nature – is the subject of Chapter 3.

***

Chapter 2: DIM | Dharma

Dharma

A profound and vitally important key term to understand in yoga is *dharma* (Sanskrit), *dhamma* (Pali), *tao* (Chinese), and *dó* (Japan).

This word permeates the entirety of ancient Indian and Asian literature: Vedic, post-Vedic, Jain, Buddhist, Tantric – you name it, it comes up everywhere in all sorts of contexts, under all sorts of guises and disguises.

The word *dharma* has come to have so many meanings in different contexts – even completely different meanings – and in the writings of different teachers down the ages, that there is no alternative but to respectfully park it to one side, and introduce in its place the best word for each of its four main meanings.

Four different key meanings of the word Dharma

After checking over a dozen meanings of the word *dharma* the proposal here in *Yoga Beyond the Thinking Mind* is to focus on four principal meanings and understand these clearly, their differences and the relationship between them:

1. *Dharma* as Nature, the Real World of Nature, Reality
2. *Dharma* referring to '*mental constructs*' i.e. all images/all **codes**/all concepts
3. *Dharma* as teaching or doctrine
4. *Dharma* referring to *homeostasis*, and the *homeostasis tendency of Nature*. This meaning is extremely important to grasp and may be new to many readers.

The first three concepts you are no doubt familiar with. The fourth needs careful attention/explanation as it is fundamental to Life in general and to yoga practice in particular.

This way confusion can be avoided and clarity gained!

Imagine a house with 17 people in it all called 'Smith'. How on earth can anyone be certain who is being called out at any given moment? So, let's be sensible and practical and have one clear word for each key concept the word *dharma* stands for.

1. Reality; the Real World of Nature
This meaning of dharma will be further illustrated in Chapter 3, Real World vs Artificial World. It refers to the entirety of the Real World that sciences are studying and trying to get to grips with through the use of the scientific method and tools for probing beyond what we can perceive with our ordinary senses.

2. Mental constructs i.e. images, codes and concepts (which are all codes)
The second meaning refers to the entirety of our *mental cinema* whose images, codes and concepts together constitute what is called 'knowledge'. There is a whole science of knowledge called epistemology. In the context of yoga, Patanjali defines seven kinds of knowledge: knowledge from direct experience, deduction, testimony, illusion, fantasy, memory and dream.

It is interesting to note here that etymologically the word *dharma*'s most literal meaning is 'carrier' or 'bearer' and that fits precisely with what an image, or a code, or a concept does, which is act as a *carrier* of a specific meaning.

Both a picture of 'apple' or the word 'apple' carries us in our mind to the real apple. And 'apple-ness' is englobed by the concept 'apple' though neither the picture, the word nor the concept is the Real World apple. They are only different forms of representing apple.

3. Teaching | Doctrine
This meaning is clear so whenever the word *dharma* is used in this sense, the word 'teaching' can be used instead.

4. DIM | Dim Tendency
Right away in this chapter we need to make clear this fourth meaning by introducing a new modern word, DIM, pointing to a clear concept with clear connections to the Real World.

> Immense gratitude here to my godfather Dr Nebojsa Dimovic (b. Serbia 1904 – d. London 1993) whose lifelong research into physics, mathematics and philosophy yielded a synthesis full of innovative insights, in which the realization of the OMNIPRESENCE of DIM and Dim tendency plays a vital role. The word DIM is not chosen because his name is Dimovic nor because those close to him affectionately call him 'Dimmy', but because DIM stands for a '*dimensionless dimension*' of quality, of optimization, and allows for a-dim (out of dim), dim-over and dim-under, as well as being an anagram of 'mid'. Moreover, its sound is close to the sound of *dhamma* and *dharma*.

In ancient times most transmissions of knowledge were made orally and to a select few students at a time. Even discourses to gatherings of monks (*sangha*) at the time of the Buddha or his contemporary Mahavir (Jain *sangha*) went unrecorded and were only written down hundreds of years later. During those early generations of followers the discourses relied on memory and transmission down the line orally through repetition and rotation.

So, it is truly amazing what has survived and come down to us over 2500 years later, and we must be grateful for that!

Most students of yoga do not have the luxury of enough spare time to go back thousands of years to check whether the reporters or commentators recorded correctly, and above all whether they made a right interpretation or a wrong interpretation of the meaning attributed to key words and phrases.

It is also possible that differences in pronunciation at that time provided listeners with the clue as to which meaning the speaker was referring to.

Moreover, we know from our own experience in life that words change meanings over time, and in different contexts, sometimes even in a single generation. And the same words (vocabulary) can vary in meaning in different geographical locations.

Even in different branches of science – which tries to be clear and precise – the same word can and does have different meanings.

The Spanish spoken at the time of Columbus has little resemblance to the hip slang of today's Spain. The English spoken 200 years ago – let alone Shakespeare's English! – is quite unlike that spoken in North America today. Even in the last 40 years languages are changing quite rapidly because language is not only a pointer to concepts and images but also a carrier of emotion, an expression of sentiment and feeling. And these change over time according to cultural shifts in perception.

Already Aristotle pointed this out in ancient Greece. The ancient Greeks were fussy about precision, and quite rightly so, because if we are not precise in our language, how can we be precise in our thinking? And thinking to a large extent is talking to ourselves.

So, with apologies, we now introduce this new word DIM together with a clear definition of its meaning and connection to the Real World and by doing so, we help resolve the monumental confusion surrounding *dharma*, *dhamma* and *tao*.

DIM | Dim tendency

The Chinese concepts of *tao* 陶 and harmony 和諧 come closest to what we are pointing to with the new terms DIM and Dim tendency.

> There exists in Nature, in the Cosmos, a general law or tendency which has been spotted and studied both by ancient and modern researchers. It has been given many names.

In some sciences the name given to it is *homeostasis*. But homeostasis is not confined to physiological situations and equilibrium mechanics (Newtons laws). Its action is basic, fundamental, all-pervasive and omnipresent. The force of its action, its intelligence, its influence, its push, as far as we can determine, is as constant and relentless as the force of gravity or the tides of the oceans. In fact, gravity is one of its most obvious manifestations.

It is the force in Nature which tends to guide things into the best position, to the position of least conflict, to what we call "normal", to a position of optimum 'balance' within prevailing circumstances and conditions. And then maintain this best position.

Bear in mind though that what this "best" or "optimal" really is may have little or nothing to do with human value judgments or concepts about what is "best".

For example, the DIM temperature of the human body is 37° C. We have not chosen this through any intellectual assessment of what is best for us. It happens to be that way because the overall DIM of Nature has made it that way for our body. We may ask why or how but we cannot question the fact of it.

If our temperature rises above 37° we have a fever (dim-over). If our temperature falls below 37° we feel chilly (dim-under). Either way we are 'disturbed' and if the disturbance goes too far in either direction it is dangerous for our health – for the continuity of our existence – and may result in death and disintegration.

It is called DIM because it tends towards the "dimensionless dimension" of relational optimization. As such it is qualitative rather than quantitative.

It tends towards what we commonly call normal, better, balanced, best, optimum or correct.

Dimensions of length, height, depth, duration, weight and so forth are all measured in a quantitative way. DIM is a **dynamic**, qualitative *dimensionless dimension.* It can be measured as in the case of our body temperature. Or as in the case of gravity.

The Dim tendency actively corrects imbalances and disturbances unless prevented by a superior force. DIM can be seen to operate throughout Nature at every level – vibrational, elastic, mechanical, chemical, electrical, electromagnetic, nuclear, gravitational – and is therefore also observable at the psychological, biological, neurological and organic level.

The Chinese word and concept **tao** comes close but it became too vague, and the writers who use it seem to forget or overlook that *yin* and *yang* are no more than deformations of tao. Yin and yang down the ages somehow got conceptually disconnected from tao, and tao got separated conceptually from yin and yang, to such an extent that their useful meanings and application got lost.

Let's stay now with DIM and Dim tendency!

Dimover | DIM | Dimunder

dimover and dimunder can be expressed simply as a-dim (out of dim).

So, there is a position or state in all things and in any *aggregates* of things which human beings can rightly describe as best or optimum or normal or harmonious or balanced or correct and such similar terms. All these terms and concepts point to a *dimensionless dimension* of quality. Because of this the easy, clear and short word DIM is chosen to cover this vital concept.

DIM is the fundamental force inherent in Nature which always guides or tends to guide and push things to their best position, to what we can call normal, to the position of least conflict (harmony) within any given prevailing conditions and circumstances.

Every single thing in the Cosmos is continuously acted on by the Dim tendency, and therefore is either now in a DIM state or in an out-of-dim state (dimover | dimunder) but tending back to DIM.

This applies at every level: from the most micro level of very minute things all the way through the spectrum to the macro level of the very biggest things. It applies near at hand and far away. It applies inside us and outside us, and to the interaction between the inside and the outside.

It operates sometimes very slowly, sometimes very quickly depending if there are obstacles preventing its action. Myriad things, large and small, all jockeying for a better position, all traveling at different speeds and in different directions, causing endless collisions, conflicts and disturbances, all the while each bearing inherent Dim tendency – all pushes – driving everything along a path to a better overall position and better state.

Amazing mind-bewildering complexity. But the fundamental principle is simple, clear and apparent.

> Important to repeat: *Nature's own inherent intelligence or understanding of what is "best", or what is required to re-establish order, to re-establish equilibrium and harmony may have little or nothing to do with human value judgments and conceptions of what is best or not best. Humans simply do not have enough information to know the full picture.*

A sudden avalanche or a mud slide is not a happy circumstance for human beings in the wrong place at the wrong time. Neither is it nice to be caught in the path of a typhoon or a hurricane. Sitting for long hours immobile in meditation can be agony as blockages are confronted by the Dim tendency. More about this in Chapter 5, Asana.

You will see in later chapters that the understanding of 'DIM and Dim tendency' becomes incredibly useful for yoga practice (*raja yoga, gnana yoga, kriya yoga, hatha yoga* etc.) especially when practicing stillness *asana*.

It also greatly enhances awareness and understanding about what is going on in daily life outside ourselves, inside ourselves and the interaction between the two. It can greatly help you get through tough moments in daily life knowing that the presence and action of the DIM is ever present, never absent. DIM can be prevented and delayed – but only provisionally – by a-dim forces.

Aligning with DIM is the essence of all yogas

What is called the body's defence mechanism – also called immune system – is a manifestation of DIM. Every single cell in the body is guided by its own inherent DIM.

> "...an important principle of homoeostasis (is) that the corrective mechanism is triggered by the very entity which is to be regulated.
>
> In other words, homoeostasis involves a self-adjusting mechanism, the control process being inbuilt into the system..."
>
> Michael Roberts (Biology – A Functional Approach)

If not interfered with – if allowed to – this inbuilt Dim tendency will tend to settle conflict and disturbance. It will tend to cool conditions down. This aspect is seen, for example, in the laws relating to thermodynamics. Its tendency is to calm things down, to settle them into an optimal relatively steady state, guiding them towards harmony, non-conflict, ease, quiescence, stillness, nirvana.

Gautama Buddha's emphasis on avoiding extremes, on temperance, on the MID reflects exactly this understanding. Indeed, this tendency of Nature always tries to find the mean, the norm, the neutral, the middle path, the best position given available circumstances.

***

"As you know I keep on opposing – as a system for teaching and for acquiring usefully applicable knowledge – the oriental way of expression because they always end up confusing the specific and saying things like 'night and day are the same thing!'

"As to Yin & Yang, most of the contemporary writers miss the point. There is something in yang and yin. The original discoverers thousands of years ago must have been fairly clear as to their meanings. But all of the authors that I have come across manage to make it all so weak, so vague and so all-inclusive that little if anything is left. I recently pointed out the mis-connectoring to you and showed you the need for a precise definition of yang and yin. And that this definition cannot leave out the neutral – what they probably meant by tao, the DIM."

Nebosja Dimovic, from a talk on yin and yang

The concept of entropy in science – if extended to include all kinds of changes – is related to the DIM or Dim tendency but the concept 'entropy' itself seems to be confused by human value judgments – prejudice/bias – about what constitutes *order* and *disorder*. Same with chaos theory.

Certainly, Nature seems to have her own inbuilt sense of ordering and arranging based on what we can only term "best". From the above it becomes easier to accept that each moment in Life is in fact a DIM moment, however grim *it* may appear in comparison to other real or imagined past or future DIMs since *it* – in its particular context of relativity – is the *best* given prevailing conditions and circumstances.

"Don't confuse DIM with Dim tendency!!" – Dimovic

If we consider this carefully and deeply, we can go on to see that each subatomic particle, each atom, every molecule – in fact every component making up the our-size tangible Reality of Nature – each of them individually and all of them collectively carry a Dim tendency. And therefore at every moment things are either in a DIM state or tending towards one. Each component of whatever aggregate or process, whether large or small, far or near, dense or subtle, fast or slow, however interfered with and disturbed, carries its own inbuilt DIM mechanism, its own Dim tendency.

Millions of tiny little DIMs jostling around together somehow end up making a new collective DIM and then lots of those collective DIMs combine together with others to make up a Big DIM and so on.

This means that COOPERATION is intelligent and looks far more fundamental to the inherent behaviour of the Cosmos than conflict or competition.

And because all things are not going in the same direction, it is only natural that sooner or later things start acting as obstacles (preventors) to the Dim tendency of other things. Therefore there will inevitably be conflict and struggle going on between DIMs. But *providing* it is not further interfered with – in which case the "Big DIM" is delayed – it all works out for the best sooner or later. The patience of the DIM is unfathomable!

> By interference I mean fresh new obstacles entering the picture and colliding.

From the observation of specific instances of DIM visible in everyday life and confirmed by science, we can make a reasonable assumption that the Dim tendency of Nature extends throughout all orders of Reality. However, the biological growth of the code interacting with the human being's own mind-made coding can make this difficult to spot.

> We can see that there seems to be a direct link between the Dim tendency and gravity mentioned in Chapter 12 (Consciousness | Ether).

In the realm of *thinking* and *feeling* we can see how psychologically the human organism is pushed by this Dim tendency under the influence of a basically fourfold compulsion:

1. Overcome disturbance (a-dim disturbance) which arises in the present moment (by disturbance is meant *any* perceived dimover or dimunder) (here feeling comes in with its momentary wisdom of the present)
2. Avoid disturbance not yet present
   (here the DIM of intelligent practical thinking/forecasting comes in)
3. Maintain the state of ease and harmony which is present
   (scope of feeling)
4. Cultivate states of ease and harmony not yet present
   (scope of thinking)

We can furthermore see that in present moments of feeling, the feeling itself has undeniable DIM-related wisdom but only a momentary wisdom valid for each instant.

> The P and the F of thinking however is the one which brings in – by comparison – the consideration of (remembered) past DIMs and (imagined or predicted) future DIMs.

This means that the DIM operates even through to the thinking which in turn implies that causality may not be completely lost in the arbitrary connection between the similar representation and the non-similar representation discussed in Chapter 1, Language & Code.

> (This assumption could perhaps be applied with advantage to quantum mechanics.)

Making artificial connections – wrong connectoring – is therefore bound to cause interference in the Dim tendency and upset the natural sequence of things, disturbing the harmonious flow of the life force, whose intelligence, if left unimpeded, is to move towards an ever better position (greater harmony as a whole).

But we need to remember and not forget that Nature's sense of *better* may have little or nothing to do with our own self-centred, biased, ignorant, prejudiced ideas of better!

The Dim tendency therefore is **omnipresent** and operates at every level – vibrational, elastic, mechanical, chemical, electrical, electromagnetic, nuclear, gravitational – and therefore also at the psychological and emotional levels.

Recorded TALKS with Dimovic, London, 1987

Talk 1

S: I'd like to discuss this evening this question of *pain* and *pleasure* and *like* and *dislike*. I'd like to leave the question of neutral feeling and *neutral states* out of it for the time being. Afterwards we can come back to that. I would like to hear your views on this question of pain and pleasure because, as far as I can see, they are already a reaction, already an interpretation by something in the nervous system. It's already a reaction. And then comes the reaction to this reaction which we can call a secondary reaction, which is us liking the pleasure and disliking the pain. Do you follow my question?

D: I follow you.

S: Whenever we are not in the neutral we seem to be swinging like a pendulum between pain and pleasure, dislike and like. We are chasing after pleasure and running away from pain. This seems to be the only mechanism which drives sentient beings onwards. How would you analyze deeply this question of pain and pleasure already being a reaction, already being an interpretation?

D: Well, at the beginning of this long sentence of yours you said that you wanted to leave out the neutral...

S: I want to come to that afterwards.

D: What I'm saying is that you cannot leave it out. It is the basis of pleasure and pain. In fact pleasure and pain are no more than a *defor-mation* of the neutral. And by neutral – it's the wrong word in this connection – it is really some sort of a best state, what the ordinary language uses the word 'best' for. Or the 'correct' or 'right'. There is in everything in the universe, depending on the location and the timing of it, a 'best' for that particular location and that particular time. We discussed it in a different way about two hours ago when we said that this best or neutral is there only for a moment or for a little longer period of time but, because of the changing context and the changing circumstances, this *best* changes, and because of that *change,* that best is also all the time changing.

Nevertheless, at any particular time, it exists. And any deformation of that *best* is what in the East has been called the *yin* and the *yang*, what we in chemistry and physics call *ions* and what in ordinary language we call *incorrect* or *wrong*. But it's all very vague. In the universe there is one precise mechanism and this is that, because of the different forces and the different conditions that at one particular time exist at one particular spot, there is a *best* condition for them. And during that period, that particular system we are looking at this moment, wants to be in the *best* condition. If it is under or over or bigger or smaller, it wants to come back to the *best*. And it will do that if it can and if the circumstances around have not yet changed to alter it to a different kind of neutral or different kind of best.

S: Yes. I see what you mean.

D: So you can't separate the pain and the pleasure, which is only an aspect of a particular *yin* and *yang*, particularly in the case of human beings or animals or any living being that has a nervous system. Because pain and pleasure is not experienced as pain or pleasure *unless* there is an awareness of this *best*. Once there is the awareness of this best – what I call the DIM – not because of Dimovic but because it's the dimension which is the Number One Dimension.

S: Yes, dimensions are different from measures or quantities.

D: Yes, measures are always connected with numbers but you can have dimension-less units like in the case of a circle. A circle as such is dimension-less because it can then go on to have any size depending. So, you have this principal dimension which I call the DIM and anything that is out of DIM is either a dim-over or a dim-under. This concept applies to the whole universe and does not relate only to some narrow part of it. It happens in anything and everything. It is the homeostat of everything but in a most general term. It's really a dimensionless homeostat, which then always tends to the neutral or to the DIM or to the best or to the correct.

S: This applies to all areas of physics too?

D: In everything, everything, everything.

S: In metals?

D: In everything, absolutely everything.

S: In every operation.

D: In everything, in everything, in everything. In every thought, in every feeling. We always tend to...

S: Would you call it the tendency towards non-conflict?

D: Yes, yes, yes, yes, yes. That's correct. So, you can't leave out the neutral.

Talk 2

D: As there was no name to describe exactly what I mean ...

S: There's no name for it, is there? That's a problem.

D: When there is no name for something that is a problem.

S: You call it DIM?

D: I call it DIM. But the only thing I have against this word is that people will say, "Aha, he did it because of Dimovic!" It's not. It's because it's the number one Dimension. And I used a short name for it in order to distinguish it from the word homeostat or homoeostasis to which people are already used and in order to make it possible to make dim-over or dim-under or whatever we decide we will use for the state that is too much or too little. For instance, when you pump up your football as a child or your bicycle tyre, you go on pumping,

pumping, pumping – it's still dim-under, dim-under, dim-under, dim-under until it's just right to play the game or to ride on. Then it's in the DIM state. But you can go on pumping, then it becomes too hard and finally it bursts.

S: Yes. So what do you call that state? The one that goes beyond the...

D: Well, I call the right state 'DIM', too little of it I call dim-under and the other one I called dim-more or dim-over or something similar – I've forgotten now – it was some continuation of DIM, I can't remember which now. It's not important. The point is that certain new names, with apologies, are going to have to be brought into all this. To stand for certain new concepts.

S: Of course.

D: We should try and give names which are easy to remember and which are not confusing with other things, if we can.

Talk 3

S: One of the things I have spotted very, very clearly recently is the *push mechanism* in the brain. The whole brain is geared for a single purpose. I have seen in a very general way that the whole brain mechanism is geared to advantage, to the seeking of advantage. Every single thought, every single movement, every single mental process seems to be – whether consciously or not so consciously – with a view to advantage.

D: Well, you remember our conversation when you told me about this girl? I was saying exactly that, wasn't I?

S: Yes, perhaps in different words.

D: I was saying, look, you can't do anything else. Don't blame her, because it wasn't...you didn't love her because of *her*. You loved her because you love to feel the feeling of love. Because you like to feel

fine and I kept repeating to you and saying, "there is no other way, there is a homeostat in us and the Dim tendency is such that we must feel better all the time and no matter what you do, when you do it or how you do it, you only try that one thing".

S: That is right.

D: You always think you do it for some other reason but in the end it's always that.

S: Yes, fundamentally we are chasing pleasure and running away from pain.

D: That's it.

S: That's the only mechanism...

D: DIM is the only mechanism Nature has given us. Yes.

S: That's the only mechanism.

D: Yes, because out-of-Dim, if it goes too far or to a large extent, can destroy you.

S: If there's too much or too little of whatever?

D: Yes, if it goes too far either way it destroys you. So you resist it. And you don't resist it for any particular reason. You resist it because it is the basic intelligence we carry because, as Newton said, to every action there is a reaction. The Third Law.

S: Equal and opposite reaction. Equalizing reaction. So Dim is related to Newton's Second and Third laws.

D: That's right. Newton two and three express that fundamental and immediate reaction towards a new DIM for each party involved in a collision.

Talk 4

D: We don't know exactly how the DIM works but it must be...you know, we can only deduce it.

S: I can't see anything else being the case, can you, unless memory of pleasure and pain.

D: Well that's basic.

S: Our memory of pleasure and pain seems to be our basic compulsion (along with the tendency to ignore what is neutral).

D: That's the basic difference and then you go on differentiating from there. That's our final judge.

S: That's the basic push-mechanism inside us, isn't it? Our basic compulsion.

D: Whoever made us, whatever made us, whatever part of the universe made us, it has gradually evolved.

S: It's chasing after feeling better and running away from feeling worse, isn't it?

D: No, it's our homeostat. The DIM inside us. It simply tells us: "Look, if you allow this to go on happening, you are in danger. You've got to stop it."

And the other way around. The DIM guides us away from danger towards safety. But feeling, which is also a guidance, can also be a wrong guidance if you exaggerate the pleasure side of it and ignore the DIM. I told you of that case of those rats who have a special lever that gives them enormous amounts of wonderful feelings of pleasure and they went on pressing it and ignored eating in order to have that feeling.

S: I remember you telling me. The same as an alcoholic will ignore eating and go on drinking.

D: Exactly. Very good example. And sex, alcohol and pleasure of it, all these things may be useful up to a certain point; up to a certain limit and the feeling cannot tell you when to stop, it can only be the thinking brain that is able to do that, because it can judge the past and to a certain extent predict the future.

S: The feeling has no wisdom as such then?

D: It has momentary wisdom for a second, it has wonderful wisdom for a second when there is an immediate danger.

S: Yes, maybe it has a self-preservatory wisdom but it does not have a...

D: No, it has not got a thinking wisdom.

S: It's not able to compare really.

D: That's what we are saying. It deals with the now and that particular now. It cannot deal with thinking although it *can* judge the thoughts, you follow?

S: Yes.

D: The same way it can judge any other disturbances, why should it judge all the other disturbances and not the thinking disturbance? It judges because its function is to deal with disturbance.

S: And we can say that the DIM's function is likewise to deal with disturbance.

D: From what you are saying you can see how closely related they are.

S: Yes, of course. But some feeling derives from thinking doesn't it? If you think about certain things this produces a feeling.

D: The final judge of all disturbance is what you call this emotional feeling, which must be connected with our awareness of DIM and it tells us, 'look! whatever is happening at this very second is good or bad for you or in between'.

S: Or neutral.

D: Or neutral, of course.

So there you have it! The thinking mind conditioned by coding and an often mistaken sense of advantage has programmed itself into chasing after pleasure and avoiding discomfort, while ignoring the DIM, the **neutral,** which it often considers boring or dull or empty.

The yogi however moves in exactly the opposite direction! The path of yoga is to confront pain and pleasure with impartiality, equanimity, and unmask both as impostors – to penetrate deeply into the bliss and calm of the neutral, the normal, the balanced.

So, we see there are two forces which whenever out of alignment will be in conflict: on the one hand Nature's DIM and Dim tendency and on the other hand the thinking mind's idea of what *should* be happening. This is a conflict generated by the thinking mind's codes and images, a conflict between *should* and *is*, between what we want at that moment to be happening and what Life is actually presenting us at that moment.

Therefore, whenever confronted by distress, disturbance, discomfort arising from such situations of confrontation/antagonism, go for the Real and allow the DIM do what the DIM is capable of doing. It can and will re-establish order and harmony.

Give it time to ripen naturally.

***

Chapter 3: Real World Vs Artificial World

"Monks, I will teach you the All. Pay attention and listen carefully to my words."

"So be it, lord," the monks responded.

The Blessed One said, "What is the All? Simply the eye and sights, the ear and sounds, the nose and smells, the tongue and tastes, the body and sensations, the mind and mental constructs.

"This, monks, is called the All. Anyone who would say, 'Rejecting this All, I will describe another All'. If questioned on what exactly might be the basis for this statement, would be unable to explain, and furthermore fall into confusion. Why? Because it lies outside their scope."

Sabba Sutta: The All

"Outside the thinking mind of the human being everything in Nature is perfect." – assumption

Yoga means sticking to what is Real, adhering to the Real and jettisoning overboard the entirety of internal cinema and mental tennis.

All the libraries of the world, past and present, the lost volumes of Alexandria and Constantinople, all modern paper and digital books as well as mountains of microchips – the entirety of it – are no substitute for the direct intelligence/insight/perception of the Real World of Nature available to any of us.

Our body – and Nature's Mind which governs it through the DIM and Dim tendency – holds the secrets of the universe.

"...it is just within this fathom-long body, with its perception and intellect, that I declare that there is the World, the origination of the

World, the cessation of the World and the path of practice leading to the cessation of the World."

Rohitassa Sutta

Furthermore:

"There is no disappearing of the Real World
until a counterfeit world appears in this World;
when the counterfeit world arises,
it makes the Real World to disappear."

Samyutta Nikaya ll, 224-227 Saddhamma Sutra

Since ancient times men and women have sought to understand the Reality of Nature which is ever presently and never absently penetrating us and surrounding us.

That venerable and worthy search is the search to know, a search for **self-knowledge**.

Curiously, animals – the life forms most akin to us on this Earth – seem not to have this need. It seems to be a trait peculiar to and unique to humans which arises from inside the thinking mind. It does not arise from any other part of our mindbody nor from outside it.

The rest of our mindbody carries on much the same way as the mindbody of those animals closest to us in appearance, characteristics and function. The rest of our mindbody carries on under the natural influence of DIM and Dim tendency same as it does in animals, each according to its unique natural coding/programming.

As shown in the previous two chapters, the *thinking mind* – the artificer of codes, images and concepts – is a *difference* hunter and at the same time a *merchant of connections*, both of these activities motivated by a *sense* of 'advantage', of making things better, of improving something somehow.

On the one hand this peculiar thinking mind of humans differentiates and divides through establishing differences and then on the other hand it engages in putting things together again by establishing identities through similarity. Having eliminated some aspects of difference it connects non-similar things together again by establishing similarity and sameness.

This continuous process _in-the-thinking-mind-only_ of chopping things up and then putting them back together again, in the course of time generates what can be called our *internal cinema* whose nourishment and maintenance requires tremendous investment both in time and expenditure of energy.

> Yet despite all efforts – all the King's soldiers and all the King's men – Humpty Dumpty cannot be put together again.

And the attempt to do so causes all sorts of ramifications externally in the Natural World and internally inside us. This propagation of ramifications in ancient India was called *prapanca*.

From the time we are born this internal cinema gets gradually built up and we grow up thinking, speaking and behaving to a large extent as if the internal cinema were the Real World when it is only a representation of the Real World – a tool for understanding it and navigating it.

This mistaken notion inside our heads then travels outside our heads interacting with other peoples' heads carrying equally mistaken notions and affects every aspect of human life and interaction – oneself, personal, domestic, social, national, economic, international, legal, scientific, health – you name it, it affects every walk of human life. You can't get away from it.

But we can at least recognize and acknowledge that this is what is happening. And that to get thoroughly Real again this has got to stop. That recognition and acknowledgement is the first step of ancient yoga, and is as important today as it was then.

> All else is delaying tactics: making mischief while having fun making wrong guesses.

This mistaken notion inside our thinking mind results in thinking and feeling we are something separate, instead of indivisible, from the Real World of Nature.

The word *individual* means that which cannot be divided or separated, something indivisible. Anybody who thinks deeply enough about the nature of numbers will soon realize that One in essence always remains One however much division or addition is applied. Half an orange is no longer an orange yet it remains one: *one half* of an orange. Similarly for one quarter and any other fraction. Likewise, the aggregation of two oranges together becomes one pair or *one set* of two oranges.

There is no separation from the Reality of Nature for a human being or for anything else. The Reality of our individual Nature together with the Reality of Nature as a whole is inseparable/non-dual. This is what the yoginis and yogis of ancient times – those original shrewd and wise observers of Nature – discovered for themselves. Or more correctly put – *rediscovered*.

But one thing is intuitively understanding and feeling the indivisibility of our own nature with the Nature of Reality and quite another thing being able to make a map which can accurately and intelligibly show others how this Reality of Nature might be structured.

> You will have noticed I have switched the phrase around from Nature of Reality to Reality of Nature. *Are these two phrases 'Nature of Reality' and 'Reality of Nature' pointing to exactly the same thing?* Or do each point to different aspects of the Structure of Reality? Words are *so* tricky.

The issue of *structure* is far more important than it may seem. The understanding of fundamental structure has been and continues to be a key component in the quest for knowledge, both self-knowledge and knowledge of the Cosmos.

> "...it is just within this fathom-long body, with its perception and intellect, that I declare that there is the World, the origination of the World, the cessation of the World, and the path of practice leading to the cessation of the World."
>
> Rohitassa Sutta

So, which *world – which order of Reality* – is the Buddha referring to?

Knowing he is teaching solely about *dukkha* and how to bring about the complete cessation of *dukkha*, it seems more than likely this sutta refers to the Artificial World concocted by the thinking mind – the internal cinema – which in yoga is called Maya, a counterfeit world, which *"makes the Real World to disappear"*.

***

Since at least several thousand years ago there have been careful observers of Nature – ancient Indians, ancient Greeks, Jewish kabbalists and more recently Western philosophers of science – fussy about precision, who pointed out that there are several different levels or orders or layers of Reality, which are interconnected *but not the same*. Neither do they necessarily occur at one and the same time. These different orders of Reality are qualitatively different and perform different functions in the conjoint scheme of the total Reality.

> There are either three or four orders of Reality depending on whether similar representations (images) are classified separately from non-similar representations (codes).

Such divisions are mentioned in the recorded teachings of the Buddha (*patisambhida*), in the Jain texts about Mahavir (*anekantavada*), by Patanjali (*yogasutra*), by Aristotle, by Shankaracharya, by Bishop Berkeley, by Korzybski (in *Science and Sanity*) to name a few of the most significant.

> What they discovered, being very subtle, *for whatever reason* has never become general knowledge, and even today is not taught at schools or universities.

Using the terminology of *samkhya* – the theoretical foundation of Yoga – in chapters 1 and 2 we have already looked at the four orders of Reality in terms of:

- *purusha & prakriti* (see Chapter 12)

- the Reality of Nature (Cosmos) that sciences are busy studying and all of us are daily perceiving through the five senses – sight, hearing, taste, touch and smell
- code & image including all mental constructs, which constitute the 'bits' of our thinking mind's internal cinema.

Gautama Buddha refers to the invisible, unmanifest level as *asankhata* which means *codeless/unconstructed/un-assembled/un-put-together* and therefore lying outside the scope of the thinking mind – beyond language to describe it. This level potentially extends beyond even the *purusha/ prakriti* duality which can at least be conceptualized, and perhaps even one day verified directly with ultra-sensitive scientific instruments.

> In our modern era, ultra-sensitive electronic instruments have already detected the ether or at least the ether's carrier disturbance in the form of cosmic microwave background radiation – what some physicists are calling the quantum field in recognition of its non-emptiness.

The Buddha taught not to waste time theorizing until the priority task of erasing the thinking mind's coding from the mindbody has been completed.

> "The Tathagata has no theories."
>
> Majjhima Nikaya, I

Mahavir the great Jain yogi taught the doctrine of *anekantavada*, which is an early reference to Relativity Theory. The word *anekantavada* is made up of *an-* meaning *not*, *eka-* meaning *one*, *kanta-* meaning *sides, angles, facets, corners* or *aspects*, and *vada* meaning doctrine or theory.

Mahavir taught that Reality is multi-faceted and can be viewed from many angles which cannot be simultaneously expressed in language. To this great insight Mahavir added another: namely, that though the Truth of Nature flows into language (code) it does not travel backwards the other way. By this is meant that language (code) being part of Nature is real and true but that it cannot express what is outside its own order of reality. Language can never express what is beyond its scope.

Certainly not absolute or ultimate truths because any perception of Reality depends on the standpoint of the viewer – on what in modern language can be called *the connectoring*.

> *Connectoring* needs to be distinguished from simple *connecting* because connectoring takes place over three-dimensions in space as well as over time, and involves jumping across different orders of Reality.

Connector is a term borrowed from electrical engineering: *connectoring* is the action of connecting up several connectors or groups of connectors and fitting them into a pattern. Such patterns are interpreted as meaning or given a meaning. Most meanings are inevitably arbitrary and made by consensus. As such they continue to be codes.

In terms of psychemechanics, connectors are anything the mind latches on to in order to construct and concoct bits of its internal cinema. Connectoring therefore englobes the whole process of connecting and assembling sets of connectors into codes, images and concepts.

The four orders of Reality referred to above are in themselves qualitatively different "worlds" or "orders" or "levels" or "layers" of Reality, which function together, interpenetrate each other up to a point and interact with each other up to a point. These have already been described with examples in Chapter 1. Chapter 12 describes Purusha & Prakriti in terms of Consciousness & Ether, as the fundamental basic structure underlying the manifest Real World (Cosmos).

> The fact that these different orders of Reality, as far as humans are concerned, are functioning together simultaneously makes it extremely difficult at times to distinguish one from the other and so easy to fall into the trap of mistaking one for the other.

Untangling the mess is the primary purpose of *yoga*

None of the mental cinema we have inside our heads representing reality is the Real World. Our built-up imaginings of what we think we are and what we think the world is, are neither the world nor us, let alone the words "I", "me", "we" or "us", which are no more than codes and images standing in for perceptions, sensations and feelings about ourselves which too are *also codes standing in for something fundamental most humans are ignoring.*

Each person during her or his life builds up a mental picture of what he or she is and what the world is, and we can talk together and discuss it all over a cup of tea without getting too lost because enough of us have sufficiently similar pictures in our heads owing to prior consensus and agreement to together go on pretending and perpetuating collective illusions and fantasies. But to the extent the concepts (and the words standing for them) become more and more complex and **ab**stract – with many of them lacking any clear link to the Real World of Nature – then the trouble, muddle and serious mischief begin.

Shankaracharya's three propositions

> Brahman is Real
> The World is unreal
> Brahman is the World

is not as clear as it could be. Korzybski was much clearer in his declaration, "*the map is not the territory!*" Yet Korzybski misses how the code is constructed. And Shankaracharya, *unlike the Buddha,* likewise makes no mention of the code, nor the central role it plays in fabricating and conditioning our perception of Reality.

To make this difference absolutely clear, let's call thinking mind-made representations of reality "*internal cinema*" and all thinking "mental tennis".

> Samkhya is one of the six orthodox philosophical systems of ancient Sanatana Dharma that follow the Vedas: the others being Yoga, Nyaya, Vaisheshika, Mimamsa and Vedanta. The so-called unorthodox systems such as Buddhism, Jainism and others share common roots, concepts

and practices with the orthodox six but follow the authority of their own line of enlightened teachers rather than the Vedas.

Valid Knowledge

In the quest for knowledge, whether self-knowledge or knowledge about the structure of the Cosmos, a tremendously important consideration to serious researchers has always been: *what constitutes valid knowledge?*

Meanings may be related to valid knowledge or maybe not – it depends on our definition of 'valid'. Patanjali's Yogasutra echoes most of the main ancient Indian philosophical systems of his time in enumerating various kinds of knowledge – both valid and invalid:

- valid knowledge from direct experience
- valid knowledge from deduction/inference
- valid knowledge from reliable 3rd parties (reliable testimony)
- memory
- dream
- illusion
- fantasy (make-believe)

MEMORY blends valid data into mental cinema. Most of the memories we have are not of what was objectively happening then at that moment in time but mostly how we were affected by some aspects of those past events – our impressions – and what we made of them.

That means since childhood we actively build up a store of memory pictures into our internal cinema and never stop updating it. That is how our internal cinema works – it gets built up and proliferates over time. The ancient yogis already were on to this and both in Sanskrit and Pali they called this *prapanca* – proliferation of mental cinema.

Prapanca both in Pali and Sanskrit is mentioned in Mahayana as well as Theravada (Madhupindika Sutta, MN 18), signifying proliferation of codes, images and concepts thereby exponentially expanding mental cinema.

Because of not understanding *sankhara* as code, and no inkling among people at that time in history of what code is nor how it operates, it is not surprising that none of the early texts are able to give a precise definition of what the word *prapanca* stands for. 'Mental cinema' seems to be a most apt rendering into English given the times we live in.

ILLUSION has a basis in reality but the interpretation is faulty. An antelope in a field seen from the side can appear to have a single horn, and so the onlooker may believe she has seen a unicorn.

FANTASY is where there is no antelope in the field yet a unicorn is seen – imagined out of thin air with no foundation whatsoever in Reality.

DREAM takes place during sleep or during moments of inattention when the awareness and thinking mind drift off and get provisionally disconnected from events of the outside world. At those times the connectoring – partially disturbed or disturbed differently than during waking – nonetheless goes on making connections and generating some internal cinema.

In DEEP SLEEP there is usually only experience of absence, which becomes known after waking up again, although some people claim to a degree of awareness even during deep sleep.

VALID KNOWLEDGE

- from direct experience
- from deduction/inference
- from reliable 3rd parties (reliable testimony)

These three sources of valid knowledge are clear and most *darshanas* have the same or similar three forms of valid knowledge. These three are of course the ones mainly used by both sciences and yogas. In ancient

India as well as nowadays, there exists a science of knowledge called epistemology with varying criteria but none of them go into the precise psychemechanics of how knowledge is acquired, developed and stored.

To say that knowledge is acquired by the various means listed above (direct experience, deduction, reliable witness and so forth) is correct as far as it goes *but it does not explain the psychemechanics of it at the level of mindbody.* And this is probably why the human being remains permanently stuck in a loop of ignorance, unable to see what the code is doing to the life-force intelligence.

This is clearly pointed out by Gautama Buddha in the terse formulation of Dependent Origination discussed in Chapter 8, Satipatthana.

Imagination and the Game of Pretence

Yoga is about getting Real, it is the exact opposite of escapism. It is the opposite of running away into some different new kind of illusion or fantasy. Yoga is the opposite of running off and away into any new belief, hope or doubt system.

Ever since humans started to think about things by inventing internal and external languages, we began to imagine things that were not really there, and as a consequence act and behave *as if they were there.* Thus pretence, fabrication, make believe, imagination and confusion entered the world picture obscuring what is Real.

> "There is no disappearing of the true Dhamma
> until a false dhamma appears in this World;
> when the false dhamma appears,
> it makes the true Dhamma to disappear."
>
> Samyutta Nikaya ll

"Il come si fosse" – Dr Michele Salmeri, Catania 1986

Interestingly, the words pretend, pretender and pretending carry the connotation of 'role usurpation' in addition to the meaning of simulation and deceit.

Pretence takes place in the human thinking mind but its effect (consequences) travels and spreads (*prapanca*) outside the mindbody affecting the Real World of Nature. That's the astonishing thing about the psychemechanics of it and the reason why it is so pervasive, so subtle and so difficult to spot. It's so easy to get caught in the meshes of its ramifications!

> There is no fire like lust, no grip like hate,
> No net like self-deception, no stream like craving.
>
> Dhammapada 251

We are surrounded by effects caused and created by imagination many of which are tools of one kind or another. The Artificial World is laden with all sorts of tools of all shapes, sizes and functions.

> What is a tool? A precise definition is needed because any time we *use* something tools can come into it. (see Glossary)
>
> Codes, images and concepts are all tools if used as tools. So it is how something is used – the action of "usage" – that makes something a tool.

That means that the motivation, the intent and the implementation are what determines if something becomes a tool or not.

Pretence and make-believe together with tool-making and tool-use profoundly affect the human being's own internal body, brain, chemistry and nervous system, conditioning and compromising the flow of life force in its natural intelligence (Chapter 9, Nadis).

For whatever fundamental reason this was initiated – whether by chance, by accident or by inbuilt design of Nature herself – it is reasonable to assume that it happens in a similar way to the DIM that it is imitating, namely, in order to secure some real or imagined advantage.

Whatever the reason, and whenever the starting point in Time and Place, of this co-development of coding and imagination, the result is a degree of **disconnect** between the natural Dim-propelled unfolding of events in the Real World of Nature, and the **ab**stract events of ideas, concepts and images unfolding within our thinking mind.

This **disconnect** necessarily involves to a greater or lesser extent significant sacrifice of the Real on the altar of the **ab**stract. This happens whenever ideas are valued more than real things. And this is the source of the sorrow we carry collectively and individually as humans. This disconnect is what has been defined as viyoga, which is the opposite of yoga. It is the source of our misery, in**sati**sfaction, despair and sense of impotence.

Realizing this, wise humans of a remote past in ancient India (and also other ancient cultures in different parts of the world) sought a way back from the state of *viyoga* to the state of yoga. They sought the way back with steadfast determination because they intuitively sensed none of the labyrinthine artificial alternative constructs of *viyoga*, however tinkered, tankered, tweaked and fine-tuned, can ever fully **satis**fy.

What about tools and shelter, clothing and medicine, you might well ask. The answer is with each tool the human being has paid a price in limiting its inherent power, capacity, life force and natural intelligence. Mick Jagger's famous hit "(I Can't Get No) Satisfaction" despite trying and trying and trying says it all. All great art points the way back home to the core – to the heart – to what is Real and of Real value.

Whatever the school in ancient India – and there are nine main ones with many branches and sub-branches – they all have in common an acknowledgement and recognition of the paramount necessity to return to a state of Oneness and conscious integration with Real Nature in order to achieve **sati**sfaction and release from frustrating limitations.

Thinking and imagining has resulted in tool use. And this means tools which in some way or other **force** Nature to behave in a particular manner other than she would if left to her own devices. And tools which force changes on Nature have karmic consequences – this is the basic meaning of *karma* and *karma vippaka*. Action and the consequences of action are expressed in Newton's second and third laws. In fact the third law is almost the same as the second law but expressed from the other side's perspective.

First law states, absent collision absent disturbance and change. The second and third law describe what happens when collision takes place. Put into the human context of psychemechanics, the second law describes the mechanical aspect – but only the purely mechanical aspect/s – of what happens when you interfere with the natural order of things in Nature. What happens when codes are used as tools is what the Buddha rediscovered and formulated in Dependent Origination (*paticcasamuppada*, Chapter 8).

To quote Milton Friedman – "There is no such thing as a free lunch!"

Another way of putting this is that all striving to secure advantage is ultimately self-defeating because the game of mental tennis is a zero-sum game. Not only that, but if the intention and motivation behind the coding is incorrect, the karmic consequences are bound to be negative causing suffering (*dukkha*) here and now or later on.

***

Garden of Eden story

I am sure to many of you, as it is to me, the story of the Garden of Eden is as intriguing as it is strange. If we look at it through a modern looking glass lens of yoga, it is both revealing and instructive.

Linear Evolution theories of mainstream modern science stand in complete contrast to an abundance of ancient myth, legend and culture recounting repeating cycles of Gold, Silver, Copper (Bronze) and Iron ages. During the Golden Age humans endowed with a full panoply of paranormal powers (*siddhis*) roam the Earth as gods and goddesses and to a lesser extent in the Silver Age during 'the decline of shine'. In the early Copper Age gods and goddesses are still recounted as interacting with humans, most of whom by then have lost the remnants of psychic powers.

No reference whatsoever is there in ancient literature to any linear evolution from earlier primitive humans or from any prior primitive life form. Quite the contrary: past records and references invariably hark back with veneration and nostalgia to a past state of humanity as quasi-divine, as belonging to a 'higher order', and all ancient cultures of the world seem to acknowledge in their drawings, paintings and writing a process of degeneration from nobler to baser mettle (metal).

Nowhere is this divergent view on human origination more evident than in the ancient Indian culture, which describes in great detail and precision vast repeating ages of Cosmic inbreath and outbreath, where at the end of the Great Unfolding comes the Great Dissolution, called *pralaya* (*mahapralaya*), wherein everything of value is taken up, preserved in seed form and carried forward to the next Cosmic Unfolding.

The Garden of Eden story is to my knowledge not found in ancient Indian texts but there are other versions of a similar story in other cultures. Let's take a look at the story as described in Genesis because it provides insights into yogic alchemy such as arose in medieval India and elsewhere.

The story about Adam and Eve can be seen as a window through time and space into a moment of transition of man and woman from living in the Golden Age of perfect harmony (*satya yuga* – the age of truth and harmonious interaction with Nature) – to the start of the Silver Age (*treta yuga*).

Also, it seems too much of a semantic coincidence that the sound of the names Adam and Eve (as *adharma* Sanskrit, *adhamma* in Pali) and Devi/Eve are so strikingly similar.

The jury is out on whether the cyclical decline of shine is a true reflection of the past unfolding of events on Earth but it is certainly a huge coincidence that all the efforts of technology seem bent on restoring exactly those same lost psychic and paranormal powers through the symbiosis of the human with ever more sophisticated tools and machines.

The exponential progress of artificial intelligence – unless derailed by an incapacity to match Respect-for-Life with cleverness – could be on track to complete this process of recovery of *siddhis*.

Meanwhile the Garden of Eden story highlights the invisible chasm between yoga and vi-yoga, and how such a transition from one state to the other might have taken place.

Interpreted in the light of what we know about yoga, the several key elements and actors take on the following principles and attributes:

- Adam, the male principle as *Pingala-nadi*
- Eve, the female principle as *Ida-nadi*
- The Serpent – the X factor as *Kundalini*
- The Tree of Eternal Life as *Sushumma*
- The Tree of Knowledge of Differentiation as "forbidden"
- The Garden – the MindBody – as the paradise where all takes place.
- Instructions from "the Almighty" regarding rules of behavior and nourishment i.e. 'keep to Nature's original CODE!'
- *Prana*, the life breath, as Sustainer
- *Dukkha* as signposting the way back to the entrance/gateway to *Sushumma* (Harmony)

> The Almighty commanded the humans, saying, 'You may surely eat fruit of every tree of the Garden, but of the fruit of the Tree of the Knowledge of Differentiation (opposites) you should not eat, otherwise the moment you do so, you are bound to die.' (Genesis 2:16–17)

The ability and freedom to interfere with original coding is a priceless gift in both senses. A two-way gift. Note that in German '*gift*' means poison.

Paraphrased

There is no problem to harmoniously interact with and to fully enjoy the Real World of Real Things but once the human being starts making her or his own images and codes – by thinking and guessing about it all, making images of how things *could* be or *should* be, by inventing meanings, by valuing certain images more highly than the realities they represent – then progressively *siddhis* and perfect vision will wane and become lost. *Siddhis* become lost because access to *siddhis* is not located in the ordinary thinking mind (brain), and woman and man will suffer and die along with all their concoctions and fabrications (mental cinema), because the knots these programs generate in our brain and nervous systems, obstruct the free flow of the creative life-force intelligence and prevent it joining and flowing up *sushumma* – the central channel – the Tree of Eternal Life. Thus is lost the conscious connection to the Cosmos. Hence yoga becomes vi-yoga.

> We have literally 'lost touch with Reality' – lost touch with our true Nature, with Nature. Thankfully not completely, because **the DIM's action can never be diminished** (no pun intended), **only ignored, diverted and delayed.**

The Garden of Eden was a beautiful paradise of fruit trees, lush vegetation and crystalline streams. Among the multitude of different fruit-bearing trees there were two singular trees quite unlike the others: The Tree of Eternal Life and the Tree of the Knowledge of Differences.

The Almighty (Mother Nature) had placed Adam and Eve in the garden with inherent instructions (inbuilt codes).

> "You may certainly eat of every tree of the garden (including the Tree of Life), but of the tree of the Knowledge of Differences you should not eat, because the day you do so, you will surely lose your immortality." (Genesis 2:16-17 paraphrased)

Adam and Eve lived in harmony enjoying the bliss of the senses, endowed with *siddhis*, free from the need for thought and self-reflection, free from the need for clothing and tools, free from the need to cultivate anything because sunlight, air and the garden provided all nourishment, all sustenance.

Unclothed, uninhibited, free from complexes, complete in perfection, in full control of the serpent power (*kundalini*)...completely at ease with their physical bodies and attributes, free from dis-ease and enjoying perfect health and long life. Natural in Nature, passively holding dominion over the Natural world through harmless interaction – humans, animals, insects, plants, each acknowledging and respecting the other.

In Genesis Chapter 3, the perfect equilibrium (*satya | krita yuga* – the Age of Truth | Harmony | Perfection) comes to an **ab**rupt end when

Kundalini, the Serpent Power, the evolutionary X factor, triggers in the mind of Eve (Devi) the thought of doing something different to what the DIM of Nature had until then been doing.

What did Eve do? It seems she tried to make a good thing better!

As soon as thinking replaces feeling, the connection with the Real World starts to fade, eventually becoming lost. But at first only ever so slightly in the Silver Age.

The biblical story is sudden, like a snapshot of a process which most likely took a long, long time to unfold. The transition is more likely to have been mostly gradual, not a sudden development.

Plumbing does not calcify and become obstructed overnight – sediment builds up gradually, encrusting/calcifying, causing a narrowing of pipes until eventually outright blockages occur. Gradually the free flow of life-force intelligence gets more and more impeded, the natural powers of human mindbody wane and insight gets lost.

The Yugas

According to ancient Indian cosmology – whether Hindu, Jain or Buddhist – this is a process which repeats and occurs time and time again over immensely long periods of time.

Gold
Silver
Copper
Iron

Labels and the Tower of Babel

And so just as a glass of water fills drop by drop then when filled to the brim, suddenly overflows...so too change is gradual until it is no longer gradual, and then suddenly everything changes.

Adam blames Eve and Eve blames the Serpent. Responding in a typically human way, neither willing to accept responsibility for the mistake of trying to make a good thing better.

However, the good news is that the inherent guide – the DIM/ Dim tendency – is still ever present, never absent always guiding us correctly as long as we don't interfere and as long as we just let it do its job. Also, and most important to know, *metta* can never ever be lost even though *sila, samadhi* and *pañña* be lost.

> Immortality is lost because the *sankharas* compromise the life force preventing the *pranas from merging* and rising easily up *sushumma* and abiding there.

The need for *tapasya* and yoga to dissolve the *sankharas* (codes) increases in direct proportion to the narrowing of plumbing and presence of blockages.

The Garden of Eden story goes on...

> Then the Almighty said, "Behold! the man has become like one of us in knowing good and evil..." (we might well ask who is he speaking to?!)

So it is through the creation of thinking mind-made codes that the human being is able to exercise some degree of free will. By interfering with Nature's coding and programing, and making its own creations, humans become co-creators with Nature but the price of this is temporarily (provisionally) losing conscious connection and conscious access to Ether (the Tree of **Ether**nal Life).

> And so the Almighty (Mother Nature) cast out Adam and Eve from Paradise and placed a cherubim with a flaming sword blocking and guarding the entrance to the Tree of Life. (Genesis 3:22–24)

Access to *sushumma* gets sealed off hence the need for *tapasya* and yoga.

The ancient path of yoga as solution to the Fall from Grace is thus founded in *yama* and *niyama* and continues with *asana* in Chapter 5.

***

Chapter 4: Yoga

The first yogi and yogini: Siva and Sati

To understand the original meaning of the word *yoga* and the primary purpose of *yoga sadhana*, we go back to its ancient origins to a legendary time when gods are humanlike and human beings are godlike endowed with all the attributes and aspects of *siddhas*.

The great God Siva was reputed to be as powerful as all the other gods together, including Brahma and Vishnu. But Siva was mostly shun¬ned by the other gods except by his fellow Trimurti brothers, Brahma and Vishnu. The other gods, if they had to interact with Trimurti, were less uncomfortable in the company of Brahma, the creator or Vishnu, the Sustainer, than in the company of Siva, the Transformer

The notion of transformation with its implicit impermanence made them uneasy – they feared the destruction and loss transformation appears to bring. Most gods and goddesses – Kali being a notable exception – were conservative and wished as far as possible to preserve for long ages all they cherished and held dear.

So, whenever immortality was revealed as only provisional they would become anxious and uneasy. They did not like it one bit to be reminded that even the greatest gods must one day pass away at the disintegration of the Cosmos (*mahapralaya*).

Thus, they avoided contact with Siva and whenever possible overlooked inviting him to ceremonies and gatherings.

Making matters even more unpalatable, Siva – the *adi-sadhu* – had eccentric tastes and disturbing habits. Mahadev would wander around naked, smeared in ashes or dark pigments, adorn himself with necklaces of serpents, gird his waist about with belts of skulls, and spend prolonged periods in solitary contemplation high up in the icy Himalayas while most other gods and goddesses socialized together in great halls and palaces, enjoying splendour, enjoying finery, enjoying their powers (*siddhis*).

Daksha, one of the sons of Lord Brahma, had several daughters, the most beautiful of whom, Sati, had long admired Lord Siva. But Daksha did not approve of Siva, and so when the time came to invite the gods to the ceremony in which Sati was obliged by tradition to choose a husband, Siva was not invited. At the ceremony Sati would have no choice but to place a garland around the neck of one of the other gods. Or so Daksha thought. In this way Daksha sought to prevent Sati from marrying Siva and realizing her heart's desire.

However, when the moment came for Sati to make the choice, she gazed around the gathering, saw Siva was absent, and in dismay threw the garland high into the air, exclaiming:

"Om namó Sivaya!" (the main mantra of yoginis and yogis)

At that very instant Siva manifested, the garland fell conveniently around his neck and Daksha had no option but to accept Siva as Sati's husband. And thus were they duly wed.

Siva turned out to be a dutiful and devoted husband, and all went well until Daksha organized a sacrificial fire ceremony – a *yagna* – to which Siva and Sati were not invited.

Nevertheless – because it was family – Sati decided to attend the ceremony even though Siva urged her not to do so. But Sati ignored Siva's advice. This would be unusual for a wife in ancient India but let us not forget that Sati was a goddess in her own right.

At the ceremony Daksha snubbed Sati and insulted his absent son-in-law to her face in front of all the guests. As was the custom, in order to save face and uphold honour and dignity, Sati cast herself onto the sacrificial fire of the *yagna* immolating herself.

Instantly sensing something amiss, Siva rushed to rescue Sati from the flames but it was too late. Sati had perished and in his anger and grief, Siva took upon himself the fearsome aspect of *Virabhadra* summoning up the attribute of Destroyer.

Out of his mind with grief Siva clasped Sati to his chest and began the dance of *Nataraj* with such forcefulness that the entire universe began to quake and tremble forcing Brahma and Vishnu to hasten to calm their brother in order to prevent a premature implosion of the Cosmos.

Calmed down but stricken with grief, Siva moderated his dance, and as Sati's body slowly rotted in his arms, parts of her fell down to Earth, marking spots where the 12 Siva temples (*jyotirlinga*) would later be built. Some say though that it was Vishnu who, unable to bear Siva's grief, cast his disc to sever the body of Sati, thus releasing his brother from attachment to her physical form.

Either way, Sati's physical form was lost and Siva withdrew to a remote location high up in the Himalayas on Mount Kailash – there to mend his broken heart. Meanwhile, Sati was reborn in a fishing village as Parvati and as she grew up she became more and more drawn to Siva. Rather than remain a mere devotee she resolved to go up into the Himalayas and seek out Siva.

After much searching, after enduring severe ordeals and difficulties along the way, Parvati at last came upon Lord Siva, covered in white ash, sitting motionless on the ice in *padmasana*. But Siva ignored Parvati and did not look at her, his two eyes staring unblinkingly ahead absorbed in *samadhi*.

Siva was not looking at the mountain view, not admiring the snowy peaks, the blue skies, the white of the snow – he was engaged in watching the content of his mind reflected in the mirror of Consciousness.

In the attempt to get Siva's attention, Parvati practiced intense austerities of mind and body to try to force Siva to notice her. Parvati would sit motionless in *asana* in front of Siva for days at a time, fast for weeks or only eat fallen leaves but none of this was to any avail. Still Siva sat unmoved and unmoving, watching only the inner workings of his mind.

Finally in desperation Parvati placed her two palms over Siva's unblinking eyes...at that very instant the third eye on Siva's brow opened and thereupon he saw her, recognized her, remembered!

From that very moment onwards Siva and Sati again became inseparable as Shiva-Shakti. Thus the meaning of yoga and yoga's purpose as illustrated in this beautiful legend about the first yogi Siva and the first yogini Sati (*adi-yogi* and *adi-yogini*) is re-uniting with the Real by recognizing and remembering.

The final goal of yoga is not achieved by meditative absorption, nor by austerities nor penance. It is achieved through arousing such an intensity of concentration that the third eye (*ajna chakra*) awakens, sees, recognizes and remembers the true Nature of Reality as Purusha/Prakriti and Siva/Shakti.

> Acknowledging the Reality of Nature (Prakriti/Shakti) as non-separate from one's Self (Purusha/Siva), the austerities and all the rest of it are but a prelude. And so integration of differentiated realities into Wholeness can only begin by perceiving the world through the third eye which sees and realizes what the other two eyes cannot. Whatever two-eyed dualistic vision perceives is colored and conditioned by imagination – by the thinking mind, by human mind-made coding – and thus remains merely a simulacrum of the Real, a shadow of the real, not the Real itself.

The eye of yoga, the I behind the code "I", is the eye capable of seeing completeness. Paradise is lost through the thinking mind casting a veil of illusion (*maya*) differentiating the Real. Paradise is regained through re-integrating the Real.

In this story Siva's condition of **vi-yoga**, his broken heart, with all its dis**sati**sfaction and grief is completely resolved by reunion with Sati. Likewise for Parvati.

> "Outside the thinking mind of the human being everything in Nature is perfect."

***

Moving from the legendary time of Siva and Parvati to the historical time around 600 BCE in the Greater Magadha area of northeast India, *vi-yoga* had at the time become a central preoccupation inspiring thousands of men and women from all walks of life, cultures and religious backgrounds to renounce the ordinary mundane way of life to seek liberation from *dukkha*.

This liberation has been variously called *moksha, vimukti, mukta, kevalya, nirvana* and similar names. Some have different nuances of meaning but their basic idea is liberation from all forms of unsatisfactoriness by completely resolving the cause.

Those men and women who achieve liberation are variously called *arahant, kevalin* or *jina* (hence Jain), meaning victorious one. By virtue of their unsurpassable victory over delusion, confusion, base instincts and compulsion, they become *siddhas* recovering all attributes and aspects natural to the Golden Age.

Through the act of renouncing an ordinary mundane way of life, these *sramana* ascetics, yogis and yoginis, although made up of diverse pre-Aryan, Vedic, non-Vedic and Shamanic elements, had a single goal in common and became collectively known as the "renouncer movement". Even in today's modern India, a *sadhu* is said to 'renounce the world' thus showing that the traditions of that time more than 2500 years ago still endure.

According to the rules of their orders, each sramana group practiced different types of austerities for purifying body and mind (called *tapas* or *tapasya*) as well as the known mental yoga techniques of that time.

Although written records were not made until centuries later, oral accounts of that time recount the arising of a number of renowned teachers, two of whom are universally recognized as having rediscovered the ancient path to awakening, enlightenment and liberation: Mahavir (Vardhamana) and the Buddha (Siddhartha Gautama).

Mahavir

Precise dating is uncertain but it appears from later written records – both Jain and Buddhist – that Mahavir was a contemporary of Siddhartha Gautama, although 30 years older. Mahavir lived and resided in the same area of northeast India and passed away at the age of 72.

Vardhamana's background and the story of his early life, renunciation and path to enlightenment is strikingly similar to Siddhartha's. Both were born into royal families of the warrior *kshatriya* caste, both had the best education available at that time, both married a princess with the name Yasodhara, both had one child, and both renounced their family life at the same age (30 Mahavir; 29 Siddhartha) to seek a solution to life's unsatisfactoriness.

But Mahavir's parents were lay devotees of the 23rd Jain, Tirthhankara, Parshvanath, and Vardhamana embarked on the ancient Jain path which adheres uncompromisingly to five core principles:

- uncompromising emphasis on unconditional respect for all life (ahimsa)
- truthfulness (satya)
- non-appropriation of anything extraneous to the body (asteya)
- non-attachment (aparigraha)
- restraint of sexuality and sensuality (brahmacharya)

These five principles became inspirational for the *yama* section of Patanjali's eightfold yoga system in his Yogasutra and form the bedrock of Patanjala *yoga sadhana*.

It is said Mahavir practiced severe *tapasya* (austerities) together with *dhyana* meditation for 12 years after which he attained *keval jnana* – pure knowledge free from conceptualization – and liberation (*moksha*).

Jain means 'victor' or 'victory' – he or she who has fought the ultimate battle winning the supreme victory that sets the heartmind free from all bonds.

The deep impression Mahavir made on neighbouring kingdoms and rulers secured patronage and sustenance for as many as 14,000 male and female Jain ascetics at that time, called *nigrantha* meaning 'bondless', 'without fetters'.

***

The Buddha

It was within this effervescence of diverse forms of yoga practice in the Greater Magadha area of northeast India that Siddhartha Gautama too stepped forth from his palace to seek the solution to Life's woes.

Of all ancient teachers, Siddhartha Gautama – who long after his passing became world-renowned as the Buddha – looks most similar to Siva, the first yogi.

So much so that it is impossible to conceive of yoga without the role played by either Mahavir or Gautama Buddha in its development and propagation. Patanjali's yoga sutra could not have been written without the records of Siddhartha's eight fold Noble Path and the immense impact it had at that time.

For seven years Gautama wandered among the sramanas practicing austerities much like Mahavir had done – practicing the same *dhyana* meditations – all the while searching for the key to liberation.

Gautama came to study under two renowned dhyana meditation masters: Alara Kalama and Uddaka Ramaputta

Alara Kalama (Sanskrit: Arada Kalapa)

Alara Kalama was a reclusive yogi versed in samkhya philosophy who taught Gautama the meditative absorptions (*jhana/dhyana*) up to the seventh level – a non-material absorption (*arupa jhana*) known as the 'field of nothingness or empty space'.

(Pali: akincannayatana)

After attaining this same level as his teacher, Siddhartha remained unsatisfied because he experienced that whenever he was out of this highly refined subtle mental state, the fundamental problem of *dukkha* would resurface. Therefore, he saw it as only palliation – a provisional or temporary solution. And so Siddhartha decided to continue his search.

Uddaka Ramaputta (Sanskrit Udraka Ramaputta)

Interestingly Uddaka Ramaputta is said by some scholars to have been a Jain like Mahavir so it is a strange omission that no relationship between Uddaka Ramaputta and Mahavir is mentioned in the Buddhist texts, neither is there any record of any discussion between Uddaka and Siddhartha about Mahavir's attainment of *moksha*.

Uddaka taught Siddhartha the meditative absorptions one level further – up to the eighth level – an even more subtle state known as the field of neither perception nor non-perception.

> (Pali: nevasannanasannayatana).

Yet once he had attained also to this lofty state, Siddhartha still remained unsatisfied for the same reason: it only suspends but does not resolve the unsatisfactoriness of the human condition, and therefore whenever out of that lofty state of mental absorption, the fundamental doubts, conflicts and contradictions of life resurface in the thinking mind.

Siddhartha Gautama came to realize that all yogic induced meditative states, however exalted and lofty, however provisionally beneficial and calming, provide no permanent solution, no lasting release. In fact, both Alara Kalama and Uddaka Rāmaputta acknowledged Siddhartha Gautama as their equal in attainment and both requested him to stay but he declined their invitations to become co-teacher alongside them. Both admitted they had been unable to rediscover that key bit of missing knowledge leading to full emancipation known to the great rishis and yoga *siddhas* of former times. They both requested Siddhartha to come back and tell them if ever he should find it!

> The reader will note this account does not tally with the fact of Mahavir's attainment as an Arahant and residing nearby – unless the dating is incorrect.

Thereupon Siddhartha resolved to continue the quest for a definitive solution to Life's dukkha. With five companions he again took up the practice of severe austerities and penance (*tapas*) pushing his body to the point of near-death before finally abandoning such practices as counterproductive. On stopping the practice of *tapasya* his five companions disapproved and abandoned Siddhartha, mistaking his decision for a waning of resolve.

It is at this point that the Buddha-to-be seems to have taken a path different from that trod by Mahavir.

After taking food substantial, he got back his strength, found a suitable spot at the foot of a great Pipal tree and sat down resolving to remain there until the final goal he was seeking had been attained.

"Aneka jati samsaram, Sandhavissam anibbisam;
Gaha karakam gavesanto, Dukkha jati punappunam.
Gaha karaka ditthosi, Puna geham na kahasi;
Sabba te phasuka bhagga, Gaha kutam visankhitam;
Visankhara*gatam cittam, Tanhanam khayamajjhaga."*

First words spoken by the Buddha after attaining the Codeless.

"Life after life I sought the Creator of this House, in ceaseless search again and again taking on (new) birth, (new) suffering but Now I see you O Builder! – no more shall you build my house! broken are the beams, shattered is the ridge pole, freed is mind – all codes and compulsion rooted out from the body!"

Through '*sati*' – through *remembering* past lives – he finally recognized the binding thread played by the code (*sankhara*), gained insight into its construction and operation, into the intention behind it rooted in ignorance, and clearly saw the way to remove mind-made coding from the body, freeing the heartmind from all conditioning and limitation.

The understanding of the role played by the code – *sankhara* – is synthesized in the formula of Dependent Causation.

His teaching on the method of practice he called *satipatthana* which means setting up conditions for *remembering/recognizing* the fourfold Nature of Reality (*patisambhida*), comprehensive insight into which is the decisive factor enabling the untying of knots caused by codes/coding.

We can rightly consider that Gautama Buddha's yoga is founded upon *sati* and Chapter 8 will go into depth of what the Buddha disco¬vered which is profound and subtle and likely became again lost within a generation or so of his passing.

Although Patanjali's eightfold yoga system is philosophically closely related to *samkhya*, the influence of the Buddha's eightfold path cannot be overstated. The presence of Pali terminology and concepts in Patanjali's Yogasutra has been noticed and commented on by Western scholars. According to Oscar Pujol, complete phrases have been lifted from suttas in the Tipitaka and copypasted by Patanjali into his Yogasutra.

Therefore, classical yoga can rightly be considered the amalgam/synthesis of several key influences:

- the philosophy of *samkhya* as theoretical base;
- the sublime ethical conduct and tapasya of Mahavir; (yama/niyama)
- the eightfold Noble path as taught by Gautama Buddha;
- *dhyana* and *samadhi* as practiced by both Mahavir and Gautama Buddha,

and their adaptation 250 years or so later by Patanjali into the eightfold yoga system.

What Patanjali seems to have missed completely – and therefore is not included in his Yogasutra – is Gautama Buddha's insight into *samskara* as code and the *psychemechanics* of Dependent Causation. Instead, Patanjali refers cryptically to 'an untraceable step'.

Patanjali

Despite great fame as the compiler and author of the Yogasutra, not much is known about the sage Patanjali himself nor the precise period in which he lived. At the earliest it is estimated to be around 200 BCE, which would locate him in a time 300 years after the Buddha's passing, around the same time the Buddhist sutras were being written down in Sri Lanka into the Pali Canon (Tripitaka). In the latest estimate, Patanjali is said to have lived 300 to 400 CE. The confusion perhaps arises because other significant treatises on grammar and medicine were authored by someone with the same name.

Because of the clear influence of *samkhya* together with aspects of Mahavir's and the Buddha's teachings, the more likely date is the earlier period.

Sutra is a form of recorded teaching found in Brahmanism, Jainism and Buddhism.

In Buddhist texts the sutra more often takes on a lengthier and more detailed form of exposition whereas in Brahmanic and Jain texts, sutras are generally terse condensations of key points or principles.

A great achievement of Patanjali was to synthesize yoga into 196 sutras which fit onto a single wide page. This synthesis is basically a checklist in shorthand for those in the know or a reminder of subject matter for yoga teachers of that time.

The 196 sutras are divided into four chapters:

Ch 1 Samadhi
Ch 2 Sadhana
Ch 3 Siddhis
Ch 4 Liberation

I made a comparison of three translations of Patanjali's first chapter on samadhi but I have not included it in the Appendix because generally

I have found the Yogasutra less useful for *dhyana* meditation practice than the Visuddhimagga.

> (Visuddhimagga, both volumes 1 and 2, are in the recommended reading list)

Although the *citta vritti nirodha* definition of yoga in three words in sutra 1 is genius, generally the explanations of *dhyana* (*jhana*) are better described in Visuddhimagga.

The problem with the Yogasutra of Patanjali is that because of its terse condensed form of expression, the meanings cannot be properly understood unless the yogi has already experienced much of the subject matter. Therefore, additional explanation is required and has been supplied not by Patanjali but by explainers and commentators who, coming long after, may or may not have fully understood Patanjali's meanings. And then come the commentaries to the commentaries...and more cooks to the broth.

In addition, Patanjali confesses to the "untraceable step" which confirms that by his time the knowledge of *samskara* as *code*, its precise construction and operation, had again been long lost.

***

Shankaracharya

Adi Shankaracharya was an 8th century Indian yogi, *jivanmukta*, philosopher and reformer of Brahmanism and is considered an avatar of Lord Shiva as well as a "buddha in disguise".

In addition to his famous threefold proposition mentioned before (Brahman is Real; the World is unreal; Brahman is the World), Shankaracharya is famous for his 'snake in the rope' simile which provides a useful insight – but only an insight – into the first and second links in the Buddha's formula of Dependent Origination:

avijja paccaya sankhara	not seeing the snake is actually a rope...
sankhara paccaya viññanam	triggers reactions in the mindbody
viññana paccaya namarupam	conditioning the life force in its innate intelligence

Shankara's influence on Indian philosophy and *darshanas* cannot be overstated and had a major impact on the revival of *advaita vedanta* echoing the Buddha's non-dualism, and emphasizing the inseparability of *brahman* and *atman*.

Another story illustrating *forgetfulness* and the key role played by *remembering* takes place when Shankaracharya was debating with a friend on the pros and cons of the householder's life versus the *sadhu*'s life of renunciation. The friend raised the objection that Shankara was not qualified to debate on this issue because he had never led a householder's life. Shankara took his friend up on this point and decided to run a real-life test.

He was to lay his body down in a safe place with instructions to his friend to search for him after some months at the palace of a neighbouring kingdom where he knew the king was about to pass away. Shankara planned to transfer his etheric subtle body into the king's body at the moment of the king's passing. The Tibetans call this *phowa*: it is one of the *siddhis* (powers) mentioned in ancient texts.

So when the right moment came, Shankara lay down, entered *samyama* on the target (full meditative concentration together with a specific aim) and projected his subtle body into the body of the king who moments before had passed away. The king revived and Shankara awoke to find his awareness and mental faculties inside the king's body, surrounded by wives, ministers, courtiers, sons, daughters and concubines all astonished at the sudden recovery of their king. After a period of 'adjustment' which Shankara used to learn about his new environment and duties, he became so actively engaged running the affairs of state and the palace household, so totally engrossed and absorbed into the details of this new life, that he gradually forgot he was Shankara!

It was not until months later that his friend came to rescue him and remind him he was in fact Shankaracharya! At the very instant of remembering, the life-force connection broke, the king's body fell down lifeless and Shankara re-awoke in his body in the chamber. Shankara was thus able to continue the debate with his friend having acquired first-hand experience of a householder's life and duties!

***

Sri Ramana Maharshi

atma nishtho bhava
hridi visa
parana chalana rodhat
satata pratyavekshanat
manasa svam chinvata
majjatha va
sakshat bhati
aham aham iti
brahma matram
kevalam

Bhagavan Ramana Maharshi 1879-1950, Tiruvannamalai, South India

The reason for dedicating the remainder of this chapter to Ramana Maharshi is that more than any other modern historical yogi he is a perfect example of ancient rishi, with the advantage for us that his life and teaching have been well documented.

Ramana was a yogi in the true sense of having achieved the goal of yoga – *kevala jnana*. As far as is known he had no instruction in yoga from any teacher other than his own direct perception of Nature.

> *Bhagavan* literally means one firmly seated in Reality and is therefore a Reality-Knowledge-holder.

At the age of 16 Ramana had already begun to have glimpses of a Reality unlike the mental cinema of his mind, which he experienced as starting to collapse. This 'collapse' of his ordinary mind was described by him as a 'death' without physically dying. What died was the entire structure of illusions pertaining to a separate sense of 'I', 'me' and 'mine'. Reality of Nature remained.

From the age of 17 Ramana became more and more established in *yoga*, in non-separateness, in the codeless, imageless Consciousness, which he recognized as true Self-Nature. Later, checking ancient texts, he found that the expression in words of his realization tallied closely with Shankara's *advaita vedanta*.

Ramana taught mostly in silence by his mere presence although he did answer questions from some of the seekers who gathered around him. He also composed the above 10 sutras synthesizing his path to yoga, to realization.

Translation of Ramana's yoga sutras quoted above:

"Become firmly fixed in the Self
Enter the Heart
Controlling the movement of the breath
By watching it uninterruptedly
Searching for the "I"-code within the mind
By piercing beyond name and form
Directly witnessing
The "I" of the "I"
Only Brahman
Purely"

Reviewing Ramana's sutras one by one gives the clue to Patanjali's *'untraceable step'*.

atma nishttho bhava
The word *atma* means that which is really Real – the Real Nature.

Nature itself, beyond concepts, words or images. *Nishttho* means to become firmly established in the Real and not come out.

hridi visa

The heart is considered both in ancient India and ancient China as the seat of awareness. It is no accident that the Chinese character for Heart and Mind both contain the character 心 . That the heart is the seat of sensory awareness (including awareness of thinking) is demonstrated by the fact that whenever we nod off while sitting upright, at that very moment our head, unsupported by enough flow of vital energy (*prana*), falls to our chest.

Consciousness with a capital "C" is reflected in the human organism at the heart centre as self-awareness. So this sutra is saying focus on the reflected consciousness in the heart – the awareness of self – and wait for the quantum jump from the reflected mirror image to Consciousness itself. The mirror of Consciousness takes on the form of whatever the mind constructs and contemplates.

The 'how' comes in the next few sutras.

parana chalana rodhat

By watching the oscillation of breathing, its rise and fall, the pauses, the turns, watch it in every way, stay with it, flow with it without letting go of its ever-present Reality, recognizing the nature of the breath as the ever-fresh Life force. It is the ever-present gateway and bridge to Real Aliveness/Real Life.

> It is no coincidence that the German word *atmen* meaning to breathe is almost identical to the Sanskrit word *atman*.
>
> Earliest mentions of atman in the Vedas consider it the ultimate all-pervading sentient principle. In the Upanishads '*know atman as your Self*' is the central theme and is described as the *vital breath* in sentient beings.

satata pratyavekshanat
Watching it uninterruptedly. Only by keeping on top of the thief uninterruptedly, does the thief finally stop pretending to be a policeman and give up. How long the thief can hold out depends on each individual human being's accumulations and investments in mental cinema.

manasa svam chinvata
This is a key sutra. Here *'searching for the "I"-code within the mind'* means delving into the very structure of the 'I' code – the master code. And discovering that what we sense and perceive as our ordinary awareness is itself also a code.

> So, if the code is omnipresent, *how can it be escaped?* The code cannot escape from itself! The code cannot jump outside its own shadow!

The wood fire of codes and images goes on endlessly burning fed by the accumulation of action-reaction. The way for it to be entirely extinguish is by not adding more wood while using the last remaining stick (the 'I' code) to keep on prodding the fire until finally throwing that stick into the last flames.

> When the fire goes out by itself, it cools down: and that is one of the meanings of Nibbana.

majjatha va
Literally, 'dipping in' – this means making the plunge into the radiant ocean of Real Being beyond name and form. This is the quantum jump beyond thinking mind – beyond mental cinema. And the root code and sustainer of the entire edifice of codes and images, the builder and maintainer of illusion (*maya*), is none other than the I code. It means turning around 180 degrees at the 'seat' of the deep heart-mind to witness (the mirror of) Consciousness itself instead of the content of mind reflected in it. This 'turning around' happens when the time is ripe. It cannot be forced or engineered or contrived.

sakshat bhati
directly witnessed

aham aham iti
As the 'I' of the 'I' – I am that – the source of the perception of 'I'. The real sun as opposed to the sun's image reflected in a body of water. The real moon as opposed to the image of the moon reflected in a lake at night.

brahma matram
'Only brahman', means every single thing that is perceived – including perception itself – is experienced as Brahman, as Consciousness, as Nature, as Tao, as Undifferentiated, Undivided, Unlimited, Codeless, Nameless. What the Buddha called *asankhata*.

> **visankhara** *gatam cittam*   *mind gone to the* **codeless**

The superimposed mental cinema of codes and images preventing seeing what was always there, is no more.

kevalam
purely

> What remains is what was always – Consciousness, deathless and eternal, beyond name and form – beyond concepts, codes and images.

Mahavir's attainment of moksha is described also as *keval jnana*.

As Ramana said, "*each moment brings fresh ripeness*". It is not an end; it is not a beginning. It is ongoing completeness, for all endings and all beginnings are in the heartmind only.

Ramana's life is a supreme example of the yoga of enquiry (*jnana yoga*/*jnana marga*) involving prolonged periods of immobility and uninterrupted self-enquiry.

When asked about *asana* or yoga technique, Ramana would simply say, "Single pointed concentration (*ekagrata*) is the best asana." Like the Buddha, Ramana advocated uninterrupted watching of the breath as the best way to anchor the attention in the Real. He did not place any particular emphasis on any physical posture (*asana*) of the body.

Ramana gave a clear illustration of the fundamental paradox we are faced with as human beings. He tells a story about a village where a thief goes round stealing everyone's happiness.

> The mayor of the town, sick and tired of this unsatisfactory situation, and prompted by several intelligent villagers, decides to appoint a policeman to catch the thief. The mayor asks for a volunteer and the thief immediately volunteers to become the policeman. The thief is thus duly appointed as policeman, and thereafter goes round *pretending* to catch the thief, which unknown to everyone else, is none other than himself.
>
> Of course, the thief has no intention whatsoever of arresting himself. On the contrary, by pretending to be policeman he has virtually guaranteed not being caught. He therefore invents an elaborate routine – a charade, a pretence, a phoney search, a phoney investigation – to convince the mayor and fellow villagers that the search for the thief is fully 'on' and his capture is *only a question of time*.
>
> Postponed conveniently into a future that never comes.

Does that not ring a bell? It is called kicking the *can* down the road. Thus we remain stuck in the *cannot*.

Reviewing Ramana's yoga sutras one by one we can determine the clues to success: continuously focused awareness brings about one pointedness (*ekagrata*), and that intensity of continued concentration and undivided attention sets up a confrontation between that which is Real and that which is false and artificial. Eventually the thief is subjected to such pressure that he surrenders and the mind is freed from bondage to any thoughts.

> When the sun of suffering has set,
> There comes this peace,
> Lord of the quiet stars,

This peace of creation,
This place where the Garden grows,
This place where the mandala spins grey.

The fool says in his mind,
That his thoughts are only thoughts.

Saraha v.98-99

***

Chapter 5: Asana

"One pointedness of mind – *ekagrata* – is the best asana"
– Ramana Maharshi

Yoga sadhana – the path of yoga – is about removing obstacles and impediments to abiding and living in a natural state of indivisibility with Nature and the Natural World. Both ancient yogis and ancient Taoists clearly knew this; they shared this same vision and they cultivated a similar attitude.

All movements, fluctuations between opposites, of ups and downs, seasonal changes in Nature including those alterations of the body and its sensations were viewed with equanimity and clear comprehension of the DIM's action.

Stability, equanimity, non-difference and clear comprehension in the face of opposites means cultivating a mental and physical attitude – a posture of both mind and body (asana) – in the face of *oscillations* of mood and feelings, which ancient yogis and Taoists discovered to a large extent to be *oscillations of the thinking mind – citta vritti – as* much as external events in the Real World of Nature.

'Oscillation/s' is another word and concept for 'disturbance/s'.

To discriminate *between which ones* are erroneous stored mind-made coding triggered internally by images, beliefs, hopes and doubts, *and which* ones are the mindbody's own natural DIM-related response to genuine danger is the entire art of discernment.

Discerning which is which is the foundation for true insight.

The thinking mind ever trapped in fixation on opposites is powerless to bring about the 'state of yoga' which in any case, as the Katha Upanishad cautions, 'comes and goes'.

The thinking mind is bound to be confused. It is the originator of all confusion. It itself is built up from confusion. Confusion means putting two or more things together, mixing them up and then mistaking one for another. This is exactly what the artificer **sankhara** (code/coding) does, and these confusions become blockages in the mindbody to be transformed and released. This requires careful discernment.

That discernment is what is referred to as *samma ditthi* – perfect perspective and perfect attitude – occupying first place among the qualities to be developed in the Noble Eightfold Path.

Asana as an unwavering mental and physical attitude can be seen in many anecdotes:

- Siddhartha at one point during his seven-year quest immersed in the practice of austerities (tapas) gave this answer to messengers sent by his father, the King, imploring him to return to palatial duties, by declaring:
- "...it is better to die on the battlefield than to live a life of defeat!"
- At one time a group of monks on returning from an unsuccessful alms round to a nearby village, reported to the Buddha that instead of gifts of food they had instead received insults and abuse, but the great sage counselled:
- "Monks! become as sandalwood which perfumes the very axe which cuts it!"
- Jesus, as he was being nailed to the cross is reported to have had the mental posture and composure to say, "Forgive them Lord, for they do not know what they are doing"!
- The story of the Pandavas is one of the most inspiring. The five sons of King Pandu – Yudhishthira, Bhima, Arjuna, Nakula and Sahadeva who figure prominently in the great epic Mahabharata – were forced into exile by political skullduggery

to spend years on a quest in order to atone for actions committed during the Kurukshetra War. The five brothers had to again undergo another major penance (*tapasya*) by ascending the Himalayas to seek out the Heaven of Lord Vishnu. One by one the brothers perished, succumbing to the adversities of the journey. Only Yudhishthira the eldest reached the summit together with his faithful dog.

Upon their approach, the Gates were flung open and Lord Vishnu appeared in all his splendour exclaiming: "Congratulations Yudhishthira! You alone have passed the test – welcome to Heaven!"

But just as Yudhishthira took a step to walk through the Gates, Lord Vishnu raised a hand: "Wait! No dogs allowed in Heaven! Yudhishthira – you alone may pass!"

To which Yudhishthira replied, "Lord Vishnu, my faithful dog has been with me throughout every ordeal and tribulation! I will not abandon him now. If he cannot pass, I too shall not pass!"

At which Lord Vishnu smiled and said, "Dear Yudhishthira, you have now passed the final test of nobility! You may pass with your faithful companion for he too is an incarnation of Dharma!"

So Yudhishthira and his dog entered Heaven and gazed in awe at the dazzling beauty and wonders therein...but as they gazed around Yudhishthira was unable to find any of his brothers – Bhima, Arjuna, Nakula and Sahadeva – not one of them.

Concerned, Yudhishthira asked of Lord Vishnu, "But where are my brothers, Lord? – I see them not!"

"Ah, Yudhishthira, unfortunately your brothers are not as free from impurities as you, so they still need to spend some time in Hell working off past karmas..."

Whereupon Yudhishthira said to Lord Vishnu, "Then take me right away to the realm of Hell where my brothers abide,

because Heaven without my brothers will be a Hell for
me, whereas together with my brothers Hell will seem like
Heaven!"

"*That* Yudhishthira was the *final test!*" declared Lord
Vishnu satisfied, whereupon Yudhishthira's four brothers
appear in Heaven beside him.

That dear Reader is *asana*! That quality of mindbody posture is
mahamudra – the *grand gesture* which the great Tibetan yogi Tilopa
describes so magnificently in his Song of Mahamudra, which sums up
the attitude of those yogis and yoginis whose posture of body and mind
(whose *asana*) dissolves all knots generated by past mistakes, freeing
the full flow of life-force intelligence to rise to the summit (*sahasrara*)
and regain Immortality (*amata* – the Deathless).

***

Hatha yoga asanas

The *asanas* of hatha yoga are a 1500 year later development in the
known history of yoga. Patanjali's Yogasutra – the benchmark manual
of classical yoga – makes no mention of *asana* as understood in modern
hatha yoga.

> Sources of modern hathayoga asanas can be seen in the appendices'
> two charts compiled by J. Mallinson & colleagues.

In Yogasutra only three stanzas are dedicated to asana. Patanjali dedica-
tes merely two sutras to asana and one other sutra to explain the effects.
The sense of asana in Patanjala yoga is **one single asana to be held for
as long as needed** in order to still the mind, steady the body and set in
motion the arduous job of deblocking the plumbing. Ramana Maharshi
echoes this emphasis on one-pointedness: *ekagrata*.

Modern hatha yoga practiced properly is an excellent system of fitness with plenty of benefits – increased wellbeing and energy, better mood, more flexible body, agility, beauty and all the rest of a long list of advantages. But this kind of asana practice cannot lead to a thorough deblocking of the plumbing because these asanas are held for relatively such short times. By changing asana often the whole approach becomes fragmentary and partial, haphazard even. It is rather like drilling many shallow holes in a big field expecting to find deep water.

It might happen but there can be no certainty.

Since 1971 I have been practicing hathayoga asanas almost daily to complement other sports and exercize routines. I love hathayoga but I don't consider it has much to do with the original yoga. In fact it smacks of the thinking mind's favourite pastime of wanting to have it both ways, i.e. eat the cake and keep it.

In Spanish there is an even better expression to illustrate this.

"Querer nadar y guardar la ropa", meaning wanting to swim across a river but at the same time keep the clothes dry.

"Having it both ways" is not ekagrata. It's the opposite which is to remain divided. And as long as we remain divided, we remain defeated.

There is an ancient Taoist saying in the Tao Te Ching: "In making the slightest distinction, Heaven and Earth are set apart and the Ten Thousand Things appear!"

It echoes the old political expression "divide and conquer"! Well, in yoga it means divide yourself and be defeated.

The shifty, scheming, devious thinking mind goes on trying by any and every means to avoid the unavoidable confrontation with what has to be done in order to return to Immortal Life and true happiness.

Nevertheless, modern hathayoga is excellent as a foundation with which to initiate the deeper practice of yoga as envisaged by the ancients. No efforts with the right intention behind them are ever wasted.

***

At the time the Buddha began teaching, and also at the time of Patanjali around three centuries later, there is no conception at all of yoga as physical fitness. Among the yoga and ascetic communities of those times, the body was considered more of an obstacle – not part of a solution – not something to spend time and effort cultivating and improving but rather something whose limitations and precarious nature were such that the best course of action was to practice indifference towards it. This practice of indifference was often taken to extremes in the practice of *tapas*. Even in today's India living examples of such extremes can be found.

Thus, the prevailing view then, and lasting long after, was that through *tapas/tapasya* – austerity of body and mind – lay the path to liberation. And if not liberation, then at least to *siddhis*.

In the yoga path taught by the Buddha – the Nobel Eightfold Path – there are only references to sitting down asana and natural bodily asana. Emphasis is placed on uninterrupted recollection by remembering whatever is real in all stages of bodily movement and positioning: standing | walking | sitting | lying down | changing positions | attending calls of nature | eating and so forth – and the accompanying sensations, perceptions and volitions.

The view that the body is an obstacle and somehow has to be 'conquered' along with the mind had been widespread before and during the years Siddhartha Gautama and his contemporary Mahavir had taken tapas to extremes. Siddhartha had also participated in extreme penance and austerities but came to reject them as counterproductive favouring instead what he called "the middle path".

Nevertheless, the so-called *middle path* he discovered and later taught, is from our current day perspective of addiction to comforts and pleasures far from what most people would remotely consider a middle path – in fact it looks extremely tough by today's standards.

Let's take a look at what at that time the more ardent followers of the *middle path* were expected to do:

- sit upright throughout the night and never lie down;
- wear only garments sewn up from scraps of cloth (no finery whatsoever);
- eat only what is given (cultivating choicelessness in food);
- only one meal a day before noon, accepting whatever is offered as alms;
- avoid high comfortable beds, all fragrances, jewelry and bodily adornment;
- avoid any form of entertainment and distraction in the form of shows, music, dancing and theatre;
- remain outdoors in the Nature the maximum amount of time.

These practices show that the *middle path* at the time of the Buddha – and probably for centuries afterwards – was still extremely austere compared to modern day standards of yoga or vipassana practice.

Yet Jains at that time adhering to the more austere discipline of Mahavir are reported to have frowned upon what they viewed as the 'cushy', 'soft' lifestyle of the 'middle pathers'!

In the Buddha's yoga the only reference to asana is in the context of arranging a seat to sit down for *jhana* and *satipatthana* practice. Seated asana was clearly highly important for developing full concentration (*jhana*). Recollecting what is Real with regard to bodily postures, sensations, feelings, states of mind and contents of mind was uninterruptedly applied in all stages of bodily movement and position: standing, walking, sitting, lying down, when changing positions etc.

***

So asana in its broader sense means 'situation'. It has retroactively come to mean a physical posture but the original sense means 'staying in a situation', facing and confronting a circumstantial situation. It is a posture of mind as well as of body both together.

> In this sense asana is closely related to tapas. In fact asana becomes tapas – *is tapas* – if prolonged and sustained.
> Any sustained effort which pushes the mindbody beyond ordinary limits experienced in everyday life in fact amounts to tapas.

Asana therefore involves a situation or a circumstance as much as a physical posture. The mental attitude of equanimity is all-important. Asana produces confrontation with a situation until the situation is resolved by Nature – by the relentless action of DIM. So asana can be a *situational setup* in a context of circumstances, and not just a physical posture.

In the texts you will read that a yogi goes to a quiet place in Nature, arranges a seat and sits down at the root of a great tree. Or goes to a quiet cave or to the bank of a river. And there the yogi, after previously attending to calls of nature or other necessities of body such as taking adequate nourishment, arranges his or her bodily parts into a comfortable position, with spine fully erect, shoulders relaxed, arms and hands at ease, chin and face level, breathing steady, even and natural, with mind focused and attention poised for just watching.

The starting position has to be as stable and as comfortable as possible so that uprightness and stillness – non-movement – can be sustained and prolonged with the minimum effort.

Asanas before and after sitting

Badakonasana

This asana is probably the most essential and indispensable for hip opening and pelvis preparation if you are aiming to sit cross-legged comfortably for prolonged periods. This preliminary asana must surely be one of eight fundamental hathayoga asanas. It combats the atrophy caused by sitting in chairs since generations.

Janusirasana

Both sides with variants including half-lotus, which will depend on if you are preparing for *padmasana.*

Patchimottanasana

Forward bend with both legs forward as well as the variants with legs spread wide, and side stretch, is an excellent back relaxing asana and hip pivot.

> Backbends are important for compensating forward bends. I incorporate a series of spinal twist into daily routine as well as standing asanas for balance.

After sitting, use any known asana that relieves stiffness, aches and pains, remembering these manifestations are much more mental than they appear to be.

Sitting asanas

Padmasana – full lotus position – has always been considered an ideal choice because of its symmetry and stability and the fact that the pressure of the two feet on the thighs promotes circulation in the upper body while reducing congestion and stagnation in the lower body. Siva and Buddha are both depicted mostly in padmasana. Unfortunately, for almost all of us, the full lotus is not an asana option because it is either too stressful to begin with, or rapidly becomes stressful after a mere few minutes.

However, Burmese meditators discovered an effective and comfortable alternative which is almost symmetrical: fold one leg placing one heel lightly touching the centre of the body just in front of the pubic area with the other leg then bent to lightly place the other heel in front of the first heel. This asana has several noteworthy advantages. It avoids any pressure of one leg on the other leg; avoids leg pressure on any other bodily part; is almost symmetrical and equally comfortable at the base for both folded legs. Pressure on the ankles can be minimized by placing a wide flat cushion underneath.

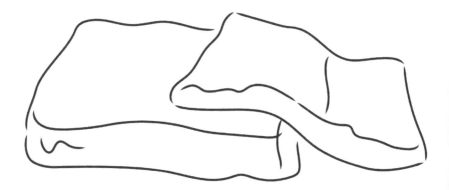

For maximum comfort at 'take-off', experienced yoga sitters use two flat square futon-like cushions, the upper one placed on the middle of the lower one so that the overlap is in the place where the heels, calves and knees rest, while the buttocks are seated comfortably on the higher double layer.

Ancient Egyptians and Chinese used specially designed high-back chairs with arm rests.

For comfortable kneeling in *yogasana,* the Japanese developed a special stool which removes pressure from the knees and lower legs.

Some of the great Jain yogis used the standing position – *tadasana.* Mahavir would remain in *tadasana* until the thinking mind was stilled. Then he would take a step forward but as soon as thoughts returned, again he would stand still in *tadasana.* Mahavir practiced this asana continuously until the thinking mind stopped entirely – until the breath became perfectly balanced and samadhi attained.

In our era Ramana Maharshi (d.1950) sat in *sukkhasana* until he attained realization. Afterwards he would mostly adopt a relaxed sitting position even propped against a rock or the back of a chaise longue.

Whatever the asana, the choice of asana is up to you and will depend on the aptitude of your own bodily structure and flexibility. Use as many cushions or supports as you want – it doesn't matter! The point is to achieve maximum comfort and ease *at the start,* with no possibility of bodily harm being caused by the asana itself.

The spine must be kept upright in a centered axis between earth and sky – with no sack-like sagging or leaning like a Tower of Pisa!

If you lie down, you will fall asleep – that is the natural reflex of the body and thinking mind – and then during sleep all sorts of uncontrollable movements and fidgeting will happen as the mindbody begins a choreography of posture adjustments to avoid confrontation with discomfort.

So *savasana* – lying down flat on one's back in corpse-like position – is not an option. *Savasana* is good for deep relaxation but no use at all as an asana for sustained confrontation with blockages because you will switch off and fall asleep.

Falling asleep defeats the purpose of confrontation so don't use savasana. The DIM cannot do the full job of de-blocking the plumbing while lying down. *It does another job instead but not the job aimed for in yoga asana.*

Immobility and Confrontation

The objective of *asana* is to remain as still and motionless as possible for prolonged periods of time because the ancient yogis discovered that changing of postures hides *dukkha* (stress) and thereby avoids most of the confrontation with what needs to be confronted.

> Stillness in asana is the open but ignored secret of yoga.

In yoga asana the aim therefore is to maximize the amount of time in immobility. It is through confrontation with discomfort – with stress – that understanding eventually dawns that discomfort is a mental, emotional phenomenon thus an *energetic* issue – *of psychemechanical nature* – not a problem of the physical body.

That means discomfort arising in sitting asana is not the result of *external* factors but the result of *internal* reactions triggered by the presence of **sankharas**. The triggering of reactions arises whenever the tapes of coding embedded in the body get 'touched' and activated (disturbed). What kind of reactions arise depends on how the sensations have been 'turned' and 'biased' through identification into pleasant, unpleasant and neutral feelings hence triggering like, dislike and ignore.

Firstly, stillness/immobility is only ever relative, never total. Obviously, because at every moment – in addition to breathing and the heart beating – there are countless processes, big and small, going on inside all the bodily systems that, working harmoniously together as a bigger DIM, enable a human lifeform to function optimally. At the micro level the amount of ongoing DIM processes runs into millions if not billions, depending on how far you go into the numerical analysis.

Therefore, the stillness/immobility we are talking about is maintaining asana as unchanging as possible. This means avoiding moving

- head, hands, feet, swaying trunk etc.,
- especially changing the position of the limbs is to be avoided at all costs;
- no fidgeting (something frequently witnessed in vipassana courses).

At the beginning the meditator thinks many of his or her problems during immobility sitting have a physical cause or origin. But anyone who has done a 10-day vipassana course or equivalent retreat in raja or gnana yoga realizes by the fifth or sixth day that the problem is mental and emotional not physical, which means the problems lie at the subtle level of prana blockage, not necessarily at the physical structural level.

Prana flow blocked by *sankhara* will bring up *dukkha* of one kind or another and this alters the breathing pattern as will be seen in the next chapter on pranayama. The Dim tendency will always work to harmonize the mindbody and it will immediately start to breathe in a particular way to combat the impact of the discomfort/distress and begin dissolving the blockage as long as we don't move.

These altered breathing patterns were observed by yogis both in themselves, in others and in animals too, and were over time systemized, that is to say *'reverse engineered'* into pranayamas that have come down to us in the form of specific breathwork techniques.

Nature was the original teacher, and through observation, practice, trial and error, her natural patterns were eventually systematized so others could use them and benefit from them.

Asana therefore sets up perfect conditions for the Dim tendency to do its work of releasing the bondage of coding, erasing the tapes of imprints, freeing up the energy pathways.

All we have to do is minimize interference with the Dim tendency's work. Therefore, in asana the strategy is simply to stay still and let the DIM do its job, which it will, inexorably, relentlessly, at its own pace, in its own time and rhythm.

> A note of caution here: this does not apply if the starting position is wrongly or unnaturally arranged – we have to be careful and discerning in order not to mistake genuine warning signals of the body from signals of discomfort triggered by the very coding that needs to be expunged.

During sustained sitting I have in the past made a couple of such mistakes not heeding genuine bodily alarm signals, in one case nearly causing serious damage to one ankle by steadfastly ignoring the pain.

By sustaining asana for three hours and longer the yogi also develops the *paramitas* of energy, patience and determination (*viriya; khanti; adhithana*). This happens naturally as a result of the DIM's action during immobility. The more these three qualities develop, the more we get into alignment with Big Dim.

So asana involves setting up conditions for a perfect storm that can be survived intact without bodily harm! It becomes the operating theatre where a deep operation on the mindbody can take place by setting up a confrontation between the Dim tendency of Nature versus our deviant a-dim nature (*asava*) originated by the presence of embedded mind-made coding (*sankhara*).

Of course, Patanjali does not put it quite like that because by the time he came to synthesize what had come down to him of yoga from the time of Mahavir and Gautama Buddha, certain key words and phrases of earlier teachings had become misinterpreted, which is probably the reason Patanjali makes no mention of the Buddha's system of yoga, even though the eight limbs of the Yogasutra closely ressemble the eightfold noble path.

It seems that the Patanjala Yogasutra are a combintion of Mahavir's teaching of *ahimsa* together with the Buddha's teaching on yoga minus the -isms. It looks like an attempt to synthesize and present the essence of the instructions in the context of yoga *sadhana*, not any religious belief system.

> It is doubtful that Siddhartha Gautama had any intention to found a new religion. In fact there is every evidence to support the contrary view which is why Chan in China and Zen in Japan in their origins and *vipassana* in its later development in Burma are all attempts to return to an 'ism-free' original teaching and practice –what SN Goenka called 'an art of living'.

Confrontation should be with relaxed determination (*adhitthana*) and perseverance. Forcing can be counterproductive.

> "Absolutely certain there is water at depth, the yogi drills a single deep hole, and not lots of superficial ones!" – Chaitanyananda

Three hours was discovered by yogis of ancient India to be a bench-mark, a crossover point because every three hours the life force (*prana*) in a human being completes one cycle of the nadi channel network in one element (see Chapter 9).

> "Just as to find water it is necessary to drill only a single hole as deep as required, and no use in drilling multiple superficial holes, so likewise a single asana can take you to samadhi sooner or later. Performing dozens of asanas for a few seconds or minutes each may be good for health and fitness but it will not take you to the final goal of yoga.
>
> "What is the purpose of performing 200 hathayoga asanas if we cannot hold still in a single posture for one hour, let alone three hours?!"
>
> Hatha yoga is for fitness of the physical body; rajyoga yoga is to undergo the death of the thinking mind."
>
> Chaitanyanda (paraphrased)

Be still, passively watch what is going on at the level of pushes and patterns and let the DIM do what it knows how to do. In every confrontation that arises, the opportunity simultaneously presents itself to discover what needs to be discovered outside our everyday scope of awareness, and deblock whatever prevents us living at ease.

The ancient Chinese word for 'crisis' contains two hieroglyphs, 危 机;
one stands for challenge, the other for opportunity.

Confrontation with any crisis requires patience, steadfastness and trust that it is a worthwhile process.

sabbe sankhara dukkha

All thinking mind-made codes are dukkha because in some way or other – because they are to some extent artificial and unnatural – they limit and restrict the life-force intelligence.

Mind-made coding is therefore the root cause of all avoidable suffering.

Changing of postures hides suffering and conceals discomfort. Therefore, holding asana will reveal what needs to be done at the deeper attitudinal level than just the physical.

"Done is what had to be done! In these conditions (now), there is no more of this or of that!"
Victory declaration of arahants

In other words no more blockages to be removed! Compulsive behaviour caused by codes made in ignorance has been rooted out!

Immobility times
The initial goal is three hours, then increasing by three-hour periods. The reason for these three-hour time periods is explained in Chapter 9.

Nature in the wild provided the ancients with clues. They observed that animals whenever seriously unwell would go to a quiet secluded place where they could remain undisturbed for long periods, and there they remained *completely still* in the least uncomfortable position they could arrange their body. And there they waited for Nature – the Dim tendency – to re-establish order and harmony and cure them. But if their condition was too far gone for the DIM to be able to effect a cure, they died.

Nature looks brutal from a human perspective but she is fair. Nature is much more a cooperation than a competition, and thus in wild nature lifeforms do not survive unless they are in perfect health, in possession of full faculties. The demise of the unwell is then taken up by other nearby creatures and organisms as food or fuel, and what is left over nourishes the earth. Nothing (no thing) is wasted. It seems humans are the only lifeforms in Nature unaware of these facts of life.

Changing of the postures hides the issues that need resolving. If we fidget and move, even if slightly, thereby changing the arrangement of parts of the body – even from one uncomfortable position to another equally uncomfortable one – then even so, the process of deblocking a particular *nadi* can be aborted.

In the form of Chinese yoga known as *tai chi* – where the practice involves a steady flow of movement instead of immobility – the aim is likewise *"to create pressure and heat in the boiler"* – in the '*cauldron*', like a modern pressure cooker – and if the pressure is released too early through a big valve or various little valves then the pressure and heat cannot build up to a sufficiently high enough level (optimum DIM pressure) to do the job of opening up the closed circuits.

> Sustaining the process is all-important. In the case of tai chi, low pos-
> ture and slow even flow of movement is sustained in order to build up
> sufficient pressure for the breathing to properly fan through the body's
> circuits.

In Chinese yoga the breath comes first. Breathing guides the mind, and the mind then guides the movement of the body or non-movement in the case of standing yoga or sitting still yoga.

Practicality and practice

It takes quite some time and practice to become comfortable sitting for an hour. Some people take to it much quicker than others. I would suggest using every sitting opportunity to sit cross-legged. This can easily be done on the sofa when relaxing or reading. You can also arrange a work chair at your desk with no side arms to sit cross-legged while working at the computer, drawing or writing.

The other day I saw a five-year-old boy in a bus just happily sitting cross-legged on his seat sucking a lollipop. Naturally and effortlessly he just sat in *sukkhasana* chatting with his grandmother. To sit cross-legged is not usual in Spain and most people have difficulty to be comfortable sitting like that so it was encouraging to see how at ease this boy was even with his shoes on.

Depending on the accumulation of blockages, most adults have considerable difficulty sitting still for even one hour. It depends on the impediments to free flow of prana throughout the mindbody.

A test of the degree to which the plumbing is blocked or unblocked is to be able to remain comfortably in a single position for three hours. By 'comfortably' is meant physically, emotionally and mentally comfortable, unperturbed by any internally arising sensation of disturbance. Thus, asana acts as a mirror which shows you exactly where you are, and in which self-deception becomes impossible.

*** *** ***

Modern day asana and tapas

Nowadays several forms of athletics and endurance sports – such as iron man, triathlon, weightlifting, ocean swimming – are modern forms of *tapas*, because they generate tremendous vital heat, and to a degree free up and deblock the bodily systems leading to increased strength, vitality, wellbeing, satisfaction and contentedness.

Difference is yoga asana = immobility

Each of these endurance modalities makes the mindbody react in specific ways and will alter the breathing to adjust its pattern in order to deal with the stress so that, if it can, it will restore homeostasis, DIM.

When the stressor is extreme, fainting becomes a possibility when the mind – especially the thinking mind – is no longer able to cope with the level of discomfort. In Spanish the word for faint is revealing – *desmayar* (des-maya – in English dis-may is from the same root) – the mind (*citta*) is expelled from illusion (*maya*) so that the DIM gets a free hand at repair work in a similar way to the surgeon in an operating theatre while the patient is under anaesthesia.

So-called 'loss of 'awareness' is only a temporary shutdown of the thinking mind to allow the *deeper mind* – we have called it heart-mind, the one that handles all the myriad different DIMs in the different systems in the human body – to do its best work possible under the prevailing circumstances, un-interfered with by any hysterical reaction of the thinking mind. The dreamer – the thinking mind, the illusionist, the pretender – is expelled from daytime dreaming while the DIM gets on with its work of restoring homeostasis.

In fact this switch-off happens every single day of our life. In every cycle of 24 hours the human being needs to switch off the thinking mind for several hours while the DIM gets on with the task of repairing, restoring, balancing and re-establishing the optimal physiological state for the next morning/day. We can think of this as a daily reset.

Sleep and dream

It is common knowledge that if human beings are systematically deprived of or prevented from sleep, they rapidly become unhinged, unbalanced and unwell.

You have probably seen footage of people sleeping. It's truly amazing the amount of involuntary movement, changing of positions and bodily contortions!

> Changing of position and posture conceals *dukkha* because it avoids the confrontation!

The limitation of the DIM is that it has wonderful wisdom in the present moment of here and now but no sense of past and future as conceived by the thinking mind.

Therefore the yogis of old had to devise strategies to prevent sleep from interfering with immobility. They realized stillness in the posture had to be maintained.

Dreaming is when the thinking mind is only partially active. The dream content is all about oneself and one's internal reactions to disturbances. In dreams there are no 'others'. Every aspect of a dream is an aspect of oneself translated into dream content of what is occurring at that moment to oneself.

Dream is mirroring different aspects of physical events like temperature changes, digestion, pressure from the position of the body's parts at different levels of oneself – physical, mental, emotions, thoughts – all of which need to be continuously integrated into coherence for overall balance. So dreams too play a restorative function but it is during the dreamless deepest level of sleep that the most restorative work is done by the DIM. Without deep sleep no amount of dreaming can do the job. Good quality deep sleep is therefore an essential requirement for a healthy human being. In yoga, the state of *samadhi* provides equally restorative and balancing benefits, probably even more so.

> "Long is the night for he who stays awake!"
> The Buddha

Conversely, no amount of tinkering with the outside world can clear anyone's inner blockages and imbalances. This rule can be applied individually as well as collectively.

Therefore, any external application of FORCE to force/oblige/coerce the external world and its circumstances to conform to an image of how things *should* be is the fruit of wrong attitude and wrong understanding of Nature. It is organized insanity. Such thinking and acting is doomed to failure and bound to create more mischief.

> Any wilful action by the human being that is not in alignment with the will of the Dim tendency is bound to cause mischief, complicate matters and delay harmony instead of promoting it.

Asana provides the opportunity to be witness to the rebalancing requirements of Nature. Therefore, we can consider any persistent manifestation of disharmony as a clear signal indicating need for a return to DIM. Such indications are like warning lights on the instrument dials of our automobile telling us what needs to be adjusted.

That is what is meant by the Four Noble Truths or the equally ancient fourfold formulation of dis-ease, its cause, its cure and the remedy. If understood correctly, the problem itself points to what needs to be addressed – the *origination* and not the symptom per se. Hence almost every stressful situation in life can be used to open up new pathways previously blocked. In alchemy this became known as transmuting base metal into noble metal (copper into silver; silver into gold) thereby reaching fulfilment of Life's highest purpose.

***

Modern yoga

Modern yoga is a long path – enjoyable and rewarding for its own sake day by day – but only giving the limited fruits it is capable of, no more.

If you are unsatisfied with the consumer society approach to yoga and unconvinced by the mainstream narrative of 'progress and development', and instead *really want to discover your full potential as a human being*, then there is no other choice but to develop asana until the fan of breathing hits the blockages.

In yoga the fan of the life-force intelligence waved by the in-and-out breathing collides with the accumulated *sankhara*, not the other way around. The yogi sets up conditions knowing full well that sooner or later an encounter will come with what needs to be addressed. By doing so, she or he comes to experience non-separateness with all fellow human beings, with all living beings and Nature as a whole, and to know what the ancient teachers were pointing to.

The quintessence of asana is therefore: "Be still and discover!"

Conclusion on asana

Did we not once upon a time walk the earth, swim the oceans, traverse the skies like gods and goddesses, resplendent in attributes, fearless and wise in aspect, in full harmony and synchronicity with Nature? Let us become so once again without need for props and crutches!

Is it not curious that all modern technologies are on track to emulate what the ancient texts exactly describe as the *siddhis* that appear to have been lost through forgetfulness and atrophy?

All that is required – *and this 'all' is a **big-ask!*** – is be still, wait and watch the DIM do its relentless work of reordering and restoring whatever needs to be straightened out. And this it will do in its own time, at its own pace, at its own rhythm, at the energetic, emotional and mental levels.

"Be still and know that I am God!" – the essence of yoga summed up in eight words in the Old Testament. Let the DIM have its way and let belief, hope and doubt be replaced by true insight-knowledge.

The beginning, middle and end of the whole story of Life is the Energy of Love, all else is mental tennis, cinema productions, delaying tactics, attempts to have it both ways, trying to swim and keep our clothes dry while indulging in the self-fascination of an imaginary "I", reeling in intoxication, inebriated, infatuated, driven methodically mad by identification with codes, images and concepts – all make believe.

Life is the meaning of Life. Life needs no further meaning in addition to itself. It itself *is* the meaning: all else is mind-bewildering games of the thinking mind. Become love of life and that leads to immortality. That is the message of the ancients.

The next chapter, Pranayama, is about what happens to the breath when asana is prolonged and the storm arrives. For that is the direct consequence of asana.

"What happens when the fan hits the shit?!"

According to ancient empirical yoga science, *prana* – the *breath* which carries not just *air* but also the 'push' of life force, its vital energy current, its DIM intelligence – travels through the network of nadis following a pathway of precise order such that prana completes one circuit in each tattwa every three hours, then switches to the next tattwa. This is looked at in detail in chapters 9 and 10.

Therefore, in any three-hour period it is guaranteed that prana will at some point be switching from one tattwa to the next tattwa. Around this transition point or changeover moment, a period of turbulence can occur where the 'shit hits the fan' or more correctly put, 'the fan hits the shit'!

The fan of prana blows into a blocked nadi – a nadi which has been narrowed, restricted or even shut down completely by a particular code (*sankhara*). In other words blocked by undigested material labelled and suppressed as unwelcome, unwanted, unacceptable, disliked, hated, feared or whatever negative meaning in ignorance was originally attributed to it.

Whatever the name – and naming it is not important, in fact naming and labelling are to be curtailed and at least put into their proper place – **it is a blockage caused by replacing a <u>real event with a false effect</u>**. A real cause encoded into a misinterpreted imaginary effect (itself an event!) triggering an inappropriate reaction/response.

***

Chaper 6: Pranayama

BREATH IS REAL   BREATH IS REAL   BREATH IS REAL

Pranayama regularly practiced while thoroughly understanding what we are doing and the reason for it, holds one of the great secrets to success in yoga. Whether through *natural* or *deliberate* breathing, the contemplation of breathing is an inexhaustible treasure trove of insights into the true Nature of Reality.

> "Stopping in and out breathing, stopping the thinking mind, transmuting the sexuak energy's passion into compassion are three paths to *samadhi*."
>
> Swami Chaitanyananda Saraswati

Prana – the Sanskrit word for *life force* – is the unique principle of vitality pervading the totality of the Natural World including so-called inanimate matter. It points to the same thing as the Chinese word Chi or Qi 氣.

> Chi Kung 氣功 is therefore an equivalent Chinese concept to pranayama, and equally ancient.

Since prana permeates the totality of the Real World of Nature it is absolutely related to Ether and Consciousness (Chapter 12). In the case of living beings its most evident manifestation is in the 'breath'.

Pranayama in Patanjali's eightfold system comes after asana for good reason. Pranayama as conceived by the ancients arises as mindbody's response to asana.

Patanjala Yogasutra has only five short sutras on pranayama even while emphasizing its importance and value for stabilizing the body, calming the mind and preparing a yogi for *dhyana* and *samadhi*.

These five terse remarks of Patanjali on breath/breathing do not explain details of pranayama. At that time pranayama was most likely focused on regulating natural breathing arising in response to asana. This is in line with the Buddha's *satipatthana* system of recollection of in-and-out breathing (*anapanasati*–Satipatthana Chapter 9). Also, the *raj yoga* of Patanjali aims directly for *keval kumbhaka* as discussed below.

The previous chapter has pointed out that *asana* in the historical perspective of the Buddha and Patanjali several centuries later, is not only a physical posture but a posture involving a situational confrontation. A circumstantial confrontation potentially able to liberate the life-force intelligence from *attitudinal* obstacles to free flow and full expression.

The yogis and seers of ancient times were sharp observers. They used the pushes and patterns of the Natural World as their direct frame of reference. They realized that in every situation in life, the mindbody reacts differently according to circumstances. And that these differences can be understood as pointers to meanings.

They noticed that the mindbody's Dim tendency automatically produces specific types of altered breathing in response to different kinds of stresses and disturbances. They observed that by means of these modalities of breathing, the overall DIM was able to be restored and, as a result, optimum dynamic equilibrium sustained.

Thus, every situation in which either an external "stress" or an internal "stress" or a combination of both, causes the mindbody to deviate from its DIM, a specific type of breathing pattern manifests naturally to compensate. Mother Nature comes to the rescue.

Reverse engineered, these different modes and patterns of breath reaction became formal pranayama – ways used to consciously influence, direct and regulate the life force through breathing and/ or suspension of breathing (non-breathing of air).

Ways to assist in the control and direction of life-energy breath were systematized over time through experimentation and became the various structured formal pranayamas outlined in the medieval hathayoga texts

– Shiva Samhita, Hathayoga Pradipika, Gheranda Samhita, Vasishta Samhita amongst others – which don't let's forget were composed around one thousand years after Patanjali and therefore around 1300 years after Gautama Buddha put yoga so firmly on the radar of human awareness.

Therefore, asana clearly precedes pranayama not the other way around because pranayama arises from Nature herself revealing what type of breathing is needed to re-establish balance in the mindbody, thereby sustaining overall DIM, harmony, health and power.

Examples of external or internal situations which induce specific reactions of altered breathing can be seen in multiple situations:

Exposure to heat and cold

Animals do not need to learn pranayama! They do not need to wear clothes nor have they any need for central heating or air conditioning. They have not lost touch with Nature or their nature and they (or rather their mindbody's DIM) knows full well what to do to regulate tempe-rature and life energy within a certain range.

From observation of how animals deal with overheating and dehy-dration, the pranayamas of *sitali* and *sitkari* were derived (reverse engineered).

Sitkari (hissing inbreath) and *sitali* (cooling inbreath) both are done with inbreath drawn in through the mouth with tongue placed in par-ticular positions. Both have similar applications: *sitkari* more focused on calming thirst from overheating; *sitali* more focused on cooling from overheating.

In similar manner, exposure to cold naturally induces an intensely vigorous breathing response in the human body from which *bhastrika* – the fiery pranayama – and other pranayama like *tummo* were derived. Wim Hof's power breathing technique to heat up the body after intense cold exposure is a perfect example in modern times.

Childbirth

Natural childbirth can be an extremely stressful situation inducing a corresponding power breathing response well known to midwives and taught to women of all cultures since ancient times. The reason it needs to be taught (re-learnt) is that the thinking mind is able to interfere with and block the body's natural breathing response. Therefore, teaching the natural way to breathe to assist dilation and natural birth can be necessary to overcome interference from the thinking mind.

Intense physical effort

All of us are familiar with how breathing alters to accommodate situations of increased physical exertion like climbing steep stairs, high intensity sports, lifting weights and so forth.

Swimmers for example develop different types of pranayama for open sea swimming than in the swimming pool. Long distance swims in the ocean in cold temperatures require a different breathing pattern than short sprints in a warm pool. Necessity and circumstance dictate the pattern, the rhythm and the force.

Calls of nature

This is an interesting one. There are natural pranayama (not usually taught but discoverable by oneself) which induce and facilitate quick and easy expulsion of stool and urine. In prehistory when the human being lived in the Nature in close proximity to wild animals and danger from other humans wandering around, the moment of attending a call of nature was potentially a moment of great vulnerability. Consequently humans had to discover a pranayama to ensure rapid completion of the task so that exposure time to danger was minimized. Fight or flight is problematic in the middle of a shit!

Pleasure and **pain** from prolonged asana has already been discussed in Chapter 5 on asana.

Hunger and **thirst** – *sitali* or *sitkari* can be used as above.

Sobbing from grief, hysterical laughter, threading a needle, performing delicate tasks needing stillness – all manifest quite different patterns and modality of breathing in order to compensate the particular disturbance/ stress of the circumstance.

All of these are real life situations that induce different patterns of breath/breathing to regulate and control the vital force.

> If breathing were just a question of the human body getting enough oxygen in, would there be so many different patterns and modalities?

Whether we realize it or not, every situation, every circumstance in life subtly alters our breathing as the mindbody automatically adjusts and fine-tunes breathing in the optimum way to maintain or restore DIM.

From the above we can see that most pranayama are reverse engineered from real-life situations. A few, such as *lom vilom,* are not (alternate nostril breathing also called *anuloma viloma*) and have been worked out through deducing potential usefulness, then by trial and error.

Therefore, pranayama can be understood as:

1. arising from natural life situations/confrontations
2. systematized over time into formal breathing patterns for methodical practice and that, through imitation, the latter are mostly derived from the former.

Etymology of pranayama

In either case, whether the two component words of **pranayama** are considered to be *prana+yama* or *prana+ayama* both have to do with control and regulation.

> The control and regulation aspect of pranayama has two key aspects: one is **active** and the other is **passive**.

The active meaning of *control* is where the thinking mind decides to impose a pattern of breathing upon the mindbody as in the case of formal pranayama. In the case it is forced ('forced' is one of the meanings of the word 'hatha' in hatha yoga) great care must be taken in learning and executing such pranayamas because if they are performed in a way that is out of alignment with the DIM of Nature, then the pranayama can cause health problems.

> The passive meaning of control is where the method *only involves watching, witnessing and remembering* (this way of pranayama is completely safe and natural).

- Watching how the bodymind breathes from moment to moment
- Remembering to notice the subtle details: pattern, frequency, quality of the breath, texture, grossness, fineness, temperature and length.

This passive form of breath control is the method that played such a prominent role in Siddhartha Gautama's own path to liberation.

In passive pranayama it is the deep mind – the bodymind, the heart-mind – that guides the Dim tendency of Nature without the thinking mind interfering. In active pranayama the thinking mind deliberately imposes a breathing pattern in order to achieve a specific result. Each have their time and place in yoga sadhana.

***

The precise relationship between vital force and breath – which ancient rishis and yogis seemed to have worked out thousands of years ago – is still not understood by modern science! Modern science persists in overlooking the truth that **the push of breath is one thing, the content of breath (its components) are another thing, and its patterns yet another aspect**, even though all three aspects are closely connected and function together.

> Breath is one thing and the force that pushes the breath into our lungs is quite another thing. Breath is a volume of air with a chemical composition entering in and going out the lungs whereas the forces that

bi-directionally push the breath back and forth have power, velocity and frequency as well as intention, energy, awareness and intelligence.

Breath can therefore be understood as the 'carrier' of life-energy intelligence'.

And because these two separate but intimately connected events happen together so close-by (in tandem) they are being confused. In this confusion the breath itself – the carrier along with its contents – is being given far more emphasis than the *pushing force,* which to a certain extent is being ignored by sciences and disregarded even by modern yoga. Likewise, the *patterns* of the breathing are not given sufficient attention.

In science neither aspect seems to have been thoroughly investigated from the above angles which is surprising given the paramount importance of breath and breathing not only to yoga practice but to Life itself.

One of the purposes of this book is to encourage research into both aspects: the carrier of the life force and the life force itself. As well as the interactive relationship between the two! In Chapter 10 the characteristic flows of prana are described in detail.

Nevertheless – despite the apparent lack of yoga-focused scientific research – renewed interest in breath and breathing techniques has happily resurfaced in recent years in the sports and wellness communities. But still little is known about pranayama in yoga, about its subtler aspects, very likely because the keys have been passed down orally directly from teacher to student and are not recorded in detail in yoga manuals.

As an early example of yoga manual, Patanjala Yogasutra is so terse it reads more like a checklist or memo for those who already have direct experience rather than a treatise for those who have little or none. Because of this, students have been condemned to suffer the guesswork of commentators!

A word of caution here. Don't practice formal pranayama without a good guide. Meantime, stick with recollection of breathing (*anapa-*

nasati) and natural pranayama as produced by the tapas of asana. The body's DIM knows exactly how to make the breathing. Just let it do its job while watching carefully and learning its secrets.

I don't recommend yoga students embarking upon the practice of formal pranayama (listed below) without instruction. Get good first-hand instruction from someone reliable with genuine experience of prolonged asana or tapas.

From our first inbreath at birth to our last outbreath at death – from first *inspiration* to final *expiration* – the in-and-out breathing always accompanies us throughout our lives. Without breathing, without prana, we would not survive more than a few minutes. It accompanies us throughout our life, is connected to every rhythm and pulsation of the body, is reflective of all states of mind and energy, and acts as a barometer of how we are at every moment.

It is connected to every memory we have ever had. Moreover, it is capable of reconnecting us to every embedded memory – even the deeply buried ones – because it has always been present with us, never absent, throughout our entire life. A perfect barometer if only we knew how to read it!

At birth the first breath is an inbreath. At death the last breath is an outbreath. *Inspired* we commence life in human form; *expired* we depart life in the human form.

Whether we realize it or not, our **inbreathing is only possible thanks to atmospheric pressure**. This atmospheric pressure in science is measured at sea level as 1 bar or one atmosphere. Every 10 meters under the surface of a body of water adds another 1 bar of pressure so that at 10 metres depth the pressure is 2 bar. So even if there is air with 1 bar pressure remaining inside a scuba diver's tank, **no air can be drawn into the lungs**. Every scuba diver knows this and may even have experienced a situation when the air pressure remaining in the tank is too low for the regulator to compensate.

But for those who are unfamiliar with scuba diving, this is extremely important to understand because it makes us realize that every inbreath is actually a *gift of life*.

As we inhale we are accepting Nature's *push* of air into our lungs. Her gift.

The mindbody 'opens up' the air passages to receive the inspiration of life – the gift of life – with every inbreath. This inbreath, which carries the lifeforce's DIM push along with the chemical components of air, is then transformed by the body through an exchange process and then given back by us to Nature in the outbreath.

In-motion and out-motion. I-motion and e-motion. It's a continuous give and take, a continuous there and back process – an oscillation, an ongoing exchange *where sensing and feeling is far more important than thinking.*

> Realize and feel that inbreathing and outbreathing is a wave-like phenomenon, the pulsation of life, the oscillating movement of life energy.

Every outbreath can be felt as an expression of e-motion. An outwards moving motion. Likewise for speaking or singing. Speaking and singing is virtually impossible on the inbreath and is possible only on the outbreath. All speaking and singing is done on the outbreath, never on the inbreath.

Singers – especially opera singers – need to learn precise breath control. Also theatre actors. What they practice too are forms of pranayama. The long form of 108 movements of Tai Chi is effectively a pranayama lasting 25-30 minutes.

> Nature gives us the gift of Life with every single inbreath, and we give back to Nature our e-motional response with every single outbreath.

Almost every sound we make with the voice and mouth expresses emotion. It tells how we are responding to the gift of Life.

So, in-and-out breathing is not just fresh air pressed into the flexible container of our lungs and transformed air pressed back out of our lungs into the atmosphere but every motion, every cycle of inbreath and outbreath, carries a 'vital push' – it's a vital dialogue – the essence of life called Prana in India, Chi in China, Ki in Japan, Pneuma in Greece and many other names in other cultures throughout history.

Fundamentals of breath control

In and out breathing has four clearly discernible phases:

- Breathing in (puraka)
- Breathing out (rechaka)
- Pausing during two turns (kumbhaka)

The two turns are where the cycle of breathing turns from inbreath to outbreath and from outbreath to inbreath. Just like waves coming in and going out on a sandy beach, there are two moments of pause – an interval or gap – in between the ebb and flow which can be clearly noticed if we pay close attention. During breathing these two pauses can be shortened or prolonged at will.

When the pause occurs at the completion of inbreath (lungs filled up) it is called *antara kumbhaka* (suspension of breath at full).

When the pause occurs at the completion of outbreath, it is called *bahya kumbhaka* (suspension of breath at empty).

Pranayama therefore means the *regulation* of these four *phases* either by making the cycle of in and outbreathing an uninterrupted continuity with minimum pausing, or the reverse – by prolonging pauses by either holding at the completion of an inbreath or by holding empty at the end of an outbreath. Either way the two turns with their pauses, whether left to a natural spontaneous rhythm of the body or whether deliberately shortened or lengthened, are called *kumbhaka*.

The word *kumbhaka* is often explained as originally meaning 'a jar' because the rib cage, chest and lungs have a jar-like shape. In actual fact because we have two lungs the internal shape is also like a figure of eight or the wings of a butterfly.

An alternative meaning of *kumbhaka* which makes sense in the context of *sushumna nadi* (the all-important central channel) is *pillar, column* or *mast,* which points to the heaven-earth axis alignment, so important in seated or standing asana.

The third meaning of kumbhaka and which is the third phase of breathwork is *breath retention.*

By retention is sometimes meant stopping and holding with effort, and sometimes effortlessly suspending the breath in which case suspension is the preferred word because retaining and holding imply effort. Also, one thing is physical tension and another thing is mental tension.

All modalities of kumbhaka accompanied by in-and-outbreathing are called *sahita kumbhaka* because the kumbhaka is associated with inhalation and exhalation.

If kumbhaka occurs unintentionally or spontaneously, as for example in deep relaxation or apnea, it is called *sahaja kumbhaka. Sahaja* means natural and spontaneous.

Thus kumbhaka itself is fundamentally of two kinds: *sahita* and *kevala.* The one associated with inbreathing and outbreathing is called *sahita kumbhaka.*

The kumbhaka free from the oscillation of in-and-outbreathing – where breathing entirely stops of its own accord – is called *kevala. Keval* means pure, alone and absolute.

When a yogini or yogi gains experience in *sahita kumbhaka,* then *keval kumbhaka* can be explored. Swami Chaitanyananda called this fourth form of pranayama – keval kumbhaka – a true goal of yoga and a certain pathway to *samadhi.*

In *Vasishtha Samhita,* a 13th century yoga text:

"When after giving up inhalation and exhalation, one holds the breath with ease, it is keval kumbhaka (absolute kumbhaka)."

Furthermore, the *Dattatreya Yogasastra* 74 states:

> "Once keval kumbhaka is mastered, free from inbreathing and out-breathing, there is nothing in the three worlds that cannot be accomplished!"

But before going into detail on keval kumbhaka – the jewel of pranayama –

I backtrack a moment and share with you some experience of formal pranayama practiced over the years and found useful.

1. Complete breath practice (also called 'full breath')
2. *Lomvilom*
3. *Kapalavati*
4. *Kapalavati* + *lomvilom* (combined)
5. *Bhastrika*
6. *Ujjayi*
7. *Sitali & sitkari*
8. Practicing effortless suspension of breathing (*kumbhaka*)
9. *Keval kumbhaka*

1. Complete breath

This begins with becoming familiar with the basic three bodily areas inflated by inbreathing which together make up a full or complete inbreath.

> Inhalation can be abdominal, intercostal or upper chest focused. Each can be practiced separately and then afterwards practiced together.

A full or complete inhalation is therefore filling these three areas in sequence beginning with the lower abdomen until it inflates like a half balloon, then filling up the intercostal area expanding the rib cage more sideways than forwards, and lastly filling the upper chest up to the neck. With practice a complete inbreath can be done smoothly and uniformly, in one full movement of inbreath without rushing it. Never rush or hurry in pranayama even when doing it vigorously! No hectic!

Exhalation is easy and only requires releasing the in-taken air. Letting it go allows the chest, ribcage and abdominal areas to relax and return naturally to their neutral DIM position.

Some action may require deliberately squeezing the lungs empty beyond their natural neutral DIM position such as in the practice of *uddiyana bandha* or *nauli*. But this is only done for a specific purpose. Squeezing the lungs empty is otherwise not usual nor recommended.

In general, avoid any forcing in pranayama. Knowing when too much vigour and power becomes forcing is the reason why an experienced guide is advised until you get the hang of it. The lungs are a wonderful instrument but their structures are delicate and must be treated with care and sensitivity.

Modalities of full and complete inbreathing:

- Full inbreathing <u>without</u> any intentional pausing after the inbreath (no retention) consciously creates a continuous cycle of full inhalation followed by relaxation, letting go on the outbreath.
- Full inbreathing <u>with</u> intentional retention after the inbreath – holding then followed by relaxation, letting go on the outbreath.
- Full inbreathing with intentional retention (kumbhaka) plus lock – holding the air locked in and slightly compressed – followed by relaxation, letting go of both the breath and lock/s on the outbreath

Locks require learning some *mudras* and *bandhas*, roughly translating as gestures and locks. The most commonly used ones applied after the full inbreath in sahita kumbhaka are:

- Mulabandha
- Uddiyana bandha
- Jalandarabandha

Immediately after taking a full inbreath, *mulabandha* compresses and squeezes the perineum area inwards and upwards. Similarly, once the inbreath is in, *uddiyana bandha* compresses and squeezes the lower belly, and *jalandarabandha* compresses and squeezes into the neck and upwards by pressing the chin towards the chest.

When these three bandhas are practiced together, the action involves two aspects in two directions. On the one hand this triple lock compresses and confines the air and prana between the anus and the neck and at the same time the compression and thrust from below pushes the air and prana upwards towards the head.

The above three seals/locks/*bandhas* seem to have similarities to the three 'gates' in Chinese *chi kung* and *tai chi*.

Mulabandha is also similar to *asvini mudra* where just the anal ring is squeezed tight in a somewhat similar manner to the Kegel exercize.

Bear in mind that formal or contrived *mudras* and *bandhas* are one thing and quite another thing is the bodymind naturally and spontaneously making such actions.

The purpose of this kumbhaka plus locks is to trap the air + prana and squeeze upwards. If all three locks are used together it is called *mahabandha* – the *great seal (lock)*.

As an analogy we can consider how a sponge is cleansed of dirt. Immerse it in water and detergent, then squeeze it and release it several times. After each release, water plus detergent is again sucked in and circulated through the sponge due to its soft elastic structure returning to its DIM position. Little by little all the dirt is washed out. Once the sponge is fully clean, no more detergent is required! Once all impurities have been cleansed from the nadi network of channels, a yogi may be able to draw in prana directly without the pumping action of in-and-out breathing.

2. Lomvilom

After learning the basics of the complete inbreath from Ramiro, the first pranayama I was taught by Swami Chaitanyananda in India in 1972, was *lomvilom*.

According to Chaitanyananda this extraordinary and safe pranayama was 'discovered' by the genius Shankaracharya who Swamiji assured me employed just this pranayama to remove all the obstructions from his nadis, thereby awakening to the realization of Advaita: the Real World of Nature as Brahman only.

How to practice the alternating nostril breathing lomvilom? (also called anuloma viloma)

Precise instructions for lomvilom are recorded in Hathayoga Pradipika:

> Sitting in Padmasana posture the yogi should fill in the air through the left nostril (closing the right one); and, keeping it confined according to one's ability, it should be expelled slowly through the surya (right nostril). Then, drawing in the air through the surya (right nostril) slowly, the belly should be filled, and after performing *Kumbhaka* as before, it should be expelled slowly through the chandra (left nostril).
>
> Inhaling thus through the one (nostril) through which it was expelled, and having restrained it there, till possible, it should be exhaled through the other, slowly and not forcibly.
>
> If the air be inhaled through the left nostril, it should be expelled again through the other, and filling it through the right nostril, confining it there, it should be expelled through the left nostril. By practicing in this way, through the right and the left nostrils alternately, the whole of the collection of the nadis of the *yamis* (practitioners) becomes clean, i.e., free from impurities, after three months and over.

Seated upright comfortably in a cross-legged asana of your choice, *lomvilom* requires using the inner part of the thumb and the inner part of ring and little fingers of the right hand to alternately close the right nostril and the left nostril. Switching from side to side automatically leaves open the unpressed nostril for inhalation.

A cycle of lomvilom pranayama always starts with inhalation in through the left nostril followed by exhalation out through the right nostril. Then without pausing, continues with inhalation through the right nostril finishing with exhalation through the left nostril (the 'unused' nostril being meanwhile alternately blocked by thumb on right or ring plus little finger on left. For left handers it's the opposite/reverse.

That is one complete round or cycle. The practitioner can do as many rounds as feels appropriate or as indicated by the instructor. In lomvilom the *sahita kumbhaka* (the two turns with their pauses) can follow a natural spontaneous rhythm of the body or be deliberately prolonged by retention. But *in lomvilom retention is only after the inbreath*, never after the outbreath, therefore every inbreath always follows on smoothly and continuously after every outbreath with minimum pause.

3. Kapalavati

Kapalavati is initiated from a relaxed neutral position of thorax and abdomen, then making successive short sharp punching exhalations through both nostrils in such a way that the lower abdomen contracts with each expulsion of air. Each inbreath follows naturally and effortlessly as abdomen and thorax promptly return to neutral position after every outbreath. The rhythm is roughly punching a bit faster than one outbreath per second. Experienced *kapalavati* practitioners can do rounds of 60 punching outbreaths with ease.

I have read explanations of *kapalavati* which do not concur with this and which instead state the abdomen is punched outwards on every exhale i.e. opposite of contraction but that is the way of *bhastrika* not *kapalavati* whose action in this sense is opposite.

4. Kapalavati + lomvilom (combined)

Kapalavati can be combined with lomvilom to great effect in order to speed up the awakening of kundalini (see Chapter 9, Nadis). Kapalavati pranayama should be learned from a qualified instructor and the combined kapalavati + lomvilom even more so.

Kapalavati often transcribed into our alphabet as *kapalabhati* is frequently translated as if composed of words meaning "skull" and "shining". According to Chaitanyananda this is an incorrect interpretation. Since ancient times 'kap' signifies 'head' both literally and figuratively (this same root word is found in many languages capisc') and 'lavati' – also surviving in many Indo-European languages – means cleaning/washing out/washing thoroughly. *Lavati* as 'washed through' in the sense of suffused was an important concept even at the time of the Buddha 1500 years before the earliest records of hathayoga in India!

Hence according to Chaitanyananda the main function of kapalavati pranayama at the physical level is to cleanse the sinus cavities inside the head. Not to polish our skulls!!

5. Bhastrika – fire bellows
Bhastrika – the fire-stoking bellows breath – is initiated from a relaxed neutral position of thorax and abdomen. But from then on both the inbreath as well as the outbreath are active, deliberate and precise:

- the inbreath consists in taking a deep inbreath and at the same time contracting (pulling in) the lower abdomen inwards so that the volume of air is taken into the intercostal and chest with abdomen contracted.
- the outbreath is a sudden forceful expulsion whose thrust descends to impact the lower abdomen from behind pushing it/thrusting it sharply it outwards. This is repeated successively at a rhythm of one bellow action every second and a half or slower.

The rhythm of one cycle per 1.5 seconds should not be exceeded, and can be done slower if more comfortable. Bhastrika pranayama is quite tiring so the number of cycles should be gauged according experience and capacity.

BKS Iyengar is reported to have said kapalavati is a milder form of bhastrika. But this is incorrect so either he has been misreported, or he himself got confused.

Kapalavati and bhastrika have more differences than similarities:

- on the outbreath the muscular action of kapalavati and bhas-trika in the lower belly is exactly opposite to each other;
- the inbreath of kapalavati is effortless and natural (automatic) whereas the inbreath of bhastrika is deliberate and powerful;
- the rhythm (speed) of kapalavati is roughly about double that of bhastrika;
- both are forceful and intense.

Bhastrika is a powerful aid to generating heat in the body. I use it often in a natural way in horse stance position to recover from the tapas of cold exposure (Chapter 11, Tapas).

6. Ujjayi

Ujjayi is a perfect example of a natural situation-induced pranayama which makes not so much sense to simulate in an artificial way. Only a person trained in martial arts or who successfully undergoes some other form of tapas can discover and realize the real *ujjayi* breathing and make the genuine sound. The body must make the sound not the thinking mind which can only fake it! This sound will vary depending on the type of tapas. It is called "the victorious" because above all it is a breath sound expressing the primal sentiment of victory and mastery of some situation. It is a sound like saying *'wa'* with throat constricted. It sometimes comes out quite naturally as high-pitched.

Exhalation with sounds, like om, hum, buzzing, or pitching the voice at different octaves is worthwhile experimenting yourself. Experiment by yourself at the end of any high intensity workout or other endurance test to find what sound/s you naturally feel like making at that moment. Without interference from thinking, just let the body express the emotion of the moment through the outbreath sound!

7. Sitali and Sitkari

Both of these can be practiced safely without a guide. These pranayama can be used to combat thirst or ambient heat. *Sitkari* (hissing inbreath) and *sitali* (cooling inbreath) are both performed with inbreath drawn in through the mouth and released through the nostrils.

In *sitali* the tongue is folded lengthwise to form a tube with lips pursed and the inbreath is drawn in slowly and evenly. You will instantly feel the cooling effect. The inhaled air is released through the nose. In *sitkari* the mouth and tongue are placed with teeth almost clenched together drawing in the inbreath as if about to undergo something painful. The indrawn breath is faster than the former but also felt as cooling. Both have similar applications and can be used in combination with each other: one is more focused on calming thirst from overheating; the other more on cooling from overheating.

8. Holding Kumbhaka

This *kumbhaka* should be performed in a comfortable sitting asana not lying down.

If you lie down you might fall asleep. In this pranayama, in-and-outbreathing is deliberately suspended to stay in a completely neutral position with abdomen and thorax just waiting while witnessing. Its purpose is to explore the state of effortless suspension of breathing/ effortless non-breathing. To prepare for this practice which is more an exploration than a technique, any of the above pranayama can be used as a prelude but perhaps the best and simplest is to do 20 or 30 rounds of complete breaths without retention. Then on the last outbreath of every series just allow the lungs to suck back an amount of air to reach the neutral DIM position of thorax and abdomen. By experimenting by yourself you will soon come to find a "sweet spot" where the amount of residual air in the lungs is exactly in neutral position – somewhere between a quarter and one-third full.

This preliminary and provisional keval kumbhaka will be discussed together with keval kumbhaka. The practice of the provisional one can lead to the spontaneous occurrence of the latter.

9. Keval Kumbhaka

Keval Kumbhaka - the jewel and goal of pranayama

Keval kumbhaka - effortless suspension of in-and-outbreathing - is the goal of pranayama. It accomplishes *samadhi* by controlling the vital force through natural suspension of breathing. It is one of the three yoga paths to *samadhi*, the other two being suspension of the thinking mind – *citta vritti nirodha* – and the transformation of sexual energy into compassion.

In actual fact these three events are separate in language only and in fact may happen concurrently although at any given moment one or the other may become the more prominent path to the 'top of the mountain' (Chapter 7, Dhyana).

Breath is Life! Key to unlocking so many secrets lost to us because of the Nature-disconnected lifestyle of so-called 'developed world' culture:

> too much clothing; too much food; wrong food; wrong beverage; avoi-
> dance of cold; avoidance of heat; living in a narrow comfort zone of
> just a few degrees of temperature variance; avoidance of physical dis-
> comfort and stress; lack of high intensity physical exertion; over-using
> the thinking mind; sedentary non-physical lifestyle; unsatisfactory
> or non-existent sex-life; way too many hours per day spent indoors;
> screen-fixation; air pollution...and so forth.

Without breathing a human being cannot survive for more than a few minutes unless he or she is a *siddha*. A siddha is a yogi or yogini who has mastered keval kumbhaka, the jewel and goal of pranayama, and can remain for prolonged periods without in-and-out breathing of air.

> This is possible because the DIM of Nature is capable of drawing prana
> – vital force – into the body through the navel as it did for all of us for
> about nine months when we were in our mother's womb.

In keval kumbhaka the prana gets drawn into the body passively, effort-lessly from our surroundings. Don't forget science has also confirmed that our skin system is part of our respiratory system, and that about 10 per cent of respiration takes place through the porous container of our skin.

I remember in the early years of yoga practice – years before the 1978 'codeless' breakthrough – while sitting in asana exploring sus-pension of in-and-out breathing with the aim of keval kumbhaka, when twice in one week, the breath stopped of its own accord! When this occurred I distinctly felt a disconnection from lung input of energy to input of energy through the navel. As if unplugging from one source of power and plugging in to another power source. This was experienced as something physiological, mechanical and energetic, nothing mystical about it at all.

On one of these two occasions out of apprehension I cut the expe-rience short after a few minutes but the other time I continued just calmly witnessing what the body was doing, and allowed what was happening to continue. I cannot say with certainty exactly how long mindbody remained without breathing while drawing energy in from outside the body through the navel. It was a comfortable, effortless sensation of a continuous inflow of energy streaming into the body from outside. It wasn't an oscillation like breathing. Whatever energy was needed, just flowed in. My mind allowed this to continue until the body seemed to indicate 'that's enough!'

Curiously, this experience of spontaneous keval kumbhaka has never repeated in all the 50 years since despite many other intense experiences during yoga practice. How come? I cannot say.

There are however preliminary forms of keval kumbhaka that arise in the course of practicing suspension of in-and-out breathing for up to three or four minutes. Through this practice some persons are even able to effortlessly reach four to six minutes.

Kumbhaka is often explained in terms of *retention* or *holding*. This is correct in the context of *sahita kumbhaka* but incorrect in the con-text of *keval kumbhaka*. There is no question of holding or retaining in keval kumbhaka because effortlessness is the essence of it. So, it is suspension not retention.

In keval kumbhaka the breath stops with no need for further inhalation or exhalation and the yogi can effortlessly retain breath as long as he likes thereby silencing the thinking mind and simultaneously attaining the state of raja yoga.

Such powers as *siddhis* are said to arise as a result of this 4th form of pranayama.

'Effortlessness' is emphasized because any path to keval kumbhaka has nothing to do with effort or forcing. Keval kumbhaka is antagonistic to any kind of forcing or tension.

Most healthy people with proper training can soon learn to stop breathing for two minutes or more. In fact, on a full breath a healthy person can train to hold breath for several minutes. But keval kumbhak is not about holding a full breath. It is about finding that 'balance-point' in between a full inbreath and its release by just letting go of a full inbreath and allowing the body to find its DIM. It is a balance point between inhalation and exhalation. Equilibrium.

Another way to explore finding this balance point, this particular DIM, is to slow the breathing down more and more, becoming more and more deeply relaxed until the breathing at the entrance to the nostrils becomes shorter and shorter, until hardly noticeable.

> Practice shortening the inbreath and outbreath until the ebb and flow seems to take place only inside the nostrils.

Swami Chaitanyananda said, "Desirelessness, timelessness and egolessness" are three clues for keval kumbhaka.

Apnea free-divers function on a full inbreath so it's not keval kumbhaka. Innate physiological aptitude combined with specific lung expansion training and repeated practice, enables free-divers to hold their breath for up to 10 minutes or longer under water *without exertion* and up to four or five minutes *with exertion* (swimming under water or diving down).

Keval kumbhaka is a suspension of breathing – there is no retention. Retention implies tension. Effortless suspension of breathing/
non-breathing is keval kumbhaka.

In approximations to keval kumbhaka, suspension of in-and-out
breathing for several minutes can be easily achieved and experienced
with a bit of practice thereby giving yoga students a clear idea and
sensation of the target.

Also, *quasi* keval kumbhaka can occur in 4th *jhana* or *samadhi*
(Chapter 7, Dhyana) where breathing becomes so subtle and refined
as to be imperceptible to an outside observer but may not completely
stop. You would have to hold a mirror in front of the nose or mouth
to spot condensation as doctors in the field do. This imperceptible
breathing can also occur in states of coma where breathing likewise
becomes so subtle and short that the in-and-out movement of breath
takes place within the nasal passages. Think of a house with open
doors (nostrils/mouth) but where there is no to-ing and fro-ing visible
at the entrances but nonetheless has some activity going on in the
passages and halls.

***

As pointed out in Chapter 1, language is a minefield of confusion. If
we don't grasp the fact that language structured as it is cannot address
everything at one and the same time, we may fail to understand that
asana, pranayama, pratyahara, dharana and even samadhi can all be
processes that overlap and are not separate, and to a greater or lesser
extent occur dependently on each other and simultaneously.

Nothing is more real than breath and breathing. Just the remembering of in-and-out breathing can enable us to pass beyond the bewilderment of the artificial world of codes and images and immediately
reconnect to the Real World of Nature, to its power, its intelligence,
its wisdom, its beauty, its magnificence and there penetrate even deeper – into what lies beyond even the Natural World's coding – into the
Codeless!

Breathwork can go to the very core of Existence. It can liberate mind from all compulsion and conditioning. It all depends on passion, intensity, focus, really feeling it, becoming one with it, making the waves more powerful and more subtle. And then stopping completely to enjoy and savour the calm of stresslessness.

***

Chapter 7: Dhyana | Samadhi

As said earlier there are three known paths in yoga to dhyana and samadhi:

- control over the mind culminating in *keval jnana* (this chapter)
- breath regulation culminating in *keval kumbhaka* (previous chapter)
- control over the sexual current culminating in *mahamudra*

As one of the three known routes to *samadhi*, *dhyana* (*jhana* in Pali) was widely practiced by the *sramana* movements of yogis and ascetics at the time of Mahavir and the Buddha as a way to stop the thinking mind, to perfect (verb) concentration and to achieve higher mental development and powers (*siddhis*).

The Buddha taught the same *dhyanas* to achieve calmness of mind (*samatha*) and perfect concentration that he had been taught by his two teachers, Alara Kalama and Uddaka Ramaputta. Nevertheless, he cautioned against considering *dhyana* an end in itself because it does not lead to decoding at the deepest level of mindbody.

He also advised against the pursuit of *siddhis* that arise from attainment of the 4th *jhana* through what Patanjali's Yogasutra calls *samyama*. If *siddhis* arise in the natural course of practice, that's okay, but to pursue them as ends in themselves is a deviation from the path of insight-knowledge. It is not the path to freedom from the bondage of coding. Instead may become a diversion into the paths of power.

In fact the way of power stands in opposition to the process of liberation from coding, because it can perpetuate delusion and ignorance.

"Getting Real" is yoga's true objective

Nevertheless, the systematic and sustained practice of *dhyana* is strongly recommended as preparation for arousing the kind of concentration needed for *satipatthana* (Chapter 8).

> "There's no dhyana for one with no discernment,
> no discernment for one with no dhyana.
> But one having both dhyana and discernment is on the verge of the Codeless."

> Dhammapada 372

This chapter looks at the successive stages of development of concentration called *pratyahara, dharana, dhyana* and *samadhi* by Patanjali in his Yogasutra, and called *jhana* 1, *jhana* 2, *jhana* 3 and *jhana* 4 in the Theravada Buddhist Canon and Abhidhamma.

The fourth level of dyana is the equivalent of *samadhi* as understood in Yogasutra whereas the word *samadhi* in Pali texts is used for the complete practice of concentration, as well as being commonly used for tranquillity, for just sitting quietly. Again, we must always beware of language creating differences where there are in fact none in real life! Both texts essentially describe the same stages practiced by yogis and ascetics at the time of Mahavir and Gautama Buddha, and equally valid today.

One problem with 'today' – and it is a significant problem but difficult to quantify with any certainty as to its impact – is that the amount of human generated electromagnetic disturbance going on in the atmosphere in addition to other kinds of "new forms" of artificial disturbances (distractions) has greatly increased in the past couple of hundred years, especially in the last 50 years or so, and is increasing exponentially since 20 years ago.

> How the 5G roll-out will impact mental concentration is anyone's guess.

My own experience of dhyana practice now spans over 50 years and I can vouch that it seems generally to be quite a bit harder to reach 'full concentration' (jhana one) nowadays than it was when I first started out 50 years ago.

Aside from electromagnetic disturbance and other kinds of 'noise' and 'interference', the location and setting make a big difference, as does time of day and a number of other factors and circumstances.

Air quality and altitude are factors to be taken into consideration as are times of day and meals. For example, the 3am to 6am time window (real sun-time not artificially adjusted time) is a more favourable time for calmness and concentration of mind than say 3pm to 6pm, because usually there is far less activity and disturbance going on during the early morning hours than during the afternoon.

The problem is that a lifestyle timetable to include wakefulness during the 3am to 6am window hardly exists in today's modern world. Nevertheless, it is not uncommon for serious yogis and monks to begin their day at that hour and end their day not long after sunset. More about 'time windows' in Chapter 9 on nadis.

Theory and practice

A popular saying is that a kilo of practice is worth 100 kilos of theory but this is not entirely true because a good map along with proper guidance can save a huge amount of time, energy, going down wrong paths and getting confused. Conversely, the absence of a good map can lead to wasting time, frittering around doing nothing, when time is so short and precious.

So, it is extremely helpful to have a reliable map so long as we do not allow the map to condition the vision of the territory to such an extent that it distorts the direct experience of the 'territory'. We have to be ceaselessly on guard whenever and wherever words and descriptions lead to the formation of images and expectations, including those in this book!

Remember 'ehi passigó' – always and in all ways test everything in the light of your own direct experience before accepting it fully. Even then, test it again a few more times until you are thoroughly convinced.

While testing, you have to provisionally accept but give full acceptance only when it passes the test of direct experience and becomes your own independent verification.

Above all, do not be a follower!

The innumerable followers who do not complete the path and do not gain their own direct realization have systematically undermined every great teaching the world has ever known. That applies equally to *followers* of many other branches of knowledge such as sciences and philosophy.

There is an apt story in this regard about a seeker who comes to the cave of a great rishi high up in the Himalayas. The seeker's very first question is:

"Master, how come there are *so many teachings, so many doctrines, so many paths to truth in this world?*"

The great rishi shot back with a stern look:

"What do you mean so many teachings?! So many doctrines?! So many paths?!

So few! Every man, every woman in this world can be a teaching, a doctrine and a path to Truth!"

Each person is unique and Nature is expressing herself in a unique way through each and every one of us – that's the beauty of the freedom of expression that is gained from Realization of Truth.

***

Patanjali's fourfold division of stages as outlined in Yogasutra into

- *pratyahara*
- *dharana*
- *dhyana*
- *samadhi*

seems to be a veiled copy of the four *jhanas* of the Tipitaka, which in any case were previously taught to Siddhartha Gautama by his two teachers, Alara Kalama and Uddaka Ramaputta the Jain, and were forms of yoga in existence and in practice since long before his time.

> Samkhya and Yoga in Rigveda are referred to as ancient in time long before the 600-450 BCE period taken in this book as the reference point for early yoga. Some say Kapila was the first teacher of dhyana; others say Lord Siva was the adi-yogi who first imparted it, and still others claim that the most ancient was the first Tirthankara of Jain Nath tradition.

Either way a case can be made for

pratyahara = jhana 1
dharana   = jhana 2
dhyana   = jhana 3
samadhi   = jhana 4 and covers the other modalities of samadhi, such as jhanas 5, 6, 7 and 8.

Patanjali may have done this in order not to over-copy the earlier Noble Eightfold system of the Buddha but more likely as an attempt to distance Yoga from any religious connotations already present in Jainism and which had also crept into the Buddha's yoga with the widely spreading -*ism* of Buddhism.

One among many of yoga's outstanding virtues throughout its long history has been its uncanny ability to remain non-sectarian, universally acceptable and usable by one and all as a system of mental and physical development. And we are grateful for Patanjali's role in keeping it that way.

Pratyahara

There seems to be a misconception that *pratyahara* involves shutting the eyes and withdrawing the mind and senses from their objects as if such a thing were possible or desirable as a first step to realizing the Real. Such interpretations are non-sense in the pure meaning of the word.

What has to be withdrawn from the senses and the deep mind is the *thinking mind* – not the senses from their objects! Withdrawing the senses from their objects would be tantamount to throwing the baby out with the dirty bath water!

Yoga is about getting Real. And what prevents getting Real is precisely the thinking mind – not the senses nor their objects! They are innocent!

So *pratyahara* means withdrawing from the artificial world of our internal cinema and paying full attention to what is the Real. And this can be done with eyes open or with eyes closed, either way – as the Buddha so repeatedly emphasizes in the satipatthana sutta, focusing on the 'Real in the Real'.

There is no need to close the eyes or try to deliberately shut down any of the senses. The need is to restrain the thinking mind from engaging in its habitual code-making and manipulation of images and concepts *in addition to* what the senses are directly perceiving (sights sounds tastes touches smells).

In this regard, there is a wonderful story about an ancient yogi who had long sought an encounter with the Buddha in order to receive his firsthand instruction.

After traveling on foot from far away the old man at last came upon the Awakened One after morning alms just as he was about to sit down and break fast. So Gautama said to the old yogi who was insistent, "Abide sir, I will first take my meal and then we will talk!"

But the old man insisted, "No, Venerable Gautama – I beg to hear your instructions right away now for I am unsure if I will still be alive much longer!"

The Buddha paused and surveyed the old yogi with the Eye of Wisdom. Seeing he was indeed about to pass away and already close to insight into the true Nature of Reality, the Buddha put down his bowl and gave the old seeker this instruction:

"In seeing sights with the eye, let there be no I, nor me, nor mine besides ...
In hearing sounds with the ear, let there be no I, nor me, nor mine besides...
In feeling sensations, let there be no I, nor me, nor mine besides...

In smelling odours, let there be no I, nor me, nor mine besides...
In tasting savours, let there be no I, nor me, nor mine besides...
In thinking thoughts, let there be no I, nor me nor mine besides ..."

Thereupon the old yogi attained that stainless vision of Truth attainable to the noble ones gaining the supramundane path from which there is no falling back to lower states of confusion and woe.

If you hear a nightingale – that's real life!!

If you use external kasina disc as support for concentration – that is one of the best forms for developing concentration (*dharana*).

So there is no need to withdraw the senses from external objects! Yoga is about coming to our senses, not going away from them and going off at a tangent into **ab**stractions and mind trips.

On the contrary, the objective of yoga is to bypass/still/stop the thinking mind with all its conceptual baggage and mental tennis. What needs restraining is the internal cinema together with its code-generated compulsive habit reaction patterns.

Remember the game of the thinking mind is to create divisions and then put things together again...this is the senseless game that has to stop, at least during *dhyana* and *satipatthana* practice. There is absolutely no such division in Real Life from the nondual viewpoint of the third eye.

All divisions arise from conceptualizations, image-making and encoding by the scheming mind.

"Sono schemo perche non capisco un cavolo...
O per che non capisco un cavolo sono schemo?!"
Michele Salmeri, Catania 1985

Visualisation in my view is inferior to real sensing in contact with the Real World of Nature.

What inner sight can match a beautiful sunset?

What inner sound the song of wild birds or a chorus of crickets?

What remembered fragrance that of real flowers or citrus trees in blossom?

What taste that of a healthy meal lovingly prepared?

What touch that of the myriad cells of the body dancing in a free flow of energy...

***

Dhyana

Dhyana (jhana) is a concept and word which has no proper equivalent in Western culture. Meditation, contemplation, introspection, reflection, pondering and similar concepts are all vague and can even be quite misleading because the aim of dhyana is precisely to restrain/suspend/ stop all activity of the thinking part of mind.

Because 'meditation' in the Western mindset is so associated with *'thinking about things'* the word 'meditation' has in the context of yoga been replaced by many writers with the word 'absorption'. But this word carries connotations of trance and **ab**straction, neither of which fit the proper meaning or aim of dhyana.

The aim is neither to encourage thinking nor fall into a glassy-eyed trance. A silent investigative fully-focused mindset is more to the point.

"The intellect has little to do on the road to discovery. There comes a leap in awareness, call it intuition or what you will, the solution comes to you. And you don't know how or why. I did not arrive at my understanding of the fundamental laws of the universe through my rational mind. I think 99 times and find nothing. I stop thinking, swim in silence, and the truth comes to me."

Albert Einstein

Thinking is founded on **ab**straction because thinking deals with the artificial representational world – our internal cinema of concepts, codes and images – whereas the focus of dhyana is on the Real, penetrating it so fully so as to become undivided from it, beyond thought.

That is the reason in tantric imagery the joining of male and female, whether deity or human, is often used to represent this. Indeed, there are few situations in human life more powerfully Real than the joining together of two persons thrilled by the embrace of the new, filled with the passion for creativity/creation.

So even though the influence of yoga over the last few decades has indeed added new shades of meaning to Western concepts of 'meditation', it seems clearer to retain and keep using the original word *dhyana* or *jhana* (if its Pali equivalent is preferred).

***

Dhyana (Sanskrit), *jhana* (Pali), *chan* (China) and *zen* (Japan) are all the same term with the same meaning. In this chapter both the Sanskrit *dhyana* and the Pali *jhana* are used interchangeably.

In Patanjali's eightfold Yogasutra, the parts describing *pratyahara* – restraining the thinking mind from interfering into the reality of senses and sensations, and *dharana,* focusing the awareness upon a single object of attention – may seem as if they are preliminary steps or preludes to attainment of steady concentration. But these steps are conceptual only, and their sequential appearance is more of an illusion created by language needing to deal in an order with distinguishable aspects of a single process.

In real-life situations, *pratyahara, dharana* and *dhyana* occur as often simultaneously as sequentially. An *emergency* can induce all three simultaneously, and a whole lot faster than sitting in yoga asana. So can the *tapasya* of cold exposure. Top level sports also provide examples showing that on peak occasions athletes can attain the highest degrees of concentration even to the point of performing feats considered impossible by conventional science.

> Even threading a needle or defusing a bomb – and similar delicate or dangerous manual tasks – require a momentary high degree of one-pointed concentration which may be accompanied by momentary suspension of breathing.

There are many cases recorded of humans manifesting superhuman strength in emergency situations which stop the thinking mind. I once read of a case of a man lifting the front end of a truck with one hand to rescue a child from underneath with the other hand. Countless such examples are recorded throughout history in all cultures and different parts of the world showing that the fully-concentrated-in-the-present deep mind has far more capacity and power than most people realize or imagine.

Kasina

As focus for one-pointed concentration there are two supports which are both highly recommended:

- one with eyes open
- the other with eyes either closed or half-closed

With eyes open, the less difficult way to develop full concentration (jhana 1) is setting up a plain white or plain light-colored disc at a comfortable angle and distance to stare at while keeping the body upright in the chosen asana.

This exercize is called *kasina* in the Pali texts. By continuing to gaze at the kasina, confining the attention solely to the area of the kasina, it is possible to quite quickly reach what is called access or neighborhood concentration.

> Transitions between degrees or levels of concentration are experienced in the mindbody as a subtle shifting of gear from grosser to more refined concentration, or vice versa if proceeding in inverse order. The transitions cannot be provoked or forced in any way. They occur spontaneously when conditions are right. They depend to a large extent

on the quality of the breath, meaning on the quality of the life-force-intelligence as it flows through the nadi network.

The other most highly recommended support for gaining one-pointed concentration – the one most frequently recommended by the Buddha, tried and tested throughout the millennia and also recommended by Ramana Maharshi – is watching the breathing (recollection of in-and-out breathing called *anapanasati* in the Pali literature). In Chapter 8, Satipatthana, *anapanasati* is further explored in detail.

Here the use of the breath and breathing as support for jhana differs from pranayama (Chapter 6) in that we pay careful attention not to interfere at all in the breathing. Just let the body breathe as the body is naturally inclined to. And watch the sensation and movement at the entrance to the nostrils.

Because breath and breathing is a **dynam**ic process continuously in motion, it is considerably harder to develop full concentration focusing on the breath than on a kasina. Nevertheless, the rewards are great whenever successful.

In the Yogasutra the practice of *trataka* – steady gazing at a light – has some similarities with kasina as focus for concentration. But in kasina practice there is no effort to prevent blinking to make the eyes water. Let natural blinking occur whenever the body requires it. Be natural. The only effort is to remain focused on the object of concentration.

Tibetan yoga seems to favour visualization for attaining *dhyana* but my teachers mostly all favoured concentrating the attention on things belonging to the Real World of Nature, avoiding the contrivance of anything artificial.

Precisely what we are trying to get free of is the superimposition of the artificial on the Real – not create more internal cinema.

One important thing to know and be aware of in relation to achieving jhana levels 1-4 is its total relationship to the quality of prana flowing in the nostrils (discussed in Chapter 10) because it is not possible to attain full concentration without the breath flowing equally, evenly and unobstructedly through both nostrils at the same time.

As Siva says to Devi in the Vigyan Bhairava Tantra, full concentration/ samadhi *"is difficult only for the impure."*
Water only flows badly in obstructed pipes.

***

Etymology of the word 'dhyana'

The Sanskrit word *dhyana,* whose etymology is said to be unknown, could be semantically related to the Greco-Roman *diana* meaning *target.* In Spanish *diana* means a bullseye. In Greek Διάνα also means bullseye – *the centre of a target.*

The equivalent Greek name *Artemis* is also of lost etymology, most likely of pre-Greek origin and related to Sanskrit *artha* (अर्थ: purpose, objective, meaning), signifying the 'sense' carried by words exchanged by people when speaking or writing.

> Whether to oneself or to others, the communication of meaning is certainly the original purpose and function of code before forgetfulness sets in.

Meanings triggered by codes can take many forms, such as connecting to an **ab**stract idea, to an emotion, or pointing to real-world 'things' such as are found in the Real World of Nature.

Diana, like her Greek counterpart Artemis, is the goddess of the chase, the huntress. The supreme tracker and achiever of her aim and target, which is the practice of dhyana's whole purpose.

Attributes of the goddess are sharp intelligence, a quiver of silver arrows upon her shoulder and bow in hand. 'Silver-tongued' is an old way of saying a person endowed with the gift of words. Like so many Sanskrit and Pali words starting with sam- or san- we always have to think of the number three, three aspects, or three things coming together, assembling together into one.

In Patanjali's Yogasutra, *samyama* is therefore achieved when the trio of observer, observation process and observed become one with the object of attention. Or where the distinction between subject, object and connectoring process no longer appears. This threefold aspect is emphasized again and again repeatedly in the Buddha's instructions on *satipatthana* practice.

Based on the oldest descriptions of dhyana in the sutras, dhyana was the core practice of early yoga together with tapas, both of which involve asana and pranayama as described in chapters 6 and 7. Single-pointed asana and what breathing is and does are fundamental to what has to be recognized and acknowledged.

A scientist engrossed in her work or a painter absorbed in his creation or an engineer pondering over a design, all such endeavours require high levels of concentration and certainly could cover Patanjali's conception of *pratyahara* and *dharana (jhanas* 1 and 2).

The stilling of thoughts by attaining high levels of concentration and suspension of the thinking mind makes way for intuition and 'perceiving outside of the box'.

Perceiving outside of the box = outside the thinking mind.

The highest levels of concentration occurs when visible movement of breathing is almost imperceptible or even completely suspended.

Keval kumbhaka, already discussed in Chapter 6 on Pranayama, may occur spontaneously in the 4th jhana.

***

Access concentration and Jhanas 1, 2, 3, and 4

Truth be told the description of the jhanas in Tipitaka is more detailed and precise, and therefore more useful as a map than Patanjali's terse sutras on dhyana, which at best, serve as reminders for those who already know the steps and progressions.

Also my own practice of jhana tallies closely with the descriptions in Tipitaka so let's stick with this description bearing in mind there are bound to be variations/differences for each person depending on accumulated coding (sankhara) and on their mental store of images. Everyone's internal cinema – while still of the essence of cinema – is unique to him or her.

To some extent we are each the producer, lead actor, crew and scriptwriter of our own particular idiosyncratic life film. This is especially evident in the dream state.

Meanwhile the One Life powers on in all its magnificence, mystery, grandeur and splendour.

Only access concentration (approximation to full concentration) and full concentration for levels 1-4 will be described here because the likelihood of anyone in today's modern world investing the time to reach levels 5-8 through methodical practice is unlikely. For those interested, the descriptions of jhana 5-8 can easily be found in the texts so no need to go into detail here. In the introductory chapter I gave a brief description of spontaneous experiences in 1978 of jhana 6 and 8.

I do not recall ever experiencing either jhana 5 or jhana 7 therefore I strongly suspect they do not necessarily occur in the order described, and that it is possible to jump from the 4th to any of 5 to 8. What occurs to a yogi at such levels of concentration seems to depend on past accumulations of actions (*karma*) as much as on efforts or circumstances at that present moment.

***

Now without further preamble, here is the nitty gritty of the states of concentration.

First, choose your meditation support, the object or target on which to direct one-pointed concentration (*ekagrata*). Either *anapana* or *kasina* as recommended.

After having attended to any needs of the body, having gone to a suitable place, quiet and secluded, arrange and adopt an asana of choice so as to be able to maintain it comfortably for as long as intended, keeping the body upright, neither too tense nor too relaxed, exactly balanced in the middle, with spinal column aligned between sky and earth. Then rouse up that degree of intensity as can manifest in the artist's mind at work, the scientist's mind in the laboratory, the poet's mind in choosing the right word, the warrior's mindset at the onset of battle.

Then direct this intensely focused attention onto the object of concentration until access concentration is sensed. Access concentration, also called neighborhood concentration, is when concentration is felt to be 'hovering almost there' but wobbles away from the object. Keep on bringing it back and sooner or later the transition is sensed.

The transition from access concentration to full concentration is experienced as a definite steadying/gelling of concentration as below.

Four Jhanas (dhyanas)

The stages of development of jhana with their distinguishing characteristics and features are paraphrased below, without similes, into easily understandable modern language and concepts:

1st jhana
"After concentrating and focusing the mind upon a single object...it happens that when a yogi's mind becomes (provisionally) free from sensual desire and ill-will, free from restlessness, sluggishness and sceptical doubt, the mind enters and abides in the first jhana, which is accompanied by conceptual thinking (*vitakka*) and discursive thinking (*vicara*), filled with happiness and contentment born of concentration and unification of mind.

2nd jhana
"Furthermore...after the subsiding and fading away of conceptual thinking and discursive thinking, and through achieving tranquillity and unification of mind, the mind enters into and abides in a state free from conceptual thinking, free from discursive thinking...the second

jhana, born of concentration and detachment (dis-identification from words and images), and filled with rapture (*piti*) and happiness (*sukha*).

3rd jhana

"And furthermore...after the fading away of rapture the mind dwells in equanimity, thoroughly aware (*sampajañña*), remembering (*sati*) and experiencing throughout mindbody that feeling of which the Noble Ones declare, '*Happily lives the person of detached and alert mind*', thus the mind enters into and abides in the 3rd jhana.

4th jhana

"And furthermore...having let go of (coding relating to) pleasure and pain, and after the disappearance of previous elation and depression, the mind enters into and abides in that state beyond pleasure and pain, the 4th absorption, which is purified by equanimity and recollection (of the Real)."

The yogi abides, permeating the body with a pure, bright awareness, so that there is nothing in the entire mindbody un-suffused by purity and brightness.

(*Anguttara Nikaya* & other suttas paraphrased)

Remembering what is Real (*sati*) is present in all stages of the four jhanas, while wisdom and confidence are balanced along with concentration and energy.

If concentration is strong and energy is weak, sluggishness and torpor will set in to prevent full concentration. You will become drowsy and sleepy.

Conversely, if energy is strong and concentration weak, restlessness and fidgeting will set in preventing full concentration. You will think of reasons to get up and do something else.

Reviewing

The jhanas, along with their specific characteristics and features can be reviewed jhana by jhana, one at a time – in other words entering each jhana, then coming out of it to review it – or they can be reviewed all together after coming out of the 4th jhana.

Either way it is seen that:

The 1st jhana is free from five obstacles and possesses five positive and neutral factors:

- The five impediments, that are absent, are sensual desire, fear/ anger/hate, sluggishness, restless and sceptical doubt.
- The five positive or neutral factors, that are present, are conceptual thinking, sustained thought, happiness, recollection of the Real and concentration.

The 2nd jhana has rapture, happiness, recollection of the Real and concentration. (In the 2nd jhana sustained thought about 'real things' is still there but we have stopped talking to ourselves).

The 3rd jhana has happiness, recollection of the Real, concentration and dispassion (the pleasant disturbance of rapture having been replaced by calmness and equanimity).

The 4th jhana goes beyond (previous) pleasure and pain and has the deepest degree of detachment/equanimity/dis-identification with full recollection and awareness of the Real in whatever it contemplates.

Reflections

Electromagnetic disturbances have greatly increased since the 1970s when I was able to frequently and fairly easily enter jhanas 1 and 2. Nowadays the electromagnetic disturbances along with other kinds of disturbances have reached a higher level of proliferation and intensity that seem to interfere with jhana access.

Nevertheless, most yoga practitioners with a stable sitting asana, calm mind and steady focus of intention should still be able to reach *access concentration* fairly easily. Access concentration is a good enough base for *satipatthana* and what some Burmese vipassana teachers call insight-knowledge meditation.

Nevertheless, to enter jhana 1 does not only depend on concentration or willpower or determination or the presence or absence of external disturbances but on the breath in both nostrils becoming free from obstruction at that precise moment – free from impediments triggered by coding (*sankhara*) – and becoming spontaneously balanced and even.

For the breath to become balanced and even, the mindbody needs to become momentarily free from emotional or energetic disturbances such as torpor or sluggishness (tamas), restlessness, anger or desire (rajas) – particularly sensual desire – because the jhanas are a transmutation of gross creative energy into higher mental and emotional energy.

Jhana 1

The transition from Access Concentration to Full Concentration of jhana 1 is palpably sensed on the entire framework of the body as a definite *change of gear*. This subtle and palpable shift in energy and awareness has been, in my experience, mostly accompanied by a spontaneous straightening of the entire spinal column bringing increased alertness, steadiness, lightness and clarity.

This experience of unprovoked straightening and lengthening of the spinal column seems to take place the moment prana enters the *sushumna* (discussed in Chapter 9, Nadis, and Chapter 10, Kriya Yoga). Sensual desire at that time becomes entirely absent.

The sensation of power spontaneously moving upwards straightening the spinal column can be likened to the feeling of power (*shakti*) moving into the *lingam* or *yoni* when these become erect through desire but in the case of jhana access, the energy moves in completely the opposite direction, inwards and upwards, instead of downwards and outwards.

The existence of this 'energy transformation' phenomenon – its 'erection' or 'empowerment' – is openly venerated in countless statues and images of Shiva-Shakti throughout India.

In the 1ˢᵗ jhana, conceptual thinking means that the thinking mind will still be engaging in concepts. By discursive thinking is meant that the thinking mind will still be talking to itself to some extent.

In the 2nd jhana both these manifestations of thinking mind subside and are replaced by sustained thought free from verbalization or conceptualization.

The 4th jhana is the condition of mind from where higher mental powers called siddhis in Yogasutra and *abhiñña* in Pali texts can be aroused and developed.

***

On the meaning of 'samadhi'

In some forms of Buddhist meditation practice, *samadhi* is equated to *samatha* which just means tranquillity, stillness, calmness. In Thailand it has even come to mean just sitting still and being quiet.

For practical yoga purposes we can consider samadhi as the precise equivalent of jhana 4.

Samadhi is the 8th part of the Buddha's Eightfold Noble Path as well as the 8th part of Patanjali's eightfold system expounded in Yogasutra. Yet of the seven jewels as factors leading to Enlightenment, samadhi comes 6th with equanimity (upekkha) coming as the final 7th, which confirms the Buddha's own experience that final emancipation from the bondage of code/coding is only achieved through equanimity, detachment, indifference towards codes (*sankhara upekkha*) and not through samadhi alone.

Dis-identification is key

There seems to be considerable misunderstanding surrounding the concept of detachment in yoga. It does not mean you become detached towards Life and Love.

Detachment in a yogic sense means literally undoing the nexuses of connections making up the code/coding. This 'undoing' happens the moment you cease to agree to pretend a specific $a \cong b$. And for this to happen, you need to remember and see how that particular knot was tied in the first place. And realize the foolish or ignorant or unwitting participation and cooperation of the thinking mind in that process of bondage.

***

Samadhi

Down the ages with Hinduism, Jainism and Buddhism each playing their parts in influencing and modifying the practice and understanding of yoga, a number of different types of 'samadhi' have been described from first-hand experiences as well as from the perspective of onlookers and commentators. This reached the height of absurdity with one commentator listing 118 different types of samadhi!

To keep it simple, all we have to do is understand what the word samadhi actually means. As mentioned several times before, whenever the syllable sam- or san- occurs in a Sanskrit or Pali word we have to be on the lookout for the number 3 or three things coming together and fusing into one single thing or process.

In the case of samadhi the observer, or observation part of the process of concentration, gets fused with the participation part of concentration. In other words the observation, observation process and object concentrated upon become fused and merged into one. The result of this is the provisional disappearance of the thinking mind and full engagement with the deep mind and will.

> As explained in earlier chapters, the awareness itself is a code, and every code is formed by three things coming together (hence samskara/san-khara).

In the case of the construction of the code of awareness, the three aspects coming together (*samyoga*) are the same three as for any other code:

- **participation** in a sensation of disturbance being experienced by *feeling* it – which we have called the "**a**"

- **observation** of a pattern of disturbance being experienced by *thinking* about it – which we have called the **"b"**
- the **equation of identity** between the observation and the participation by mistakenly perceiving the above two as identical – this connection we have called the **ab**

The **ab** arises then as *something third* and takes on an **ab**stract *life of its own*, occupying a different order of reality – a phoney, imaginary, pretence, make-believe, artificial level of reality, while **a** and **b** continue their 'lives' at the more realistic level of Real World Reality.

> **Samadhi is fusing this 'artificial' division, a division of three, back into one again. This brings deep release from agitation and disturbance (*vritti*) at that particular present moment but does not bring lasting release because it does not fully erase the code.**

It is through *satipatthana* (next chapter) that we will revisit the Buddha's yoga path, properly understand what he meant by Dependent Origination, and clear up the confusion about what is path and what is not path.

The path is the path to *visankhara gatam cittam* – mind released from the bondage of coding – a mind gone to the Codeless. That's what Buddha Gautama called *ekayano maggo*, the *only path* for the purification of beings.

> Vaya dhamma sankhara – appamadena sampadetha!
> Dissolvable are codes – conscientiously work them out!

Sariputta passed away some time before the Buddha and his last words were a very similar exhortation:

> *Sampadetha appamadena – esa me anussano!*
> Keep on working conscientiously – that's my advice to you!

The Buddha's last sentence before passing is not just a farewell remark – it is the synthesis of the entire teaching of a path lost to mankind which he rediscovered.

***

Chapter 8: Satipatthana

Remembering the Real in the Real

In this chapter the insight that *sankhara* means the *code* is applied to the key teaching of *Satipatthana* and *Paticcasamuppada* (Dependent Origination). If widely accepted, this will lead to a **mid-course correction** not only in fields of mental yoga but also in sciences. It will also show that there is no incompatibility between the teachings of Mahavir, the Buddha, Samkya and Yoga.

In this chapter we see how the key points outlined in the previous chapters fit together and are integrated into a science of **psychemechanics**, in which the Code plays a hitherto unrecognized and decisive omnipresent role.

Satipatthana is, in fact, the practical application of proper connectoring to the psychemechanics of mindbody. If done correctly and thoroughly it leads progressively to a liberation from confusion and ignorance (avijja), and provides insight-knowledge into the true Nature of Reality. This means the Reality about oneself and others as well as the World of Nature.

The three are not separate.

> "In this very fathom-long body together with its perception and its thoughts, I proclaim the World, the origin of the World, the cessation of the World and the way leading to the cessation of the World."
>
> Samyutta Nikāya, I Rohitassa Sutta

In the Preface the main proposition of *Yoga Beyond the Thinking Mind* is:

- by thinking of Reality, we have lost touch with Reality to a great extent

- the internal cinema of the thinking mind with its mental tennis prevents us from seeing the Reality of Nature as it is (sati is)
- a fundamental assumption of yoga is that *'outside the thinking mind of the human being everything is perfect'*
- *viyoga* with its concomitant disharmony/dissatisfaction tends to arise whenever the thinking mind values the **ab**stract more than the Real
- yoga is the supreme natural state
- thought is only capable of dealing in **ab**stractions and incessantly entangles itself in artificial realities of its own fabrication. This happens at the individual level, at the collective level and at the individual-collective interface.
- in every process of **ab**straction, the thinking mind creates equations of identity between dissimilar things by agreeing and pretending they are the same when they are not the same.
- this elaborate orchestration of pretence involves imagination, intent to delude, agreement and habit, all of which are at the root of the creation of codes (sankhara).

Chapter 1 tackles the colossal problem of internal and external languages, which are codes responsible for conditioning our reactions and influencing our behaviour patterns at every level.

It has been explained that the only translation of the word *sankhara* (*samskara* in Sanskrit) that makes sense and fits the picture is **"code"**.

It has taken me 44 years to realize this!

The realization that sankhara is code puts the teachings of all forms of yoga – especially the yoga of Gautama Buddha and Mahavir – into a whole new light.

What a code *is* and what a code *does* has been precisely and exhaustively explained thanks to the unpublished research of Nebosja Dimovic, a genius in my view, of the calibre of his compatriot Nikola Tesla.

This knowledge is absolutely vital for obtaining a much clearer and far more accurate picture of both mindbody and the structure of Reality in which mindbody arises, operates and belongs.

The lack of awareness of the pervasive and determining role of the code is a glaring omission in the whole of philosophy and science. The time has come for its inclusion.

As Dimovic pointed out in one of the recorded talks we had, the full acceptance of the omnipresence of the Code, and thus its central role, is not going to be added to common knowledge out of ethical or moral considerations, nor out of wisdom, nor even out of loving kindness or compassion. It will be added simply because people will suddenly wake up and realize for themselves the enormous advantages, usefulness and benefits of relinquishing the attachment and confusion engendered by codes created by the human thinking mind, and start paying proper attention to the Reality of the Real – to the Real World.

What is Code?

Code is any connection between similar representations and non-similar representations with an agreement to pretend that the non-similar can stand-in for the similar. By doing this, non-similar representations, sooner or later, end up largely replacing the similar representations in the thinking mind – otherwise there would be no point in creating a code in the first instance.

> Therefore, the code can be seen in its essence as an *agreement to pretend* and install a fictitious reality in the place of the Real Reality. The agreement can be made unconsciously or consciously, involuntarily or deliberately.

It has been shown that the construction of any code consists of a proposition that **a** is identical to **b** where **a** and **b** are not identical to each other ($\mathbf{a} \equiv \mathbf{b}$, when $\mathbf{a} \not\equiv \mathbf{b}$).

All agreements equating and identifying a non-similar with a similar involve imagination, agreement (consensus), pretence and fantasy. And a desire to preserve and perpetuate these. All of this is subsequently reinforced by habit, belief and repetition.

At the origin of all such constructions – if done consciously – **a** is proposed *as if* it were identical to **b**...later the *as-if* part of the proposition is forgotten/put aside/ eliminated from awareness and memory, and thus are installed equations of **ab**solute identity. These are consolidated through repetition and habit. And they become the chains that bind us. The "as if" (*come si fosse*) is forgotten and disappears from sight (avijja) and the code **a ≡ b** emerges as something third, takes on a life of its own and becomes embedded – as in a magnetic *tape recording* in the mindbody structure (brain and nervous system). How it is recorded depends on internal and external interactions. The psychemechanics of this is explored from another angle in the next chapter on nadis.

> Encoding can be done consciously or unconsciously, that is, deliberately or without the slightest idea or clue – without realizing – what we are doing to ourselves and to others.

avijja paccaya sankhara   *ignorance conditions code*

The human organism is thus embedded/seeded with chains upon chains upon chains upon chains of mind-made connections that create and maintain all our programming and conditioning.

In 1978, in my own mind, I perceived them as TAPES. And upon these tapes are recorded and stored the binding elements that limit us, restrict us and prevent us from the freedom to reach our full potential as humans.

These encoded tapes are the source of all our complexes, inhibitions and Pavlovian reactions. They cause obstructions and restrictions in the natural free-flow of life energy throughout the mindbody. They cause fissures and fractures in our heart, literally.

sankhara paccaya viññanam   *code conditions life-force intelligence*

What code does
The code systematically connects and adds something to something else and this action of adding things together (*karma*) automatically

brings about changes which in turn cause some sensations to become qualitatively different in some way or other. The thinking mind then *uses these differences* in sensations as code to store other meanings and then derive other meanings – thus is confusion and ignorance propagated endlessly.

Nature is not doing this to us. We are doing it to ourselves in ignorance.

The key is to **remember** that all such connections are **arbitrary** and manufactured by the human thinking mind (each $a \equiv b$ is in Reality $a \not\equiv b$) and that there are many levels or layers of coding. Like a monkey, the thinking mind jumps from one branch of coding to another, in most cases without the slightest awareness of what it is doing or what is going on. Therefore, we must not lose sight of this fact if we are to avoid confusion in our intellect, muddle in our feelings and emotions, and disentangle the literal entanglements in our brain and nervous system (mindbody).

Gautama Buddha's three key propositions about human existence can be seen as pointing specifically to a reversal of the process of encoding:

all codes are impermanent   *sabbe sankhara anicca*
This is good news everybody!
all codes are un**sati**sfactory   *sabbe sankhara dukkha*

Bound to be unsatisfactory because they are artificial substitutes that generate blockages in the life-force flow and its intelligence, hence frustration!

all mental constructs are not-the-real reality   *sabbe dhamma anatta*

How can mental constructs be our Real Nature, our real self?

Mental constructs are mental constructs – none of them can ever be the Real Deal.

This is further confirmed by the Buddha's last words of encouragement and advice:

vaya dhamma sankhara appamedena sampadetha
Codes are transitory! Keep on conscientiously working them out!

It has also been shown that the word *mindfulness* in English is an incorrect translation of Sati. Siva needs to recognize Parvati, remember her as Sati to mend his broken heart, and only then can Shiva-Shakti become whole and undivided again.

After completing 14 vipassana courses in the U Ba Khin tradition (including two satipatthana courses with SN Goenka) I realized in 1994 that one can be carefully attentive and mindful until the cows come home and still not complete the job of erasing the tapes.

What is needed is to remember the real faces...to recognize the real faces, and not merely observe an anonymous crowd wandering through the field of awareness.

Therefore, the practice of satipatthana has to involve remembering and memory, because in remembering the Real, in recognising it and fully acknowledging the Real as such...then the false, the artificial, the imaginary and all the seeds and roots of the internal cinema are exposed for the pretence they are, and are undone and erased one-by-one in every moment of such insight.

Chapter 2 introduces the DIM and Dim tendency pointing to one of the most important among the four main meanings of the Pali word Dhamma (Dharma in ancient India; Tao in ancient China).

Let's review these four main meanings:

• Dharma as Real Nature; the Real World
• dharma as mental constructs (includes every concept, image, code)
• dharma as teaching or doctrine

- dharma as DIM or Dim tendency meaning the inherent self-regulating, balancing, optimizing, harmonizing homeostasis tendency, evident and present in all of Nature, from the smallest to the largest things or processes.

Alignment with DIM is the essence of all yoga. And satipatthana is no exception, only that satipatthana delves with meticulous precision and scientific thoroughness into how to erase the codes in order to reach the codeless.

> *visankhara gatam cittam tanhanam khaya majjhaga*
> Mind gone to the **Codeless** – all compulsion eradicated from the body!

Note that the Buddha locates the problem that the code causes **in the very body itself.** Mahavier likewise. Because it is with the body, and the concerns of the body, that the mind has become entangled and bound. It is in the body that the natural flow of the DIM has got deformed through thinking mind-made coding.

Understanding the constant presence of the DIM and Dim tendency – remembering that the balancing and restorative force of Nature is always present, never absent, recognizing its action, acknowledging it, embracing it – is an indispensable part of the practice of satipatthana because it helps a yogi keep to the middle path between extremes, thereby avoiding:

- interfering too much or being too permissive
- repressing pleasant or painful sensations or indulging in pleasant or painful sensations (i.e. avoid falling into what Goenka calls '*playing the game of sensations*' instead of decoding the root of both)
- ignoring and leaving out the neutral, which is the foundation of all sensation

Therefore, the action of the DIM and Dim tendency in and on the mindbody should, as far as possible, be left undisturbed during the application of satipatthana. Let the DIM force of Nature do what it is capable of doing. We need only remember to observe and witness the Real in the Real with absolute equanimity, regardless of the codes that are being triggered moment by moment in the mindbody, with the confidence and certainty that all such codes sooner or later will dissolve and disappear.

sabbe sankhara anicca   vaya dhamma sankhara

Chapter 3 emphasizes how the Artificial World of the thinking mind, in constant interaction with the Real World, ends up partially obscuring the Real, often making it disappear from sight and memory.

"There is no disappearing of the Real World
until a false world appears;
when the false world appears,
it makes the Real World disappear."

Samyutta Nikaya ll, 224-227 Saddhamma Sutra

It is in this context that Mahavir provides a perfect example of steadfast adherence to the Real, of non-interference and harmlessness – *ahimsa* – which Patanjali would later incorporate into his Yogasutra as the indispensable foundation for yoga, for human behaviour fully in resonance with the DIM.

Furthermore, Chapter 3 explores what constitutes valid knowledge and shows that the knowledge of the thinking mind, being conceptual, is always relative and can never be absolute.

Even observing the Real World of things, all conclusions about relationships, all measurements and all meanings depend on where the observer stands (point of view) and how the observer looks and assembles in his mind what is observed. In other words, it always depends on the connections and connectoring.

We pointed out the need to distinguish between 'connecting' and 'connectoring' (a verb that does not yet exist in the English language).

Connecting is two-dimensional. It connects two or more things in a two-dimensional frame whereas connectoring is a far more complex process that can involve three dimensions of Space, three periods of Time, and links together different specifics and different orders or levels of Reality.

Proper connectoring means clearly tracing a thing or a process from its origin (cause) to its destination (effect/event/outcome/result).

This is what Mahavir pointed out in the doctrine of *anekantavada*, so far ahead of its time and whose insight has been insufficiently appreciated. Mahavir asserted that the true Nature of Reality was complex and could be described from a multiplicity of angles and viewpoints, and therefore could not be expressed in language, let alone in absolute terms. 2500 years later this has been brilliantly confirmed by Einstein in his teaching on Relativity.

> Einstein: an exceptional researcher, a good man, a sincere person, who got far more attention than he expected or perhaps deserved. He was not an especially gifted physicist, nor an exceptional mathematician. Poincaré took no notice of him. *But Einstein was ultra-precise in his connectoring.*
>
> Einstein is truly great for being on to proper connectoring, more than for any of his other outstanding achievements.
>
> Dimovic, Safari on the Fundamentals of Reality

The Buddha refused to answer questions on the ultimate Nature of Reality, and remained silent. Yet his teachings of *Patisambhida*, *Paticcasamuppada* and *Satipatthana* clearly show he was likewise on to proper connectoring in advising monks and nuns to pay close attention to the three-dimensional nature of processes and interactions relating to mind and body.

Thus we see that *proper connectoring* is the key to understanding *satipatthana*. And the key to practicing *satipatthana* successfully. The

Fall from Grace, the expulsion from Paradise, the loss of innocence, the diminishing of purity, *siddhis* and faculties are all *dukkha* arising as a direct consequence of witless manipulation of the code and thereby of humans unwittingly having become co-creator with Mother Nature.

> Truly a high price, but at the same time a genuine opportunity for free-
> dom from limitations that every human being potentially has.
> A tremendous and so far unacknowledged responsibility at which –
> due to misunderstanding the root cause of viyoga (suffering), unaware of
> the psychemechanics of code, lacking the understanding of how coding
> binds the mind to the body – we, as a species, are failing miserably.

Chapter 4 describes the intense and fervent *sramana* renouncer move-ment some 2500 years ago in northeast India, when the heroic efforts and immense contributions of Vardamana Mahavir and Gautama Buddha, and several centuries later, of Patanjali, laid firm foundations for classical yoga to be transmitted through multiple generations until modern times when great rishis like Ramana Maharshi and Anandamayi Ma continued to revive and illuminate the ancient path.

Chapters 5, 6 and 7 go into details of asana, pranayama and jhana. For the practice of satipatthana to be successful, all three must be deve-loped to a high degree.

Satipatthana can be practiced in any normal situation of daily life as well as during formal training. The Satipatthana Sutta states that the remembrance of the Real – its recognition – can of course be carried out sitting, standing, walking, lying down, attending to the calls of nature, and so on. Therefore, asana in this context can be considered a mental attitude together with whatever physical posture is assumed at any given moment. That said, it is necessary to maintain a stable asana during periods of immobility so that concentration can reach maximum intensity and be still enough to follow the action of the DIM as the life force travels through the pathways of the mindbody.

> "There is no concentration* for one who has no discernment,   *
> jhana
> no discernment for one who has no concentration*.

But the one who has both concentration and discernment
is on the threshold of the Codeless."

Dhammapada 372

In the introductory chapter, I describe the extraordinary experience of those 12 days in *sahaja samadhi*, in Mind beyond the coding of the body's DNA, beyond coding at the atomic level. However, once out of that state, I saw clearly that there were tapes to erase. That there was still considerable work to be done to unlink, untangle, unravel and unwind.

At that time, despite the vision about the tapes, I had no knowledge of the construction of the code nor of the psychemechanics of the code within mindbody.

Those insights and knowledge came years later, in the 1980s, as a result of hundreds of hours of conversations with N. Dimovic about his research into the fundamental importance of getting the connectoring right in order to achieve what he then called 'Synthesis'.

In retrospect, it has been thanks to tracing backwards from the elephant to the hunter that has allowed me to see that applying proper connectoring to the psychemechanics of mindbody is exactly the way of satipatthana practice. And how the fundamental role of the code perfectly explains both the arising and the cessation of suffering in the formulation of Paticcasamuppada (Dependent Origination).

Satipatthana more than anything else is an extremely precise way of looking at things by cultivating the habit of not confusing the specific, and instead remembering at all times and in all situations the Real in the Real (what is really happening in every situation), and by doing so putting the internal cinema to the sword.

The subtlety of what is meant by the Real in the Real is explained below, as we examine the how and why of the structure of the original Satipatthana discourse.

"Whoever understands Dependent Origination, understands the Code, and whoever understands the Code, understands Dependent Origination."

Majjhima Nikaya Sutta 28

"Profound Ananda, is this Dependent Origination, and profound does it appear. It is by not understanding, by not penetrating this Code, that this world resembles a tangled ball, a bird's nest, a thicket of reeds or rushes, and that mankind fails to escape from the lower states of existence, from the course of lamentations and losses, and suffers the round of rebirth."

Digha Nikaya Sutta 15

***

Satipatthana

So now, with this understanding of the goal and method of practice, with trust and gratitude to all those teachers known and unknown, who enabled the teaching of yoga to endure and come down to us through the centuries, we will consider satipatthana as the application of proper connectoring to the psychemechanics of mindbody.

And in doing so, we will see how the decoding – the erasing of the tapes – can be carried out consciously, relentlessly, steadily until the heart-mind is freed from all bonds.

It has already been shown that *sati* means thoroughly remembering – a recognition and acknowledgement of the Real in the Real – and not simply mindfulness. The following etymology with regard to satipatthana confirms this convincingly.

Etymology

The word *satipatthana* is a compound word combining two distinct words. Some etymologists say that satipatthana is composed of the two words *sati* and *patthana* while others claim that it is a fusion of *sati* and *upatthana*.

Sati-upatthana would translate as 'applications of the Recollection of the Real' whereas *sati-patthana* would mean 'foundations for the Recollection of the Real'.

According to scholars, the former is more likely to be correct. However, there is a third possibility. It is that *sati-upatthana* is composed of *sati* and *upadana*, meaning *identification*, and that over centuries of oral transmission the word *upadana*, which sounds very similar, became *upatthana*.

Sati-upadana would then mean, 'Remembering Identification' (**idem**-tification) which is at the root of the formation of each and every *sankhara* (code) and which is also the ninth link in the Dependent Origination formulation (Paticca-samupada**). Be that as it may, satipatthana as "Applications of Remembering the Real" is an accurate enough translation that fits the purpose.

These four related aspects can and should be applied to everything in life, not only to the examples given in the texts.

The four aspects

* bodily structure (kaya)   patterns I strains I forms
* sensations (vedana)   feelings I disturbances I waves I oscillations
* mind (citta)   mental states I internal cinema I state of mind
* mental constructs (dhamma)   concepts I images I codes

Note: all *mental constructs* can be understood as codes in different disguises.

If the reader is interested in details, you can easily find English translations of the Satipatthana Sutta. There are different versions: long versions under Maha Satipatthana Sutta, and shorter versions under Satipatthana Sutta.

The following is the introductory instruction with regard to the four aspects (in bold) as given in the Pali text.

We should keep in mind that these four aspects are connected to each other, often trigger each other and can therefore arise simultaneously.

As an example of the application of the four aspects, the text on *anapanasati* –remembering inbreathing-and-outbreathing – is shown below.

Pali texts: source Maha-Satipatthan Sutta (Vipashyana Vishodhan Vinyas, Hyderabad) and Tipitaka.org

Evam me sutam.
Ekam samayam Bhagava Kurus viharati. Kammasadhammam nama Kurunam nigamo. Tatra kho Bhagava bhikkhu amantesi 'Bhikkhavo'ti. 'Bhadante' ti te bhikkhu Bhagavato paccassosum. Bhagava etadavoca:

'Ekayano ayam bhikkhave maggo sattanam visuddhiya soka-pariddevanam samatikkamaya dukkha-domanassanam atthañgamaya ñayassa adhigamaya, nibbanassa sacchikiriyaya, yadidam cattaro satipatthana.

Katame cattaro? Idha bhikkhave bhikkhu kaye kayânupassi viharati atapi sampajano satima, vineyya loke abhijjha-domanassam – vedanasu vedanânupassi viharati atapi sampajano satima, vineyya loke abhijjha-domanassam – citte cittânupassi viharati atapi sampajano satima, vineyya loke abhijjha-domanassam – dhammesu dhammânupassi viharati atapi sampajano satima, vineyya loke abhijjha-domanassam.

Translation

Thus have I heard.
At one time the Awakened One lived among the Kurus in Kammasadhammam, a town of the Kuru people. There the Awakened

One addressed the Bhikkhus thus: "Bhikkhus," and they replied: "Venerable Lord."

The Awakened One spoke to them thus:
"This is the only direct path, bhikkhus, for the purification of beings, for the extinction of suffering and woe, for treading the path of the Real, for the realization of Nibbana, namely, the application of remembering (the Real) in relation to four aspects.

"Which four? Here, bhikkhus, a bhikkhu lives ardent, comprehending thoroughly and remembering – contemplating the body as body, abandoning identification and delusion in relation to the world of codes and images; lives ardent, comprehending thoroughly and remembering – contemplating sensations as sensations, having abandoned identification and delusion in relation to the world of codes and images; lives ardent, comprehending thoroughly and remembering – contemplating mental states as mental states, having abandoned identification and delusion in relation to the world of codes and images; lives ardent, comprehending thoroughly and remembering – contemplating mental constructs as mental constructs, having abandoned identification and delusion in relation to the world of codes and images."

The above is exactly equivalent to the synthesis of the method for proper connectoring applied to the four aspects of mindbody.**

** Nama-rupa in Pali can also be translated as code-image, as well as name-form, but the word used in the sutta is *kaya*, not *rupa*, so it definitely refers to physical, material mindbody structure.

The repetition in the text of *kaye kayanupassi* – 'body in the body' or 'body as body', means that whenever we contemplate the body as structure, we remember to stick to the body as body, to its structure as structure and restrain the thinking mind from wandering outside the scope of body, structure, pattern, form. No other aspect of reality is to be attended to by switching the connectoring to another "loke", to another of the four fields.

Thus we remember the Real in the Real in relation to the bodily structure, and the body is contemplated as it is, abandoning all identification and all deception in relation to the field of codes and images.

The repetition of *vedanasu vedananupassi* – sensations in sensations or sensation as sensation – likewise means that whenever we contemplate sensations and feelings (the Pali word is the same for both feeling and sensation) we remember to keep contemplating feelings arising in connection with sensations, and sensations arising in connection with feelings; we see how sensations become feelings and vice versa, and we remember to stay focused only on feelings as feelings, sensations as sensations, pushes as pushes, disturbances as disturbances, oscillations as oscillations, vibrations as vibrations, waves as waves, and in this way the thinking mind is restrained from wandering off into another field. No other aspect of reality is to be attended to by switching the connectoring to another "loke", to another aspect of reality.

Thus we remember the Real in the Real in relation to sensation, and sensation is contemplated as it is, abandoning all identification and all delusion in connection with the field of codes and images.

The repetition in the text *citte cittanupassi* – of 'the mind in the mind' or 'state of mind as state of mind', likewise means that when contemplating the mind, we remember to focus on states of the mind as states of the mind and restrain the thinking mind from wandering off into other aspects of mind by switching the connectoring.

Thus we remember the Real in the Real in relation to mind and states of mind, and mind contemplates itself as it is, abandoning all identification and all delusion in connection with the field of codes and images.

Likewise the repetition in the text of *dhammesu dhammanupassi* – of mental constructs in mental constructs or mental constructs as mental constructs – also means that, in contemplating mental constructs, we stick just to the content of mind as content of mind: to thoughts as thoughts, to concepts as concepts, to codes as codes, to mental images as mental images, to mental cinema as mental cinema, preventing the thinking mind from proliferating (*prapanca*) the unreal.

Thus we remember the Real in the Real with respect to mental constructs, and mental constructs are contemplated as they are – as codes (sankhara) – abandoning all identification, all deception, all confusion, all delusion in relation to the world of concepts, codes and images.

Feelings can arise in reaction to sensations and sensations can arise in reaction to feelings. Sensation is always a kind of physical, mechanical disturbance (oscillation/vibration). Feeling is more a mental-emotional reaction to sensations triggered depending on the original encoding.

About the meaning of the word 'restraint'

"Restraint of the eye is helpful; restraint of the ear is helpful; restraint of the nose is helpful; restraint of the tongue is helpful.

"Restraint of the body is helpful; restraint of speech is helpful; and helpful is restraint of thought. Fruitful is restraint in general. The monk restrained in every way is free from all suffering."

Dhammapada 360-361

The key is to watch out for the thinking mind *switching the connectoring* – how and when – from mere sights, mere sounds, mere touches, mere tastes, mere smells, mere thoughts and mere observation of these to a proliferation of mental cinema, i.e. to mere codes, mere images, mere concepts...thereby mental tennis can be avoided and the mental cinema is gradually brought to an end (to a standstill).

Before I clearly understood that the aim of satipatthana is the dissolution of codes, I did not understand what verses 360 and 361 of the Dhammapada were driving at. And the idea of such iron-clad 'restraint' seemed to be unnatural, repressive and alien to the middle way. But now I see clearly that the way to dissolve the codes is to allow the reactions triggered by the coding to surface and manifest, while restraining them from proliferating by remembering and recognizing the original constituent elements for what they are. In this way the practice is to continuously abandon any inappropriate equations of identity.

> To be abandoned is identification with regard to any arbitrary $a \equiv b$ connections that arise in each and all of the four fields of connectoring detailed above in the Satipatthana Sutta.

Anapanasati section: 'remembering in-and-outbreathing'

In a number of Satipatthana related texts, immense value is placed on the practice of *anapanasati* emphasizing its benefits to the point of asserting that it is difficult to find anything more beneficial than the practice of remembering inhalation and exhalation.

Why?

> Bhikkhus, the anapanasati that one develops and makes one's own, perfects the four applications of full remembering. The four applications of full remembering that one develops and makes one's own perfect the seven factors of awakening. The seven factors of awakening that one develops and makes one's own develop perfect Knowledge (of the Real) and Liberation (from suffering).
>
> Majjhima Nikaya 118

The recollection of in-and-outbreathing is, therefore, a supreme field in which to apply proper connectoring, because although *anapana* comes under the bodily aspect, its scope encompasses also sensations, mind and mental constructs.

Anapanasati, in covering the four applications of satipatthana, also fulfils the seven determining factors that provide direct insight and vision into the Real Nature of Reality, namely:

SATI

Remembering/recollecting/recognizing/acknowledging/admitting to oneself what is Real.

DHAMMAVICAYA

Investigating the Real World of Nature as it is; investigating the DIM and Dim tendency; investigating the code and mental constructs.

VIRIYA

Energy. Energy arises in abundance as soon as the yogi dis-engages from mental tennis and from the tremendous effort and tension of maintaining the fictitious, the artificial and the false...and instead merely sticks to observing what is really happening. If the yogi allows the DIM to do what the DIM is capable of doing, the colossal energy previously devoted to propping up the mental cinema is released and becomes available.

PITI

Rapture. As a result of the abundance of available freed-up energy 'released' by abandoning pretence and make believe, great joy in the form of rapture floods the mindbody, producing waves of ecstasy equivalent to that of jhanas 1 and 2.

PASSADDHI

Tranquillity, calm. As the waves of ecstasy subside, they are replaced by deep tranquillity, relief, calm and imperturbability as in jhana 3.

SAMADHI

Concentration. As tranquillity enables the mind to focus even more penetratingly on the Real, the trio of participation, observation and participation-observation merge into a single experience of the Real, as in jhana 4, transcending previous pain and pleasure.

UPEKKHA*

Equanimity. Here equanimity refers specifically to equanimity in the face of the triggering of any code or encoding (*sankhara-upekkha*), whatever its physical or mental manifestation.

Following on from *samadhi*, equanimity arises even towards blissful feelings and blissful states and perceptions arising from full concentration and unification of mind.

This kind of equanimity is indifference in the positive sense of the word – an attitude of non-differentiation; of accepting everything and making no distinction between this or that. Impartiality is another word that expresses this attitude.

> * 'Remembering the Real in the Real' together with this quality of equanimity become the two indispensable keys to gradually erasing sankhara (codes) from mindbody. *Upekkha* is one of the four 'Abodes of Brahma' called *Brahma Vihara* – the most exalted states of sentiment – along with *metta* (loving-kindness), *karuna* (compassion), and *mudita* (joy in the success and happiness of others).

Regarding this quality of equanimity, just before his own awakening, Siddhartha Gautama, after going in and out of jhanas 1, 2, 3 and 4, related that the blissful feelings that arose during the jhanas failed to lay hold of and control his mind or distract it so he was able to instead focus it on remembering previous existences, and to relive innumerable memories of lifetimes in which he sought what he termed 'the builder of the house' (mindbody).

Pali Text

> *Kathaṃ ca pana, bhikkhave, bhikkhu kāye kāyānupassī viharati?*
>
> *Idha, bhikkhave, bhikkhu araññagato vā rukkhamūlagato vā suññāgāragato vā nisīdati pallaṅkaṃ ābhujitvā, ujuṃ kāyaṃ paṇidhāya, parimukhaṃ satiṃ upaṭṭhapetvā.*
>   *So sato va assasati, sato va passasati. Dīghaṃ vā assasanto 'dīghaṃ assasāmī' ti pajānāti, dīghaṃ vā passasanto 'dīghaṃ passasāmī' ti pajānāti. Rassaṃ vā assasanto 'rassaṃ assasāmī' ti pajānāti, rassaṃ vā passasanto 'rassaṃ passasāmī' ti pajānāti. 'Sabbakāyapaṭisaṃvedī assasissāmī' ti sikkhati, 'sabbakāyapaṭisaṃvedī passasissāmī' ti*

sikkhati. 'Passambhayaṃ kāyasaṅkhāraṃ assasissāmī' ti sikkhati, 'passambhayaṃ kāyasaṅkhāraṃ passasissāmī' ti sikkhati.

Seyyathāpi, bhikkhave, dakkho bhamakāro vā bhamakārantevāsī vā dīghaṃ vā añchanto 'dīghaṃ añchāmī' ti pajānāti, rassaṃ vā añchanto 'rassaṃ añchāmī' ti pajānāti.

Evameva kho, bhikkhave, bhikkhu dīghaṃ vā assasanto 'dīghaṃ assasāmī' ti pajānāti, dīghaṃ vā passasanto 'dīghaṃ passasāmī' ti pajānāti, rassaṃ vā assasanto 'rassaṃ assasāmī' ti pajānāti, rassaṃ vā passasanto 'rassaṃ passasāmī' ti pajānāti.

'Sabbakāyapaṭisaṃvedī assasissāmī' ti sikkhati, 'sabbakāyap-aṭisaṃvedī passasissāmī' ti sikkhati, 'passambhayaṃ kāyasaṅkhāraṃ assasissāmī' ti sikkhati, 'passambhayaṃ kāyasaṅkhāraṃ passasissāmī' ti sikkhati.

Iti ajjhattaṃ vā kāye kāyānupassī viharati, bahiddhā vā kāye kāyānupassī viharati, ajjhattabahiddhā vā kāye kāyānupassī viharati, samudayadhammānupassī vā kāyasmiṃ viharati, vayadhammānupassī vā kāyasmiṃ viharati, samudayavayadhammānupassī vā kāyasmiṃ viharati, 'atthi kāyo' ti vā panassa sati paccupaṭṭhitā hoti.

Yāvadeva ñāṇamattāya paṭissatimattāya anissito ca viharati, na ca kiñci loke upādiyati.

Evaṃ pi kho, bhikkhave, bhikkhu kāye kāyānupassī viharati.

Translated into English and replacing bhikkhu in some sentences by yogi.

And how, bhikkhus, does a yogi live observing the body in the body?

Here a yogi, having gone to the forest, or to the foot of a tree, or to an empty place, sits cross-legged, keeps his body erect and focuses attention on the area around the mouth.

Remembering the Real, he breathes in, remembering the Real, he breathes out. Taking a long breath in, he understands thoroughly: "I am taking a long breath in." Breathing out a long breath, he understands thoroughly: "I am breathing out a long breath." Breathing in a short breath, he understands thoroughly: "I am breathing in a short breath." When exhaling a short breath, he understands thoroughly: "I am exhaling a short breath."

In this way he trains himself: "Feeling the whole breath body, I will breathe in. Feeling the whole breath body, I will breathe out," thus he trains himself.

"Calming (the reactions of) coding related to body, I will breathe in," thus he trains himself. "Calming (the reactions of) coding related to body, I will breathe out," thus he trains himself.

Just as a skilled carpenter or a carpenter's apprentice, while making a long turn, thoroughly understands: "I am making a long turn," and while making a short turn, thoroughly understands: "I am making a short turn," so the yogi, while taking in a deep breath, thoroughly understands: "I am taking in a deep breath." Breathing out a deep breath, he thoroughly understands: "I am breathing out a deep breath."

Breathing in a short breath, he thoroughly understands: "I am breathing in a short breath." Breathing out a short breath, he thoroughly understands: "I am breathing out a short breath."
    In this way he trains himself: "Feeling the entire energy body, I will breathe in. Feeling the entire energy body, I will breathe out," thus he trains himself.

"Calming (the reactions of) coding related to body, I will breathe in," thus he trains himself. "Calming (the reactions of) coding related to body, I will breathe out," thus he trains himself.

Thus he dwells observing the body in the body internally, or he dwells observing the body in the body externally, or he dwells observing the body in the body internally-externally.

Thus he dwells observing the arising of mental constructs connected with the body, thus he dwells observing the cessation of mental constructs connected with the body, thus he dwells observing the arising-cessation of mental constructs connected with body.

Now he applies the remembrance (of the Real in the Real): "This is body!"

Thus he develops the remembrance of the Real to such an extent that nothing remains but understanding, nothing but recognition of the Real.

Thus he remains detached, unidentified with anything in the world of codes and images. This is how bhikkhus, a yogi remains observing the body in the body (in relation to in).

Analysis of the four tetrads

In the Anapanasati Discourse in Majjhima Nikaya Sutta 118 as well as in other texts, 16 forms of practice divided into four tetrads are outlined, which show how the recollection of in-and-outbreathing applies to the four aspects:

- **body-structure**
- **sensations-feelings**
- **states of mind**
- **mental constructs**

In this way "remembering the in-breath, the yogi breathes in; remembering the out-breath, the yogi breathes out..."

Scope: **STRUCTURE BODY PATTERNS**

1. "Making a long inhalation, recognizing it as a long inhalation; making a long exhalation, recognizing it as a long exhalation;
2. "Making a short inhalation, recognizing it as a short inhalation; making a short exhalation, recognizing it as a short exhalation;
3. "Fully recollecting the whole body inhaling, training in this way; fully recollecting the whole body exhaling, training in this way;
4. "Calming the whole body breathing in, training in this way; calming the whole body breathing out, training in this way."

Scope: **FEELING SENSATIONS PUSHES**

5. "Feeling sensations of rapture breathing in, training in this way; feeling sensations of rapture breathing out, training in this way;
6. "Feeling joyful sensations breathing in, training in this way; feeling joyful sensations breathing out, training in this way;
7. "Feeling the (triggering of) coding breathing in, training in this way; feeling the (triggering of) coding breathing out, training in this way;
8. "Calming the (triggering of) coding breathing in, training in this way; calming the (triggering of) coding breathing out, training in this way."

Scope: **STATE OF MIND MOODS ENERGY STATES**

9. "Recognizing the state of mind breathing in, training in this way; recognizing the state of mind breathing out, training in this way;
10. "Gladdening the mind breathing in, training in this way; gladdening the mind breathing out, training in this way;
11. "Concentrating the mind breathing in, training in this way; concentrating the mind breathing out, training in this way;
12. "Freeing the mind (of codes and images) breathing in, thus training; freeing the mind (of codes and images) breathing out, thus training."

Scope: MENTAL CONSTRUCTS CODES IMAGES CONCEPTS

13. "Remembering codes are impermanent, breathing in, thus training; remembering codes are impermanent breathing out, thus training;
14. "Undoing identification breathing in, thus training; undoing identification breathing out, thus training;
15. "Stopping coding breathing in, thus training; stopping coding breathing out, thus training;
16. "Abandoning (all codes) breathing in, thus training; abandoning (all codes) breathing out, thus training."

Furthermore, in connection with remembrance and recognition of the four aspects:

- **structure I form I pattern**
- **feeling I sensation I push**
- **mood I energy state I state of mind**
- **mental fabrication I mental cinema** (codes; images; concepts)

"Here, monks, after having gone to the forest or to the root of a tree or to an empty place, a yogi sits cross-legged, keeps his body erect and his recollection in the present.

"He inhales, remembering the Real, exhales remembering the Real;

"Breathing in a long breath, he knows that 'this is breathing in a long breath'; breathing out a long breath, he knows that 'this is breathing out a long breath';

"Breathing in a short breath, he knows that 'this is breathing in a short breath'; breathing out a short breath, he knows that 'this is breathing out a short breath'.

"Experiencing the whole breath-body, I will breathe in," so he trains. "Experiencing the whole breath-body, I will breathe out," so he trains.

"Calming the coding related to the breath-body, I will breathe in," thus he trains. "Calming the coding related to the breath-body, I will breathe out," thus he trains.

Kaya | Body aggregate | Structure

"And how, monks, does a yogi live contemplating the body as body?

"Thus he dwells contemplating the body in the body internally, or he dwells contemplating the body in the body externally, or he dwells contemplating the body in the body internally-externally.

"He dwells contemplating origination factors of the body, or he dwells contemplating dissolution factors of the body, or he dwells contemplating origination-dissolution factors of the body."

Or remembrance is established with recognition: "The body exists to the extent necessary for knowledge and remembrance (of the Real), and he abides detached, unidentified with anything in the realm of codes and images. Thus too, monks, a yogi lives contemplating the body as body."

Vedana | Feeling | Sensation | Push

"And how, monks, does a yogi live contemplating sensations as sensations; feelings as feelings?

"Thus he abides contemplating feelings as feelings internally, or he abides contemplating feelings as feelings externally, or he abides contemplating feelings as feelings internally-externally.

"He dwells contemplating the factors that originate feelings, or he dwells contemplating the factors that dissolve feelings, or he dwells contemplating the origination-dissolution factors of feelings.

"Or remembrance is established with recognition: 'feeling exists', to the extent necessary for knowledge and remembrance (of the Real), and he abides detached, and does not identify with anything in the realm of codes and images. Thus too, monks, a yogi lives contemplating feelings as feelings."

Citta | States of Mind | Mental Modalities

"And how, monks, does a yogi live contemplating mind as mind?

"Here, monks, a yogi knows the mind with sensual desire as the mind with sensual desire; the mind without sensual desire as the mind without sensual desire; the mind with aversion as the mind with aversion; the mind without aversion as the mind without aversion; the mind with ignorance as the mind with ignorance; the mind without ignorance as the mind without ignorance; the limited state of mind as the limited state of mind; the distracted state of mind as the distracted state of mind; the developed state of mind as the developed state of mind; the undeveloped state of mind as the undeveloped state of mind; the state of mind with mental states above it as the state of mind with mental states above it; the state of mind without any mental state above it as the state of mind without any mental state above it; the concentrated state of mind as the concentrated state of mind; the unconcentrated state of mind as the unconcentrated state of mind; the liberated state of mind as the liberated state of mind; and the unliberated state of mind as the unliberated state of mind.

"Thus, he abides contemplating the mind in the mind internally, or he abides contemplating the mind in the mind externally, or he abides contemplating the mind in the mind both internally-externally together. He dwells contemplating factors that originate the mental state, or he dwells contemplating factors that dissolve the mental state, or he dwells contemplating both origination-dissolution factors of mental states.

"Or his remembrance is established with the recognition 'mind exists', to the extent necessary for knowledge and recollection, and he remains detached, unidentified with anything in the realm of codes and images. Thus, monks, a yogi lives contemplating mind in mind."

Dhamma | Mental Constructs | Codes, Images & Concepts
"And how, monks, does a yogi live contemplating mental constructs in mental constructs?

"Thus, he abides contemplating mental constructs in mental constructs internally, or he abides contemplating mental constructs in mental constructs externally, or he abides contemplating mental constructs in mental constructs both internally and externally. He dwells contemplating the origination factors of mental constructs, or he dwells contemplating the dissolution factors of mental constructs, or he dwells contemplating both together the origination-dissolution factors of mental constructs.

Or recollection is established with the recognition that 'mental constructs exist', to the extent necessary for recognition and remembrance (of the Real), and he lives detached, without identifying with anything in the realm of codes, images and concepts.

Thus, a yogi practises steadily and uninterruptedly the remembrance of the Real in the Real in relation to the body and structures; the remembrance of the Real in the Real in relation to feelings and sensations; the remembrance of the Real in the Real in relation to the mind and mental states; the remembrance of the Real in the Real in relation to mental fabrications, keeping in mind, remembering and never forgetting that all mental constructs including concepts and images are all codes (*sabbe sankhara*).

(*Loke* = world, sphere, order of reality, realm, field)

Furthermore, we notice that certain keywords and key-phrases are repeated over and over again to drum it into our heads!

Sampajañña
This is an extremely significant use of the word here that can only be properly appreciated in its full extent if we realize that the prefix sam- here also indicates three aspects, or three things that come together in one.

Therefore, the right application of proper connectoring which the Satipatthan Sutta instructs the yogi to apply, requires viewing from 3 angles – it's a three-dimensional process, four dimensions if Time is added.

In the texts we see the three aspects/angles constantly repeated:

• *Arising, Ceasing, Arising-Ceasing*

For example, with respect to breathing, the arising phase corresponds to inhalation and the cessation phase corresponds to exhalation. Both arising-cessation together corresponds to the two turns, from in-to-out and from out-to-in, as outlined in Chapter 6 on pranayama.

Or arising-ceasing together can refer to waves/oscillations/vibrations that can be distinctly perceived in the mindbody when awareness becomes sufficiently sharp and subtle.

Internal, External, Internal-External
Here, again, is another important trio to ensure correct perspective and attitude. It can be interpreted in several ways, all of which are essential to understanding the Real and **how the psychemechanics of mindbody works.**

Internal can mean inside the body and external as outside the body. In this case internal-external refers to the interface between inner and outer (inside-outside).

> Any structure or body located in the Real World of Nature can be seen as a Content inside a Container within a Context. It is a three-dimensional configuration. This threefold connectoring of context-container-content can be applied to any structure however large or small.

We can clearly see that connectors can come from outside the body or from inside the body, or be generated at the interface – by the interaction/dialogue between the two (as is so often the case).

Moreover, this trio can also mean subject, object and subject-object.

Or it can mean subjective, objective or subjective-objective.

Or observation, participation or observation-participation.

In a previous chapter we have already pointed out that awareness itself is a code because – like any other code – it is also a connection between two non-similar things or aspects: **a spurious equation of identity**.

> In the case of mindbody, one aspect is the subjective participating part of it and another aspect is the objective observing part of it. Awareness is the subjective-objective connection that arises as a *third thing* that assumes the false self-existence as the separate "I".

All this tangle can be resolved by carefully perceiving the Real in the Real and gradually filtering out the false connections from the valid ones.

Finally, there is another trio – not mentioned in the suttas as far as I know – which are the three Times: the present, the past and the future.

The past is not really the past, but the memory of how certain things in the past affected us and were encoded and registered as memories.

Likewise, the future is not really the future, but merely a projection of what may happen that may or may not be accurate.

The present is often thought of as the only real time – a constant ongoing past-future interface but this too might be yet another illusion of the thinking mind. Only the present seems to be real, but only if it is recognized as such by paying due attention to it. To truly understand the present, feeling is required, not thinking. If perceived through the filter of the thinking mind even the present can become as dubious and biased as memories of the past and projections of the future.

Ehi passigó!

***

PATICCA-SAMUPPADA – the Wheel of Karma
(Pratityasamutpada in Sanskrit)

Now we come to where in 12 short propositions Gautama Buddha formulates the psychemechanics of dukkha and its cessation: a vicious circle of cause and effect and its opposite, a virtuous circle, together known as Dependent Causation or Dependent Origination.

Anuloma: winding–binding

Avijja paccaya sankhara;
sankhara paccaya viññanam;
viññāna paccaya namarupam;

namarupa paccaya salayatanam;
salayatana paccaya phasso;
phassa paccaya vedana;
vedana paccaya tanha;
tanha paccaya upadanam;
upadana paccaya bhava;
bhava paccaya jati;
jati paccaya jara-maranam-; soka-parideva- dukkha- domanassupayasa
sambhavanti.
Evame tassa devalassa
dukkhakkhandhassa
samudayo hoti.

Patiloma: unwinding–unbinding

Avijja-nirodha sankhara-nirodho;
sankhara-nirodha viññāṇa-nirodho;
viññaṇa-nirodha namarupa-nirodho;
namarupa-nirodha salayatana-nirodho;
salayatana-nirodha phassa-nirodho;
phassa-nirodha vedana-nirodho;
vedana-nirodha tanha-nirodho;
tanha-nirodha upadana-nirodho;
upadana-nirodha bhava-nirodho;
bhava-nirodha jati-nirodho
jati-nirodha jara-maranam-soka-parideva-dukkha-
domanassupayasa nirujjhanti.

Evame tassa kevalassa
dukkhakkhandassa nirodho hoti.
Paticca-samuppada Sutta, Samyutta Nikaya, 12

A word-for-word translation introducing the decisive role of the **code** in mindbody psychemechanics:

Vicious Circle winding–binding

Ignorance conditions code; $(a \equiv b, \text{ when } a \not\equiv b)$

Code conditions life-force intelligence;

Life-force intelligence conditions mindbody;

Mindbody conditions six-field connectoring;

Six-field connectoring conditions sense-impression;

Sense-impression conditions sensation-feeling;

Sensation-feeling conditions compulsion/desire;   literally 'thirst', craving

Compulsion conditions identification;   IDEM-tification $(a \equiv b,$ when $a \not\equiv b)$

Identification conditions **behav**iour;

Behaviour conditions Life;

Life conditions ageing and death together with grief, lamentation, physical and mental suffering.

Thus arises this whole mass of *dukkha*.

(note: $\equiv$ identical to ; $\not\equiv$ not identical to)

Virtuous Circle unwinding–unbinding

Ignorance ceasing, code ceases;

Code ceasing, life-force intelligence is freed;   (freed from conditioning/ from limitations)

Life-force intelligence freed, mind-body connection ceases;

Mindbody connection ceasing, six-field connectoring ceases;

Six-field connectoring ceasing, sense-impression ceases,

Sense-impression ceasing, sensation-feeling ceases;

Sensation-feeling ceasing, compulsion-desire ceases;

Compulsion ceasing, identification ceases; $(a \not\equiv b \text{ remains } a \not\equiv b)$

Identification ceasing, (compulsive) **beha**viour ceases;
(Compulsive) **beha**viour ceasing, body-identified life ceases;
Body-identified life ceasing, ageing and death ceases,
along with grief, lamentation, physical and mental suffering.

Thus, all dukkha ceases and immortality is attained. *visankhara gatam cittam*

***

If you can understand the first three links of the Vicious Circle, it is enough!
You will then easily understand the next nine because the next nine are equivalent to an unfolding of the first three.

Ignorance conditions code

Ignorance of what? What not-knowing-ness is the Buddha referring to?
Avijja literally means 'not seeing'...what is it then that humans do not see
that keeps them unfailingly stuck in a loop, a wheel, a treadmill, a cul-de-sac?
That is the number one question.
The answer is – we do not see the Real World because it has become hidden and replaced by an artificial world of mental fabrications (all codes).
In a previous chapter Shankara's famous example of the "snake in the rope" was given.

A husband and wife in India return to their house in the forest at dusk. In the poor light, they mistake a coiled rope near the entrance for a cobra. This triggers a chain reaction of misconnectoring in their mindbody resulting in all sorts of unpleasantly disturbing sensations like fear, anxiety, stress, worry and so forth. However, upon closer inspection with a good lamp, they see it is only a rope, so the whole coding structure related to the dangerous snake immediately ceases, and along with its cessation, all the other propagating reactions triggered in the mindbody likewise cease.

Shankara's is just a simple illustration, but one which shows the psychemechanical consequences, wherein once a wrong connection in the thinking mind is made (a ≡ b, when a ≢ b), that encoding action sooner or later has repercussions in compromising the life-force intelligence.

> What we think, say and do has specific consequences (repercussions) on the mindbody. The ancients referred to this as *karma* and the result of *karma*.

The moment this psychemechanical interaction of mindbody is seen with true insight, thereafter all codes, all images, all concepts, are seen only as such, while the true Reality of Nature is revealed as something pure and undivided – *keval* – capable of being lived and experienced, but inexpressible in language.

Code conditions life-force intelligence

To put it bluntly, we have tied ourselves up in knots and more knots, creating restrictions and blockages in the free flow of the life force and its natural intelligence throughout our mindbody. This is further discussed in chapters 9 and 10.

Also, remember that intrinsic to the intelligence of the life force is the DIM and Dim tendency. The life force is precisely the carrier of the innate intelligence of DIM, of Nature's impulse to optimize. Therefore, any embedded artificial coding is bound to interfere to a greater or lesser degree in the life-force intelligence's natural order and flow.

How could it be otherwise?

Hence all embedded mind-made codes are un**sati**sfactory and potential problem-causers – *sabbe sankhara dukkha.*

Life-force intelligence conditions mindbody

Inasmuch as the DIM flow of life-force intelligence is compromised by codes, it becomes restricted/constricted and conditions the mindbody, limiting it from its full potential.

Mindbody conditions the six-field connectoring

This is also clear. A mindbody with compromised life-force-intelligence naturally will reflects these limitations in some way in one or more of the six-field connectoring (eye/sight/seeing; ear/hearing/sound; tongue/savour/taste; touch/sensation/feeling; nose/odours/smells; mind/intellect/understanding).

The six-field connectoring conditions sense-impression

Well of course it does! All our impressions depend on how we interpret things. And how we interpret things depends on our six-field connectoring. Both links are mutually dependent. How the thinking mind chops up and again connects together all the sensory input from the six-field connectoring results in all our meanings.

Thus (next link) depending on the connectoring, bare sensations or mere sensations, are turned into pleasant, unpleasant or neither-pleasant-nor-unpleasant feelings.

Each person's thinking mind gradually constructs its own idiosyncratic artificial reality that hides the true Reality of Nature (as discussed in previous chapters).

Sense-impression conditions sensation-feeling

Depending on the meanings triggered by sensation-feeling, the 'by-the-code-deformed' DIM naturally has us compulsively running away from what we don't like, running towards what we do like. And meanwhile ignoring what we don't pay attention to, which is a lot, because we are so busily engaged focusing on like and dislike and ignoring the neutral!

Sensation-feeling conditions compulsion-desire

The 'by-the-code-deformed' DIM makes us compulsively run away from what we dislike, run towards what we like and ignore what we are indifferent to.

Compulsion-desire conditions identification

We identify with what we are inclined to, to what we like and wish to preserve and repeat.

Identification conditions behaviour

This is obvious, isn't it?

Behaviour conditions Life

Also obvious.

Life (in a body) ***conditions ageing and death***; together with sorrow, lamentation, physical and mental distress.

Thus arises this entire mass of un**sati**sfactoriness.

Yes, but let us not forget that life is not only suffering, sorrow, grief, lamentation and despair and other negative aspects. No doubt all of these exist to a greater or lesser extent depending on one's circumstances (*karma*).

But there is a lot more to Life than its negative aspects!

What about love, happiness, pleasure, joy, contentment, sense of humour, curiosity, creativity, arts and sciences, poetry, music, dance, beauty, the magnificence of Nature. All that also exists!

Gautama Buddha spoke of three things he had thoroughly experienced and understood in relation to Life: satisfaction, misery and escape.

He did not recommend a compulsive, conditioned state of mind, identified with mental cinema even for the interval of time between two finger snaps! Hence the urgency to wake up, get Real and come out of ignorance, wrong views and misalignment with Nature.

> He whose desires have been extinguished,
> Who is independent of root,

Whose pasture is emptiness, codeless and free
His path is as unknowable
As that of birds across the sky.

Dhammapada

I hope that by now the reader has realized that the so-called three marks of existence are not such at all, but are **three extraordinary keys to the decoding process.**

Change and transformation are an essential and necessary part of Life. In fact, most aspects of Life are inconceivable without change/impermanence. The transformations involved in change are necessary to keep everything fresh, new, vigorous and alive. The fact that codes are impermanent and can be dissolved is truly great news and the central point!

The knowledge of impermanence as we witness the dissolution of codes within the mindbody framework is essential in order to withstand the process. Moreover, the abandonment of concepts, codes and images includes abandoning those of the senseless debate that has been going on for over 2500 years between self and not-self (*atta* and *anatta* in Pali; *atman* and *anatman* in Sanskrit).

Sabbe dhamma anatta simply means that all mental constructs, including all mental fabrications about self and not-self, about *atman* and *Brahman*, about whether they are separate or not – all of it is mental tennis, just guesses leading nowhere. All such discussion is meaningless and a waste of time and energy.

Direct insight into Reality annihilates all such conceptualizing.

Meanwhile the magnificent and unfathomable Real Reality of LIFE continues to exist and shimmer like a diamond mostly unnoticed, unremembered, unacknowledged, unappreciated.

One day, when both the Buddha and his elder cousin and constant companion Ananda were well-advanced in years, Ananda remarked to his great friend and teacher:

"Today, during my meditation, the insight arose in my mind that the love we share between us is half of the entire Noble Eightfold Path – half of this entire path we walk together – it's about love!"

To which the Buddha, the supreme teacher of proper connectoring, of Satipatthana – who taught only about *dukkha* and *dukkha*'s complete cessation, replied:

"Never say that dear Ananda, never say that. It's *not half* – it is the entirety of it – the whole sense!"

So let us bear in mind that outside the thinking mind of the human being, there is a Real World of Nature to be discovered and a boundless love that is immortal.

> *Yato-yato sammasati*
> *khandhanam udayabaya,*
> *labhati piti-pamojjam,*
> *amatam tam vijnanatam.*

> Whenever, wherever there is perfect recollection
> Of the aggregate's arising-and-ceasing,**
> The mindbody is washed through with bliss,
> This the Deathless for those who understand.

Dhammapada 374

** Udaya-bhaya 'arising-ceasing' here means vibration, waves, oscillation of mindbody particles at the atomic level (*kalapas*).

***

Path and Not Path

A few words of caution here on the deviousness of the thinking mind. During the course of satipatthana practice – of applying proper connectoring to the psychemechanics of mindbody – with a view to freeing heart-mind from the misconnectoring of the thinking mind, from its internal cinema and from its layers upon layers of artificial coding embedded on the framework of the body, there may arise a number of lures and enticements which have been variously depicted down the ages as *temptations* to seduce the hero or heroine away from completing the task.

> These distractions from continuing steadfastly and unwaveringly on the path to distinguish the specifics of what is Real from what is not-real may take on all sorts of guises and disguises according to the accumulated coding of each person.

During the course of prolonged, sustained satipatthana practice, there comes a point where the yogi's concentration has become sharp, subtle, penetrating and refined and is capable of experiencing the body as oscillating, vibrating waves of energy or vibrating particles. At this stage the yogi feels so bodily and mentally light and at ease that she or he is capable effortlessly to continue sitting in asana contemplating structure, sensations, states of mind and mental constructs.

However, it is at this juncture that the yogi must be on his or her guard because the thinking mind – the thief of the Real disguised as policeman – in order to avoid getting caught and exposed can here conjure up a number of side-tracks (non-paths) which are to be carefully avoided if the yogi does not wish to get bogged down and slip back into winding-binding instead of continuing steadfastly with the unwinding-unbinding process.

> Remember the game of snakes and ladders!

White light or other manifestations of *inner light* may arise internally causing the yogi to think, "Aha! So this is illumination! This is what enlightenment is all about...!"

At the same time various kinds of *knowledge* may arise of such an apparently profound and sublime nature as to make the yogi forget that all conceptual knowledge, however valid, beautiful and apparently useful, is still fundamentally thinking-mind-concocted and therefore triggered by the very coding to be dissolved.

Rapture, bliss, calm and ecstasy likewise can arise and become distractions from equanimity towards codes, concepts and images. The sensations and feelings that at those moments engulf a yogi's mind and body are such that they may generate great confidence, enthusiasm and energy, and the yogi in his thinking mind then goes off at a tangent thinking, "Aha! With such knowledge, energy, confidence, enthusiasm I can become a teacher; tell the whole world! I must right away tell such and such a friend or relative this and that," and so forth!

Here again, all these various thoughts and emotional reactions – which appear to be nothing but good, beneficial and positive – in fact depend on particular accumulations of coding that are also to be steadfastly dissolved, not pumped up and propagated.

The yogi may even seem to have within his or her grasp various kinds of supernormal powers...even amazing *siddhis* like those enjoyed by the great *siddhas* – such as capacity to see the future; hear at a distance; rise up into the air; jump from a great height without injury. But such powers are like those experienced in the dream state, and thus are also manifestations of past actions triggered from the storehouse of codes/memories.

The thinking mind is so devious – so bent on its survival at any cost – that it can even produce states resembling equanimity towards codes and coding!

How to tell the difference between the genuine and the false? Between identification with codes, images and concepts and adherence to the Real only?

Fortunately, Real Nature has provided us with two barometers as litmus test:

1. In the absence of blockages in the nadi network, the breath/prana at the entrance to the nostrils will remain long, cool and even.

   (to be described in detail in the next chapters)

2. Any mental state imbalance – either elation or negativity – is a sure sign that there is still something in the yogi's mind that has to be straightened out, transformed or dissolved.

***

Chapter 9: Nadis

Background

Nadis, chakras and kundalini are three developments to the conceptual yoga framework that only began to be added around 1000 years *after* Mahavir and Gautama Buddha. To put that time gap into perspective, that also means around 700 years *after* Patanjali, and about 300 years *after* Shankaracharya.

Dating in ancient India is notoriously imprecise but it seems that the concept of a network of nadis – with chakras acting as hubs or centres and kundalini 'awakening' to travel up the spinal column activating them – emerges in the framework of *tantra* around the 11ᵗʰ century AD. Thus the concept of a network of nadis, with chakras acting as hubs, and kundalini energy, coincided with the arising of tantra not yoga.

> Tantra teaches how to dissolve coding without repressing or re-submerging any material whatsoever. All elements are included in the grand alchemy.

Tantra is another word with so many diverse nuances and meanings according to time, place and context that there is no universally accepted definition. Swami Chaitanyanda claimed the origin of the word *tantra* is an amalgam of *mantra* + *yantra*. Thus tantra is sound, shape and shade (vibration, pattern, color frequency) – characteristics which make up all manifestations and sustain them.

At the time of Mahavir and the historical Buddha the physical body was viewed by their contemporaries and followers more as an obstacle than as a vehicle for reconnecting to the Real in spite of the fact that the Buddha is reported to have declared that the World, its origin, its cessation and the path to its cessation – all four aspects – are to be found within the physical body (*kaya*).

> In this very one-fathom long body along with its intellect and its thoughts, do I proclaim the World, the origin of the World, the cessation of the World, and the path leading to the cessation of the World.
>
> Samyutta Nikaya, 1 Rohitassa Sutta

And we have just seen in Chapter 8, *kaya* – the physical bodily structure – is the starting point for satipatthana, and indispensable to its application.

The essence of tantra is fundamentally Shivaic in its acceptance and uptake of absolutely everything we see around us and inside us, good as well as bad, with no discrimination whatsoever, transforming all of it through the chrysalis of intense heat (*tapas*) into a single immutable substance.

> "Transformare non eliminare!"
>
> Michele Salmeri, Catania 1986

Dr Salmeri's leitmotif in three words sums up the entire spirit and essence of tantra, which is to bring to light, re-experience and transform whatever 'essential material' has been repressed/supressed/ignored/ undigested/forgotten/dismissed and which, through inattention and neglect – both deliberate as well as inadvertent – has generated what Jung calls the *unconscious*. In fact, Jung equated this unconscious with the 'sleeping' *kundalini* energy.

It was within this climate of willingness to include the physical body with all its aspects and functions that various tantric movements began to arise in India during the 8th century and by medieval times had gained considerable momentum and influence among systems of Jain, Hindu and Buddhist yoga practice.

A complete alchemical body theory did not exist in India before medieval tantric movements began to exert their influence. During the early millennium of recorded yoga, despite the odd hint here and there in ancient texts (Patanjali's Yogasutra mentions the navel chakra), teachers and students of yoga seem to have had no need nor inclination for such theorizing.

> Or, such theories were passed down only orally from teacher to student. If this is the case, it is unlikely to have gone unrecorded for so long but the possibility cannot be completely excluded. The kriya yoga technique discussed in the next chapter, could be an example of such closely guarded oral transmission.

During medieval times, *nadi, chakra* and *kundalini* became established parts of tantra, hathayoga and alchemical yoga among Hindu, Jain and Buddhist sects. Each had their own descriptions. In China, Taoist alchemical yoga also had such maps of their own. It is outside the scope of this chapter to disentangle the conceptual threads within all these similar currents, including those from Ayurveda and Chinese Traditional Medicine.

The main practical focus here and the next chapter is the relationship between **breath, prana** and **nadis** in order to show how the decoding process can also be carried out using another method of breathwork/breath control to those described in Chapter 6, Pranayama and Chapter 8, Satipatthana (under recollection of in-and-out breathing/ *anapanasati*).

But first a few words about *chakras* and *kundalini* from direct experience, including the experience of fellow meditators.

Chakra

The word chakra (also written *cakra*) can stand for both 'wheel' and 'lotus', and abundant references to both these meanings can be found in early Upanishads 700-800 BCE in the context of kings, palaces and chariots but it took another half a millennium, around 200 BCE – 200 CE, for later Upanishadic texts to even mention chakra in a tantra yoga context.

Then there is big gap until Guru Gorakhnath in the 10th century and then a further 500-year gap until the 16th century when Sri Tattva

Chintamani's chapter 6 describes six centres. (See the 2 Mallinson charts in appendices)

John Woodroffe, a British High Court judge in Calcutta (now Kolkata) translated the 16th century Tattva Chintamani manuscript and published it in 1919 as *The Serpent Power* under the pen-name Arthur Avalon. This was to become the benchmark text in Western languages on chakras and kundalini. And is still influential today among yoga schools.

The Serpent Power was one of the first reference books recommended to me in 1971 by Ramiro Calle. While it was an enjoyable and interesting read, neither of us found it of much practical use, nor ever saw a way to apply it to any yoga practice other than visualization.

> Nevertheless, the encounter with the dangerous dog described in the introductory chapter showed me first-hand unequivocally that there does indeed exist a powerful force which can arise in the body when the mind abides naturally in the 4th jhana/samadhi. This force seems to be capable of protecting a yogi from harm. There are many accounts of such incidents in ancient Pali texts. It is good to know that what they describe is a real tangible energy phenomenon – perhaps electromagnetic or electrical in nature but more likely a force related to *prana*.

In the wake of the interest generated by the publication of *The Serpent Power* the Theosophical Society made much of the subject of chakras and kundalini, and some of its members came up with their own elaborate pictures and descriptions. It should be emphasized here that all such 'folklore' was rejected by J. Krishnamurti who had no use for it. Neither did Ramana Maharshi nor Nisargadatta Maharaj ever mention chakras, or even nadis or kundalini.

> Descriptions are only descriptions after all, and the more precise, the more to the point and of practical use, the better. The way things are described always depends on perspective, on historical context, on the influence of peers, and on individual experiences and states of mind.

Nevertheless, the conceptualization of seven levels of Reality has been around for a long time, and there is something valid and useful in it.

The earliest reference to seven levels is likely that contained in India's most revered and well-known mantra – the Gayatri mantra.

> *om bhur bhuvah svah*
> *tat savitur varenyam*
> *bhargo devasya dhimahi*
> *dhiyo yo nah prachodayat*

Rigveda 3.62.10

The Gayatri also has a longer, less well-known version specifically naming the seven levels:

> *Om bhur, Om bhuvah*
> *Om svah, Om mahah*
> *Om janah, Om tapah*
> *Om satyam*

Thus the long version of the seven levels Gayatri Mantra is

> *Om bhur, Om bhuvah*
> *Om svah, Om mahah*
> *Om janah, Om tapah*
> *Om satyam tat savitur varenyam*
> *bhargo devasya dhimahi*
> *dhiyo yo nah prachodayat*

For yogic purposes, the seven levels can be understood as seven different levels of mindbody vibration, energy and frequency.

Satyam	Consciousness (as in Chapter 12)
Tapah	Mind
Janah	Ether (as in chapter 12)
Mahah	Air
Swah	Fire
Bhuvah	Water
Bhur	Earth

The top three levels resonate with the human being's most refined expressions and aspirations:

- **Universal Consciousness**   no mind I beyond mind I at-**om**-ic level
- **Third eye**   nondual mind I e-mergence DNAIRNA (Chapter 10, Kriya yoga)
- **Higher e-motion**   creativity I art I science I music I dance I song I literature I poetry

- **Heartmind**   In-and-outbreathing I Life force I Sustainer of Life

Heartmind is the seat of *awareness* in humans, and situated according to ancient Taoist texts 'exactly in the mid-point' between Heaven and Earth participating in all fields depending on the focus of attention. According to yoga it is located in the *hrid* – in the heart centre, slightly to the right of the physical heart. It is here that the light of Consciousness described in Chapter 12 is reflected in the mirror of the Mind as the subjective participating "I" part of the awareness-code.

The lower three energy levels deal with basic functions of bodily survival, lower e-motions and instincts:

- **digesting** I assimilating I distributing food energy
- **procreating** I grabbing I fighting I fleeing
- **excreting** solid and liquid waste I recycling

Neither at the beginning nor at any moment of the 12-day *sahaja samadhi* described in the introduction did the Mind's eye see any chakra or any wheel or lotus in connection with any of the above seven levels of awareness.

The quantum shift in awareness to the third eye (6th level) was experienced as a shift to looking through a diamond located above and behind the two normal eyes. This diamond vision instead of refracting and differentiating shapes, colours, sounds – even thoughts – into differences, integrated everything into a single essence while the attributes and characteristics of each individual *thing* continued to be visible through the two ordinary eyes.

The 7th level was experienced as a second quantum shift of perception from the 6th level of Nature's DNA I RNA coding to Nature's atomic level.

Chaitanyananda never spoke of the lower chakras or lotuses. He only ever discussed nadis and kundalini.

Kundalini

Carl Gustav Jung considered *kundalini* to be equivalent to what he called *'the personal unconscious'* which he understood as connected to *'the collective unconscious'*.

If you think about it in Jung's terms, an awakening of kundalini – any so-called movement upwards – is no more accurate than saying the 'sun is rising' or the 'moon has risen'. Both *appear to rise* because what has been hiding them moves away and withdraws.

> Neither sun nor moon nor *kundalini* rise up as such, only what has been keeping them hidden from ordinary awareness withdraws. What has been keeping kundalini concealed is the veil of the thinking mind – the internal cinema.

That withdrawal of the veil of ignorance generated and maintained by the thinking mind coincides with the quantum shift in awareness to the third eye, experienced in yoga as a turning around 180 degrees whereby the thinking mind – along with its entire 'mental cinema' – becomes 'dormant' (hidden from view; out of the field of ordinary perception) and in its place 'arises' that awareness of Consciousness which perceives all things as of a single nondual essence even though appearances and characteristics retain their diversity.

> Samsara is then seen as Nirvana
>
> Nagarjuna

During *preludes* to such radical about-turns in the seat of perception, the ordinary thinking mind's coding is perceived as collapsing and dissolving. This collapse and dissolution is well-described in satipatthana/ vipassana manuals under *bhaya* and *bhanga*.

Bhaya and *bhanga* are both equally unpleasant, disturbing experiences. *Sankhara-upekkha* aided by knowledge of their transient nature (*sankhara-anicca*) enables safe and calm passage through such upheavals in perception and feeling.

So, let sleeping dogs lie! Do not disturb the sleeping dog of kundalini – let the time come for it to awaken naturally! Continuing steadfastly on the path of yoga, let the time ripen naturally, which it will if effort is sustained and steady. When the time comes apply satipatthana to undo and dissolve the maximum amount of coding in the safest and surest way.

Nadis

The nadis or nadi network is something well worth knowing about for any yogi or yogini interested in delving deeper than physical aspects of hathayoga. The nadis are the location of the deposited, accrued, embedded coding (*sankhara*) which causes all restriction and blockage in the free flow of life-force intelligence (*viññana*).

Mahavir taught that any action (*karma*) out of alignment with harmlessness and truthfulness (*ahimsa* and *satya*), out of harmony with Nature, literally causes an in-flow of *particles* to accrue onto the *jiva* and encrust in the framework of the body. Interestingly, the great genius Nikola Tesla seems to have had a similar insight into 'shadowing particles' which dull the reflected light of Consciousness inside us.

Gautama Buddha taught *sabbe sankhara dukkha* – that all codes *are* dukkha (suffering; un**sati**sfactory) – because codes created in ignorance condition and compromise the life-force intelligence, directly affecting the mindbody and limiting its potential.

Kriya yoga – the subject of the next chapter – is an additional method allegedly attributed to Shankaracharya for deblocking the nadis through sustained *anuloma viloma* pranayama.

***

"Blissful abiding here and now is whenever prana and the life-force intelligence flow through blockage-free plumbing!"

That may not sound like yoga's ultimate secret but it is!

Probably most ancient cultures knew this. Certainly ancient Indians and ancient Chinese did. The Chinese still to this day have a wonderful expression preserved in everyday language which perfectly expresses the essence of this knowledge.

> 沒關係 *mei kuan shi, which* literally means *"it is not closed"*, *"there is no restriction"*, *"it is not constricted"* and nowadays is still frequently used in China to express *'it's okay/no problem/it doesn't matter/never mind/no big deal!*

This ancient Chinese expression must have come from either Taoist yoga or ancient Chinese medicine, whose understanding of meridian pathways bears a close resemblance to yoga's concept of the network of nadis. In both systems, overall DIM is restored through the process of *freeing up constriction* and *blockage* of ch'i (Chinese word for *prana*) in its natural flow and progression through the network of channels (nadis) throughout the body.

> Whenever, wherever there is absence of obstruction to prana circulating through the body's nadi network, this is reflected in the breath flowing freely and easily in both nostrils. This is accompanied by waves of blissful lightness and ease throughout the mindbody.

> *"Labhati piti-pamojjam,*
> *amatam tam vijanatam."*

> "Washed through with bliss,
> This the Deathless for those who understand."

> Dhammapada, XX 15 (374)

Whenever the flow of prana meets an obstacle in a nadi, this is reflected in a restriction or constriction in air flow in either one or both nostrils.

Any such *narrowing* is experienced as some degree, however minor or major, of physical or emotional discomfort, un-ease, distress – in short, as dukkha!

Encoded, forgotten memories deposited and embedded along the pathways of the nadi network are the cause of any narrowing or outright shut down.

The breathing at the entrance to the nostrils is therefore a precise barometer reflecting the overall energy state inside the mindbody at any given moment

So, if an ancient yogi were to be asked, 'What is happiness? Can you define happiness?' the answer would likely be, 'Happiness is here and now whenever prana and breath flow simultaneously without obstruction through both nostrils long, cool, and even.'

Because of the thinking mind's habit to search outside the body to find external causes for its internally-experienced disharmony, the unresolved inside problem is missed and instead transferred onto an external scapegoat. The inside dukkha remains unremembered, unrecognized, unacknowledged-as-to-its-cause and instead in compensation a projection is made onto something external.

But the 'external' is innocent!

The cause of dukkha is invariably inside the mindbody! This is extremely hard to accept and acknowledge because in a multitude of instances, it does not appear to be like that in everyday life. Thus, **compensation has become the name of the thinking mind's game**, probably because compensation somehow mimics the DIM's own natural tendency to compensate!

The fundamental problem is that the thinking mind's coding interferes with and deforms the DIM's ordinary response to natural cause and

event in unpredictable ways causing *prapanca* leading to further disorder.

***

Both the path of decoding – dissolving past conditioning, complexes,
neuroses, hang-ups, unwholesome negative behaviours, habit reactions
and accumulated ignorance – as well as the final goal of reaching the
end of the unwinding, unbinding process (the Buddha's *visankhara
gatam cittam* and Patanjali's *citta vritti nirodha*) – can be undertaken
and carried out without any knowledge or discussion of *chakras* or
kundalini or even of *nadis*.

Nevertheless, *nadis* in their manifestation at the entrance to the
nostrils are a tangible, easily accessible-to-everybody, most valuable
barometer that is certainly well worth learning to read and use.

The word '*nadi*' can be translated as pipe, channel, tube or conductor. In attempts to justify the existence of what is deemed 'invisible'
to scientific scrutiny (at least currently), 'nadi' has been equated with
nerves and blood vessels or other physical tubing. On a physical structural level the human organism contains tens of thousands of miles of
different elastic pipes, channels and tubes without counting nerves and
fascia. The network of fascia – the intricate multi-layered web of con-
nective tissue – that reaches throughout the human body to every cell
could be a location for the nadis owing to its connection to the nervous
system and central channel (sushumna).

Nadi as a concept in ancient India predates Mahavir and Gautama
Buddha by several centuries* and therefore knowledge of nadis was
likely shared by the nine main ancient Indian *darshanas* (philosophical viewpoints), six of which followed Vedic authority (Samkhya,
Yoga, Nyaya, Vaisheshika, Mimamsa and Vedanta) and three of which
followed their own lineage of world teachers (Jainism, Buddhism and
Ajivika).

* Chandogya Upanishad (800-600 BCE and Prasna Upanishad 500-
100 BCE)

During the five centuries 600 BCE to 100 BCE the Brahmin and Kshatriya classes of northeast India enjoyed a high level of education. Many of the ascetics and yogis in the *sramana* renouncer movements of that time came from these social classes and this led to intense debates and exchanges of ideas. This makes it almost certain that the concept of *nadi* was known both to Mahavir and to Gautama Buddha yet neither are reported to have mentioned nadis in their teachings nor did their later followers describe a theory of nadis as part of the map for attaining liberation from dukkha. Yet nadi as channel, pipe, tube or conductor is a tangible, existing structure evident at the entrance to our left and right nostrils, as well as evident in the nameless upper lip furrow, which nobody talks about and yet is staring us all in the face every time we look in the mirror or at another person.

> **No other primate** – from whom we are said by science to be directly related or indirectly descended – **has an upper lip furrow**.
>   *How can its absence from primates be explained if we are so closely related? Where did the furrow come from? What is its significance?*

These questions in the course of time will no doubt be answered by science but only if proper research is undertaken into the 26 modalities of breath/life force at the entrance to the nostrils, and a map drawn up of what all these modalities mean.

Furthermore, the way we humans move on our feet and run, and the great affinity of so many of us to water and swimming is striking.

> "...no animal walks or runs as we do. We keep the trunk erect; in walking, our knees are almost straight at mid-stance; the forces our feet exert on the ground are very markedly two-peaked when we walk fast; and in walking and usually in running we strike the ground initially with the heel alone.
> No animal walks or runs like that."
> Alexander, R M (2004) "Bipedal animals, and their differences from humans," *Journal of Anatomy*, 204

***

If as yogis we had to single out the most astonishing omission in human physiology and medicine, without doubt it is the failure to make a proper and thorough investigation into breathing and the vital force that breath carries.

In the early 1980s I made several unsuccessful attempts to bring this to the attention of Salk Institute, California and other organizations who could have been interested in making a proper study, including influential people in the field of wellness at that time but was ignored completely.

The reason is perhaps because there is hardly another area of yoga more fraught with hocus pocus and mumbo jumbo than the medieval tantric yoga narrative about chakras and kundalini, which includes nadis. It seems that professionals in the various fields of yoga either do not know because they have not been taught by a person who does have some knowledge, or it could be that the few who do know, remain silent and opt to keep it to themselves.

This calls to mind the famous stanza out of the Tao Te King.

"Who knows, does not speak
Who speaks, does not know."

Lao Tze

The translation of this verse can however be given a different and deeper meaning, namely that Lao Tzu is saying it is the 'deep mind' (heartmind) that knows, yet functions in silence. And it is the thinking, talking mind that does not know and is ignorant. The deep mind has no need to chitter and chatter (speak) – it just gets on with the 24/7 full-time job of orchestrating the countless different jostling and colliding DIMs into an overall ongoing **dynamic BIG DIM**. The deep mind engages solely in the present moment silently getting on with multi-task optimizing.

"That (part of us) which knows, does not speak
That (part of us) which speaks, does not know."

Lao Tze

Relationship of breath to the 5 great elements

Scientific physiological studies made so far do recognize a certain periodicity in breathing but they seem to have no notion yet about the 24-hour cycles in relation to the four great elements (earth, water, fire, air), nor about the sun-moon connection to DNA/RNA, nor the connection of sun-moon to breathing, brain, brain-hemispheres, sides of the body and nervous system.

They have observed that periodic alternation of breathing occurs between nostrils, and they have spotted degrees of openness or closedness in left and right nostrils but given no satisfactory explanation as to how or why or when. From a yogic perspective, the tentative physiological explanations so far proposed seem not much better than incomplete guesses.

> Every yogi and professional athlete knows that breathing and most especially the quality of breath is of utmost importance to performance. In fact, hardly anything is more important because without breath and prana, life quickly comes to a standstill.

The quality, texture, temperature, length, speed, frequency of natural unforced breath is a moment-to-moment indicator of the state of the vital energy – the life-force intelligence – as it circulates in specific time cycles through the **nadi** network.

Although some ancient texts give 101 and 350,000 as the number of nadis, the ancient consensus* is the nadi network consists of **72,000** nadis originating in the heart centre.

> * Brihadaranyaka Upanishad 2.I.19

Modern science has confirmed that after fertilization the first thing to develop in the human embryo is the heart with all nervous connections branching out thereafter from the heart-centre.

> Some texts say *about* 72,000 – perhaps to conceal the key number is 72072. Either way number 72 is an extra-ordinary number. As an

example, the constantly cropping up 1/137 which so fascinates scientists is *about* 0.0072.

I leave it to mathematicians and numerologists to have fun with number 72 and its manifestations in multiples of 100s, 1000s and higher, but 72 sure is an amazing number showing up again and again in Nature, in sacred geometry, in the structure of ancient monuments, and in many of the ancient world's records related to Time, Space and Structure.

***

Traditional Chinese medicine has gone to great lengths to map those parts of the nadi network relating to organs and chi (prana/vital force) but does not seem to emphasize its connection to breath's quality, power, length, texture, frequency and temperature.

In India the more complete map specifically linking prana to breathing to specific blockages to specific types of coding either never existed or has been lost long ago.

In this regard the complex Ayurvedic maps are inapplicable to yoga as their focus is on health and wellness, not on decoding (dissolving *samskara*).

From the practical yoga-usefulness point of view all that we have of a map of the structure of the nadi network is the **three main nadis** out of 72,000 and little else, although in some texts a total of either 10 or 14 nadis are mentioned. In either case these additionally named nadis bring little to the table as they are described as ancillary to the main three.

Yoga map of 3-fold structure of 72,000 nadi network

Breath quality at entrance to nostrils is precise barometer reflecting the general energy state inside mindbody at any given moment

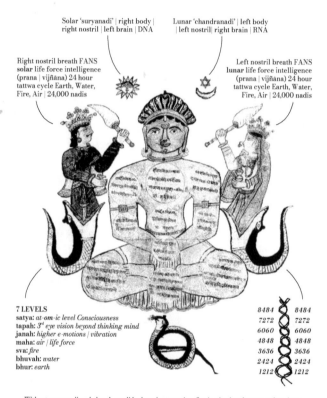

Solar 'suryanadi' | right body | right nostril | left brain | DNA

Lunar 'chandranadi' | left body | left nostril| right brain | RNA

Right nostril breath FANS solar life force intelligence (prana | vijñana) 24 hour tattwa cycle Earth, Water, Fire, Air | 24,000 nadis

Left nostril breath FANS lunar life force intelligence (prana | vijñana) 24 hour tattwa cycle Earth, Water, Fire, Air | 24,000 nadis

7 LEVELS
satya: *at-om-ic level Consciousness*
tapah: *3ʳᵈ eye vision beyond thinking mind*
janah: *higher e-motions | vibration*
maha: *air | life force*
sva: *fire*
bhuvah: *water*
bhur: *earth*

8484	8484
7272	7272
6060	6060
4848	4848
3636	3636
2424	2424
1212	1212

Without suryanadi and chandranadi both at the same time flowing in chandratattva, there is no possibility for the two breaths to join, merge and enter the central channel sushumna, thus for the life force intelligence (vijñana) to travel back up saraswati and re-awaken to Real Knowledge | 24,000 nadis | 72,000 nadis becomes 3 at triveni

Again a threefold structure

The three main channels are called **sushumna** (central), **ida** (left) and **pingala** (right).

Other names were mentioned in an earlier chapter relating the three principal nadis to three mythologically significant Indian rivers:

• **Saraswati**: centre of spinal column – hidden except for the visible upper lip furrow

- **Ganges**: left body-side I left nostril I right brain hemisphere
- **Yamuna**: right body-side I right nostril I left brain hemisphere

However, in this chapter I have chosen to use the three names Swami Chaitanyananda used, thus linking them directly to the sun and the moon, and thereby to two of the four great elements (*mahadhatu*):

- **Sushumna**   (central)
- **Chandra-nadi** (moon I left)
- **Surya-nadi**   (sun I right)

Chandra means the 'moon' and *surya* the 'sun'. Sushumma corresponds to Ether/ Aether (*prakriti*). All mindbody structures, however subtle, are therefore material according to Samkhya. And all its interactions are psychemechanical owing to the participation of the thinking mind's coding.

Searching in libraries and on the internet under yoga – aside from the countless mentions of *ida, pingala* and *sushumma* – there seems to be nothing on how prana and breath precisely reflect what is going on inside the mindbody's nadi network in regard to coding (*sankhara*) nor how coding's resultant obstructions compromise the life-force intelligence (viññana).

Avijja paccaya sankhara
Sankhara paccaya viññanam
Viññana paccaya namarupam ….

Ignorance conditions code
Code conditions life-force intelligence
Life-force intelligence conditions mindbody...

Yet as can be seen from its prime positioning in the Buddha's formulation of Dependent Origination (Chapter 8), this is an extra-ordinarily important field to study in depth now that we have scientific method and ultra-sensitive instruments.

***

The 24 hour Cycle of Prana
through the Elements

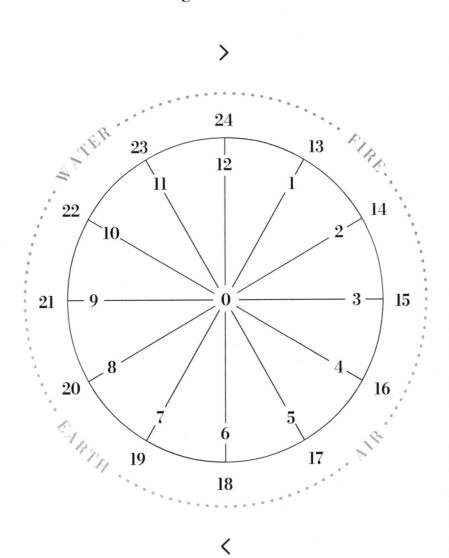

The 24 hour Cycle of Prana
through the Elements

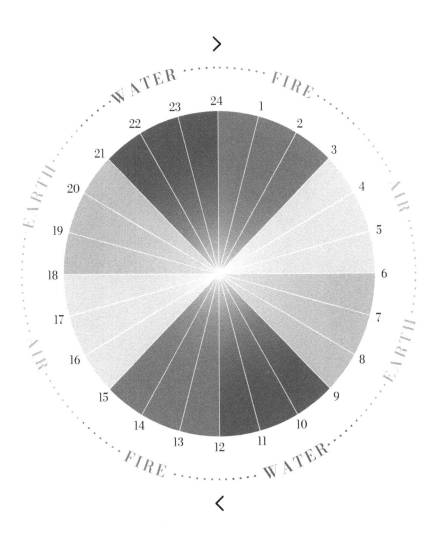

Chapter 10: Kriya Yoga

Firstly, to clarify a possible confusion.

In some yoga circles there seems to be a confusion between *shatkriya* and *kriya yoga*. *Kriya yoga* has nothing to do with the hathayoga *shatkarmas*, which are six physical purifications. The reason for the confusion is probably because the hathayoga *shatkarmas* are also called *shatkriyas*.

The hathayoga *shatkriyas/shatkarmas* are a collection of six physical mechanical exercises given in the 15th century Hathayoga Pradipika manual to help prepare the physical body for asana and pranayama.

From the head down these six shatkriyas are:

- *Trataka* – gazing steadily with unblinking eyes at a fixed external object till the eyes smart and water. Not to be confused with *kasina* exercise in Pali Buddhism for attaining full concentration and *jhana* (compare kasina in Chapter 7, jhana)
- *Kapalavati* – a blasting explosive outbreath through each nostril individually with the other nostril blocked; this is done alternately and to finish off then blasting through both nostrils simultaneously. Its purpose is to forcefully expel mucus from the nasal passages one by one, then together. Its effect may also aid in cleansing part of the sinus cavities (not to be confused with *kapalavati* pranayama, Chapter 6).
- In the 1970s I remember once being stuck in a traffic jam in Bangkok. I was fortunate to be in a taxi with aircon whose driver had garlands of jasmine hanging over the rear-view mirror. While we waited in this cool fragrant atmosphere, in stark contrast to the steaming Bangkok heat and pollution outside, a motorcyclist drew up beside us, calmly removed his helmet and unabashedly closing off his right nostril, blasted out a jet

of snot from his left nostril onto the pavement. He then closed off his left nostril and likewise blasted out a jet from the right nostril. I was so impressed by this expedient and spontaneous demonstration of *kapalavati shatkriya*, that I immediately took mental note of its efficacy for future use.

- *Neti* – with head tilted sideways running tepid salt water (purified sea water is best) in turns through each of the nostrils and out through the mouth. Or performing a similar cleansing action by passing an oiled thread through each nostril and out through the mouth or gently pulling the thread back and forth like a seesaw.
- *Dhauti* – swallowing a long strip of cotton cloth soaked in milk until pulling it out and thereby removing excess mucus from the throat and oesophagus. Vegans can use vegetable milk!
- *Nauli* – abdominal left and right rotation of inner muscles after mastering *uddiyana bandha*. I once demonstrated this powerful exercise to a learned doctor professor of gastroenterology in Madrid who was so impressed he declared everyone should be taught this exercise, especially women. This shatkriya not only benefits all the internal elastic structures of the stomach and abdomen but also massages the other nearby internal organs.
- *Basti* – using *uddiyana bandha* to suck in water (or herbal infusion) directly into the vagina or through the rectum into the colon, the intaken water is then rotated alternately left and right by means of *nauli* and then expelled.

Useful as these exercises are, this is absolutely not the *kriya* meant in this chapter on *kriya yoga*.

Kriya yoga

According to Swami Chaitanyanda, this technique has been handed down from teacher to student individually since 8th century Shankaracharya (Adi Shankara). Whether or not Shankara invented *kriyayoga* himself or whether it too came down to him from long before, is not known. What is important is that it is works.

The Sanskrit word *kriya* (also pronounced and transliterated as *kariya*) means *action*, the kind of action that brings about a specific result. In the context of yoga this action results in a cleansing and purification of the nadis, wherein what I figuratively call the *subtle plumbing* is freed from obstructions, and what I saw in 1978 as *the tapes* are wiped clean of dissonant* recordings.

*Dissonant means 'at variance with harmonic melody'

As such the meaning of the word kriya in *kriya yoga* is closely related to the meaning of the Sanskrit word *visuddhi* transliterated into English as *vishuddhi* or *visuddhi* meaning *purification* in both Pali Buddhism and in tantric branches of Hinduism such as Shaktism and Shivaism, as well as in Jain yoga.

> In Jain yoga, Mahavir taught that the accumulation and embedding onto the *jiva* (spirit) of *particles* generated by negative karma (actions) can be removed through the supreme action of non-identification whilst living according to the great vow of Protector of all Life.

According to the teaching of Mahavir, the *jiva*'s inherent, stainless purity (*visuddhi*) is revealed upon the removal of the attached particles of impure matter (Tattvarthasutra).

Kriya = action

Kriya therefore means action, a specific kind of *action* directed at removing impurities. In the case of kriya yoga this results in deblocking the subtle nadi network described in the previous chapter, freeing it from accumulated coding and conditioning caused by negative past actions (karma) and events, including trauma.

The nadi network is clogged with thinking-mind-made codes (*sankhara*). Or the action of the encoding process has in some way altered the structure of the nadi by causing deformations such as kinks, bends, twists qnd knots that restrict or outright impede the flow of prana down specific pathways.

> Research needs to be carried out in mapping the precise relationship and connections between the pathways of energy flow throughout the human body and the body's other branching networks:
>
> brain I nervous system I circulatory system I lymphatic system I fascial system.
>
> This can lead to a more complete understanding of what constitutes health, how it can be preserved and how it can be restored to optimum whenever out-of-DIM.

The issue of *structure* is far more important than may seem at first glance.

Structure

Several of the human body's systems have similarities in structure to a tree. And this applies to all mammals and probably most creatures roughly our size that move around unrooted to the earth. Most people have probably not thought much about our similarity in structure to a tree, if at all, but it's worth taking a look at what these general similarities in structure are.

Of course there are many different types of trees, of varying shapes and sizes, but here we are ignoring the differences and focusing only on the main general similarities in order to get a clear picture and not get lost into details.

A tree has three obvious parts to its structure:

- a root-system below the earth spreading and branching downwards and outwards into the earth
- an upright main trunk or stem connecting earth with sky
- and from the trunk – mirroring its below-earth root system – it has branches and branching off branches spreading upwards and outwards into the air, upwards into the sky unfolding a leaf-system.

Because a tree has no need to move around, navigate obstacles and hunt for its food or procreation partner, it remains rooted staying still* in one place for its entire lifespan obtaining its sustenance right there where it is (sunlight, air, water, minerals, organic and inorganic nutrients).

* Exceptions to this would be in the event trees are artificially transplanted or grown in a pot, shifted around by humans, or displaced by natural calamities such as a landslide or earthquake.

The human body is far more complex because it has evolved systems which enable it to enfold and carry its root-system within it, move around, navigate obstacles and hunt for part of its nourishment as well as hunt for procreation partners, all of which require some degree of skilful thought and thinking. Yet a tree nevertheless is interestingly similar in structure with regard to its upwards and downwards branching-off and spreading-out networks.

We have only to look at sketches of three of the body's main systems to realize striking resemblances:

- nervous system
- circulatory system
- lymphatic system

In addition, trees have bark and humans have skin both of which form part of their respiratory systems.

The nadi network is said to reach to every cell of the human body so it must be related to the nervous system. Every inbreath and every outbreath fans energy through the network in a wave-like i-motion and e-motion.

Now we come to the main reason for bringing the analogy with trees into the picture. Next time you go outside into Nature, look carefully and silently at a tree with its branches and leaves. If there is no wind, the entire tree will be still. But even then that stillness is always relative and only still to the naked eye because at rest it will still be invisibly vibrating, and its parts invisibly oscillating. It all depends on the motion of the wind. If there is wind, even a slight breeze, you will see its leaves trembling, at least some of them. If the wind is stronger, you may see branches swaying as well as leaves trembling. And if the wind is very strong then the entire trunk may sway from side to side like a pendulum.

Waving, swaying, swinging, undulating, trembling, vibrating and all such similar 'there-and-back' movements are in fact words pointing at a similar event, namely **oscillation**.

> *Uddayabhaya* repeatedly stated by the Buddha in the Satipatthana sutta means arising-and-ceasing like a wave, oscillating.

And every oscillation great or small is in fact a **disturbance** – a 'there-and-back' movement just like breathing – like so many of the other movements our bodies make.

Wind disturbs branches and leaves away from what has already been defined in Chapter 1 as their DIM (normal) position, and when the wind lets up, the branches and leaves return to where they were before (their normal DIM 'resting' position).

Same for the lips on our mouth or the fingers on our hands – they move away from their normal or DIM position to do things such as speak, knit or play guitar but then have to come back to their resting or normal position.

Likewise, the branches and leaves of a tree. Wind disturbs them and moves them away from their rest position, makes them tremble/oscillate and when the disturbance of wind stops, they then return to their DIM position.

On the surface of the sea, if we carefully observe the intricate details, we see waves upon waves within waves, of different sizes and shapes, all jockeying around, moving in different directions, colliding, causing diffraction and interference.

But wind unlike water is invisible to the naked eye. It can only be felt through the sense of touch. Yet wind, though invisible to the eye, is not nearly as uniform as we may think. There are as many subtle differences in air disturbances (currents) as in water disturbances (waves). If wind were a liquid fluid, we would be able to see more of these different disturbances directly.

But although we are unable to spot such differences in air disturbances – unless they are also touching our body – if we watch a tree carefully enough, we can spot those parts of its branches and leaves that are momentarily disturbed and oscillate. It's not a uniform trembling of parts which happens at one and the same time. Sometimes in a heavy wind the entire tree sways along with its branches and leaves. At other times, some parts may be at rest while other parts are trembling. And different parts can tremble in different ways and in different directions at the same time or at different moments, depending on the **dynam**ics of the currents and their relative directions. Whatever the case, all such invisible disturbances create particular PATTERNS.

The key point of the analogy to a tree, and how wind 'disturbs' and oscillates such elastic structures as branches and leaves, is to add this knowledge to the knowledge we already have from watching the disturbances of water. We can then better visualize something of what is going on inside our human mindbody with its <>72 per cent water content, branch-like structures and nervous system.

Every human being has the innate capacity to both feel the sensations of disturbances (pushes) going on at every moment as well as perceive their patterns.

***

Yogis are fond of trees not just for shade and shelter but to sit at the base of a great tree to resonate with its energy – with its stability – and align with its axis between sky and earth. In the case of Mahavir he stood like a tree. The Buddha became enlightened at the base of a great Pipal tree. In Chinese chi kung we have "Stand like a Tree" chi kung. Holding the horse stance is also a form of static chi kung.

The fanning motion of breath

Chapter 6, Pranayama, discusses the action of in-and-out breathing. How the action of inbreathing enables movement of the air current IN, and how outbreathing reverses the direction of the current. Waves going in and waves going out similar to how they do on the sea shore. And there are subtle moments of stillness, of pause, of 'pause in the air current' at each turn of the natural breath from in to out and from out to in.

A yogi whose nadis at a particular moment are open and free from obstruction, can feel the current fanning the entire framework of mindbody with every inbreath and every outbreath. Breathing in and breathing out the entire mindbody can be felt suffused, trembling, tingling with prana, with life force energy reaching every component part, every cell. The inbreath takes in the Life energy, the outbreath gives back the Life energy transformed: the process is one of continuous exchange, conversion, transformation and renewal. Whatever is unused is returned and recycled by other parts of Nature. It's all about dialogue and energy exchange.

every inbreath bringing in and creating the new	BRAHMA	A
every pause in the breath sustaining existence/life	VISHNU	U
every outbreath transforming the old into the new	SHIVA	M

In a silent place the vibration – the subtle sound A U M can easily be heard or felt whenever the nadis are free and clear. All invisible currents (pushes) whether external or internal create perceivable patterns.

***

To refresh what was explained in earlier chapters, there are basically three types of connection-making going on inside the mindbody, not all of which by any means result into embedded coding:

- frequent ones – often many times a day – are like 'a line drawn in water' rapidly passing away without leaving a trace.

- the second kind is like 'a line drawn in sand' – the water or the wind rub out this kind of fragile trace within a short period of time.
- the third kind is the enduring, encoded type persisting as a recorded pattern, mark or trace

In terms of duration, this third type – be they marks or traces accumulated or registered on the nadi or be they kinks, bends, twists in its structure – are the troublemakers. These are the ones that condition and compromise the free flow of the life force through specific pathways in the circuitry causing a vicious cycle of disharmonious behaviour (inappropriate action and reaction patterns).

The sense behind the English or Spanish word *vice* and its adjective *vicious* closely resembles what is meant in Buddhist and Jain yoga by *asava* (Skt. ashrava). As mentioned before, Mahavir saw this as an actual accumulation of physical particles onto the *jiva* obscuring its clarity and light.

***

> "When the five senses and the mind are still, and the reasoning intellect rests in silence, then begins the highest path. This calm steadiness of the senses is called yoga. Then one should become watchful, because yoga comes and goes."
>
> Katha Upanishad

The *yoga* referred to in this key passage from the Katha Upanishad is the momentary and provisional *yoga* that occurs whenever prana flows evenly in both nostrils in *chandra tattva* (moon–water element as below). In a healthy person this can and does occur naturally and spontaneously from time to time in daily life.

The breath along with accompanying life force described in Chapter 6 (Pranayama) can manifest in each nostril in any of five elements.

The five great elements (*pañca mahabhuta*) are those given in the previous chapter on nadis:

- **Ether**
- **Air**
- **Fire**
- **Water**
- **Earth**

In decreasing order of subtlety and increasing order of density, each element has an attribute (tattva) of the same characteristic nature as the element itself. The *tattwas* cause energy to flow in cycles throughout the human mindbody in similar manner to those macro-flows the *tattvas* cause in the Earth as a whole, evident in ocean currents, tides, trade winds, monsoons and similar periodic patterns of ebb and flow of Earth currents.

- **Akash**   **(Ether tattva)**   **– invisible/no colour**
- **Vayu**   **(Air tattva)**   **– sky blue**
- **Tejas**   **(Fire tattva)**   **– red**
- **Apas**   **(Water tattva)**   **– turquoise/emerald**
- **Prithivi**   **(Earth tattva)**   **– saffron/orange**

> Ether tattwa is omnipresent but imperceptible in Nature except indirectly at dawn and dusk for a few minutes each day at the two transition periods when the Earth seems to pause her own breathing as she switches from outbreath to inbreath at sunrise, and from inbreath to outbreath at sunset.

This pause which seems to last for 15 minutes or so is perceived relative to location and is reflected in the behaviour of Earth's creatures in the wild who in synchronicity seem to suspend activity as if in *keval kumbhaka* – ether element – just for this brief period at dawn and dusk. This is more noticeable in spring and summer when the wind drops at dawn and sunset. These precious moments of transition from night to day and day to night present the yogi with an opportunity for *keval kumbhaka* and *samadhi*.

Thus, including the possibility of spontaneous suspension of breathing (as in keval kumbhaka or 4th jhana) there could potentially be 26 permutations of breath combinations discernible by the different sensations around the entrance to the nostrils (*parimukha* in Pali). Whether or not all 26 are actually able to arise in real life situations is something science needs to check out.

The word *parimukha* – around the entrance to the nostrils – is significant and of utmost importance for understanding the precise instructions given by the Buddha for applying recollection of in-and-out breathing (anapanasati) as a key part of satipatthana practice, wherein the yogi recollects and recognizes the length of respiration as *long* or *short*. We have no way of knowing if this was recorded as shorthand for all the possible lengths and modalities of breath quality as described in this chapter but it is likely.

> **The five modalities of *prana* around the entrance of each nostril can be known subjectively by means of the signature characteristics of the breath's length, texture, temperature, speed and frequency**.

The descriptions below apply to the body sitting or standing or during slow, natural, unforced movement.

- **Water element**: 16 digits length | effortless, powerful full flow | cool | even | smooth | deep as if breathing into and out from the heart-centre itself | optimum mindset
- **Earth element**: 12 digits length | flow easy and comfortable | temperature unnoticeable because same as core body temperature | rhythm still slow but less deep | neutral mindset | positive practical mood
- **Air element**: Eight digits length | partly constricted flow | warmer | begins to be uncomfortable | shallower | slightly faster | mood duller and fractious

- **Fire Element**: Four digits length I hot I constricted I short flow I uncomfortable I negative mindset & mood I feverish at physical level I breathing fast I panting without physical exertion
- **Ether element**: Zero digits lengths: breath at standstill I minimal ebb & flow within only nasal cavities I coma or samadhi I unconsciousness or full concentration (4th jhana – samadhi) I icy cool

Four digits length is measured as the width of four fingers of one hand placed together horizontally against the juncture of the nostrils at the top of the upper lip furrow.

For eight digits add another hand of four fingers width placed horizontally below the other hand, for 12 digits add another hand of four fingers width, and for 16 digits add a fourth hand of four fingers width.

This means that whenever prana is flowing in either or both nostrils in the moon/water element (*chandra tattva*), the outbreath will of its own accord effortlessly reach to the navel area – to your lap – and will be felt as a pleasantly cool touch even at that distance from the nose.

> What all the potential permutations and modalities of right and left nostril breath/prana mean in terms of what is going on inside the mindbody and its subtle plumbing is up to science to investigate and work out.

If breathing were just a question of the human body getting enough oxygen in, would there be so many different patterns and modalities?

As far as **kriya yoga** is concerned, the sole aim and focus of interest is to fully clean out the subtle plumbing so that breath/prana can thereafter always and naturally flow in the appropriate tattwa as Nature intends. In other words, the nadi network needs to be restored to the pristine, unobstructed 'wild' state whereby the DIM of respiration + prana always flows in the element that corresponds to the life situation.

From this you might be guessing what the original *hatha yoga* was attempting to do or was designed to do, which is to *force* the prana/breath into balancing sun and moon energies. But unfortunately *forcing* – especially forcing without knowing what one is doing or why – can often be counterproductive to DIM and Dim tendency.

> The fine balance between forcing and effortlessness has always been an issue of concern in yoga practice. Effort has to be *right effort* in order to be successful which means it has to be in general alignment with the DIM and Dim tendency.

Ultimately the active part of yoga is to set up conditions for allowing the DIM to do what the DIM knows how to do, with minimal or zero interference from the thinking mind's **ab**stract images about *how things should be*.

Without surya nadi and chandra nadi both at the same time flowing in chandra tattva, there is no possibility for the two breaths to join, merge and enter the central channel sushumna – for life-force intelligence (viññana) to travel back up sushumna and re-awaken to Real Knowledge (keval jnana).

In Chapter 7, Dhyana (jhana), it was said, and this needs to be emphasized here once again for the record, there is *zero possibility of reaching full concentration (samadhi/4ᵗʰ Jhana) unless the two breaths (moon and sun) flow, join and merge*. And this can only take place in the water element (*chandra tattva*). No other element.

This is the great secret and truth of yoga. The 'locked portal', *Kundal*, at the base of the spinal column only allows for a single non-dual key to immortality, and no other.

As Shiva says to Devi in Vigyan Bhairava Tantra:

"This is difficult only for the impure."

So purification (visuddhi) has to be the yogi's path and priority.

***

The 24 hour cycle of prana

Returning to the 24-hour Vital Energy Cycle Chart above...

The vital energy moves through each of the four 'derived' elements earth, water, fire and air every three hours during the above quarters of a natural day and night. Thus in every 24-hour full day-full night cycle, prana passes through *each element twice* for a three-hour period in each tattva. It's a 'there-and-back' trip, an oscillation.

Ether, as underlying 'underived' primordial element, is always present and therefore potentially accessible to the vital energy at any time prana flows in both nostrils evenly in water-moon tattva.

Starting at time 0 a.m. midnight (Real Natural Time, not what we are told is the time on clocks and watches!) **fire** element is predominant until 3 a.m. when the vital energy transitions into **air** element, which for yogis is the appropriate time to awaken for the first three-hour sitting in *asana* for *dhyana* practice. Then 6 a.m. to 9 a.m. comes the first passage through predominance of **earth** element, during which would be an appropriate time for some tea plus physical and mental activity.

During the 9 a.m. to midday 12 p.m. window in **water**, tattwa predominance, the main meal of the day should be taken and completed *before* the sun reaches its highest point in the sky so that digestion takes place during the second **fire** element 12 p.m. to 3 p.m. If food is taken during the second **air** tattwa 3pm to 6pm, digestion will not be ideal and flatulence and indigestion may result. Best time for going to sleep is when it is dark not during the day in spite of the siesta habit of certain peoples in the 3 p.m. to 6 p.m. window.

The above are merely a few pointers. Find your own rhythm which feels best. The modern world's daily timetable seems to be out of sync to a greater or lesser extent with the natural 24-hour cycle.

```
        24
Water   12      Fire
        0
21 9            3  15
        ••
Earth           Air
        6
        18
```

Because the human body's vital energy circulates twice in each of the four elements as shown in the two charts, this means to stand or sit still for three hours plus a few minutes – regardless of starting off time – absolutely guarantees sooner or later experiencing *at least one transition* of the vital energy from one tattwa into the next tattwa.

> In Chapter 6, Pranayama, we saw that as inhalation and exhalation fans the movement of the vital energy through the nadi pathways – providing immobility is maintained – sooner or later an obstacle in the form of a closed circuit is bound to be encountered, and when that happens *the fan hits the shit!*

From experience in satipatthana and vipassana courses, acute confrontations of this intense kind are likely to happen during the transitions out of one element into another element. The precise location on the framework of the body depends on where the unresolved obstruction is embedded. The nature of the obstruction – physical, emotional, mental or a combination of all three – may have to do with the tattwa at the time the original code was recorded.

We do not yet know enough about it all but it certainly is a field worthy of in-depth research.

***

"Impermanent are all codes;
When one perceives this with true insight,
then one becomes released from suffering;
this is the path of purification."

Dhammapada 20.5 (277)

In Chapter 1, Language, we saw how a code gets constructed and what a code (then) does.
To refresh,

- code is made by **arbi**trarily connecting two completely different things together in one's mind, and agreeing that the connection is as real as either of the two things separately. The 'things' can belong to any order of reality, real or imaginary, mental, emotional or physical. By connection is meant attachment/identification/association.
- thus every such equation of identity **a ≡ b** is based on *agreement to pretend* and is therefore make-believe and **abstract**. The code is then perpetuated by habit, which is a previously taken decision to agree to pretend, postponed into the future, and then used again and again. Repetition reinforces the illusion that the **ab** codes belong to the same orders of Reality as **a** and **b**, which may themselves belong to different orders of reality.
- any time such a connection of identity is made by the thinking mind between two dissimilar things this creates a code (sankhara) – a concoction – which can get embedded in the nadi circuitry.
- every embedded/recorded/registered code has a repercussion on the framework of the body because what every embedded code does in some way or other is **make certain specific sensations *different* from what they would otherwise be without the presence of the code.**
- in doing this, the code alters and deforms Nature's natural mechanical cause and effect. The codes alter cause and event.

- differences in sensation, caused by the presence of coding, are *used* **by the awareness – the "I" and master code – to disturb our nervous system differently.**
- we *use* these artificially created differences in disturbances of our nervous system to make, trigger and access all our thinking-mind meanings.

***

How then do codes (sankhara) get recorded and registered on the framework of the body?

How does the psychemechanics actually work?

According to what we know of Mahavir's teaching, negative actions (which means all actions out of alignment with DIM and DIM tendency) run counter to Nature's fundamental Law of Harmony, and cause *deposits of particles* to accrue and obscure the light of Consciousness.

> Unfortunately, it seems the most ancient Jain records have been lost and there exist only later texts referring to older ones – much the same situation to Samkhya's lost earlier texts (to be discussed in Chapter 12).

All that has come down to us is summed up in the Jain understanding of seven aspects of Reality. These provide important clues:

- Only *'jiva'* is truly sentient and alive, and is equated to Consciousness (similar to Purusha as understood in Samkhya).
- All the rest – mind and matter – is *ajiva* (non-sentient) (equivalent to Prakriti in Samkhya).
- *Asravas* (biases generated by timeless revolving in ignorance birth after birth) cause an inflow and accrual of particles onto the 'jiva', shrouding the Light and Nature of omniscient Consciousness.
- *Bandha* (bondage) is caused by the **connection by way of identification** between jiva and the actions of the mindbody

(karma). It is very significant that Jainism uses the word '*yoga*' for this and this tallies with Patanjali's usage of the word '*samyoga*' for connection and connection-making.

- *Samvara* (stoppage) is the counter-habit of dis-identifying which stops and prevents further accrual of karmic particles of matter onto the 'jiva'.
- *Nirjara* refers to the process of gradual detachment and disassociation of karmic particles from the jiva.
- *Mokṣha* (liberation) takes place when all karmic particles have been completely removed and erased from the jiva, which then abides in *keval jnana* – pure Consciousness.
- Keval jnana is also translated as perfect understanding or supreme wisdom.

In the light of the insight of summer 1978 into the presence of **tapes** on the framework of the mindbody that need to be wiped out, it's interesting to review how a cassette tape recorder works.

Tapes store patterns of particles which play back the same original inputs whenever triggered.

As the tape collides with the head of the recording device, it stores a magnetic field SIMILAR (proportional) to the input signal.

This signal orients magnetic particles in a specific PATTERN which then acts as indicator (TRIGGER) to the **pattern of signal stored**. This holds true for every pattern of particles originally 'imprinted' by the connectoring into a particular configuration of code.

Hence, it's all about **pushes** and **patterns** and the creation of **abs**tract meanings from **arb**itrary connections of identity between them.

When the playback head *collides* against the tape, **the signal is reproduced** since now the particles induce *similar* magnetic *patterns* in the *playback* head (brain and nervous system).

The similarity to how significant parts of the nadi circuitry in brain and nervous system may have become biased, closed down, blocked, obstructed by undigested, unaccepted (suppressed) *painful* memories seems striking.

To de-block (**purify from bias**) all that needs to be done – and it is a Big ALL! – **is to reproduce the MEMORY of the sensation,** accept it and properly process, digest and transform the original memory.

In other words not only can any of the discordant tapes be rubbed out by playback in SILENCE but every 'noise' can potentially be transformed into melody.

The above hypothesis fits completely with the methodology behind the Buddha's satipatthana practice, in both its forward and reverse operation of binding/ unbinding (i.e. recording/rubbing out) leading either to bondage and misery or to detachment and liberation.

In all the above cases encoding involves ignorance (avijja), a-dim and negative karma whereas decoding involves SATI (remembering) + realignment with DIM + detachment and non-identification with SANKHARA (codes).

According to Nebosja Dimovic, once direct insight has been gained into the Reality that **the awareness itself is also a code** – the 'master code' – and that '*codes are only codes* not to be confused with the Real Reality' – this inevitably brings about a radical shift in outlook and behaviour.

> Proper connectoring brings about the ending of craving and compulsion (*tanha*) and in its place arises wisdom. SN Goenka aptly calls this transforming *tanha* into *pañña*.

Once the thinking mind's game of proliferating concepts, images and codes (all of which are codes) is seen as a zero-sum game there is no further advantage to be had in anything to do with internal cinema and mental tennis games. Then we can wake up to start to fully live the Real Life Nature intends.

Where on the framework of the body do the codes causing obstructions to the life-force intelligence get recorded, registered and stored?

Well, Dimovic's best guess is in the circuitry of the brain and nervous system in the form of connections between similar and non-similar pushes and patterns. The findings of his research have been indispensable for understanding what both Mahavir and Gautama Buddha were driving at in the language of their time.

And lastly and most importantly, how do they get rubbed out?

So far in *Yoga beyond the Thinking Mind* several traditional ways have been shown, all connected:

- The first way is through the tapas of prolonged immobility. By not changing postures, sooner or later all blockages will be confronted and pierced through.
- A second way is through keval kumbhaka which may achieve a similar result provided motionlessness and equanimity is maintained.
- A third way is through the systematic application of proper connectoring – satipatthana – recollecting the Real in the Real with regard to the four fundamental aspects of mindbody: bodily structures; sensations of physical and mental disturbance; states of mind; mental constructs. Whatever comes up on the framework of the mindbody is to be seen **as it is**...abandoning all mental cinema and mental tennis.
- The fourth way **kriya yoga** as passed down since the time of Shankara is a pranayama based on *anuloma viloma* (lomvilom described in Chapter 6). It is also related to *anapanasati* because once the conditions have been set up, the yogi merely watches and takes note of what takes place in the body.

According to Swami Chaitanyanda, Shankara purged all 'impurities' by practicing anuloma viloma uninterruptedly until the job was done. But because sitting uninterruptedly doing anuloma viloma pranayama for long hours is as arduous a process as prolonged immobility, Shankaracharya devised and taught a variant which does not require so much prolonged sitting. One of the purposes of this book is to propose a proper study be undertaken with a volunteer group carrying out this *kriya yoga* over a minimum 10-day period.

It requires time, patience and willingness to watch in silence, meticulously noting the characteristics of breath and breathing, watching for the transitions when the breathing moves in and out of different tattvas. This system is the one that has been allegedly handed down from guru to chela since the time of Shankara and its details are not something to be divulged anonymously in a book.

Kriya yoga can be undertaken with proper supervision and guidance. The minimum recommended time is 10 days but far better would be 40 days, or better still to set no time limit and strive until the final goal is attained.

If a volunteer group of experienced meditators is interested to make the attempt, let's set up the conditions and do it!

Vaya dhamma sankhara! appamadena sampadetha!

***

> Indeed, there is no greater tapas than the tapas of sustained confrontation, calmly resisting the impulse to move while remaining aware and awake.

This has been discussed in Chapter 5, Asana, where a yogi develops and perfects a single asana of his or her choice with the aim to maintain it for longer and longer times periods until reaching the goal of 12 hours, then if determination and capacity are sufficient, a complete 24-hour day-night cycle can be attempted.

Such prolonged holding of asana sets up a total confrontation between DIM and a-dim, between what is Real and what is imaginary (concocted/fabricated by the thinking mind). In yogic terminology we can say it sets up a direct confrontation between what is Real and Maya.

Savasana is excluded as an asana option because lying down sooner or later induces drowsiness and sleep. Lying down the yogi will be overpowered by Maya. Whether standing or sitting, the asana of choice has to keep the spinal column on a vertical axis between sky and earth.

The way of it is to build up sittings in three-hour segments. Each successive three-hour segment of the first 12 hours will reach progressively deeper layers of coding for reasons to be explained below.

Once three hours has become do-able in relative comfort, the yogi can begin to attempt six hours, then likewise when six hours has become do-able in relative comfort, then nine hours and finally 12 hours at a single sitting. To sit a further 12 hours totalling a full 24-hour day-night cycle is said to be the scope of only the greatest of yogis. Once 24 hours is attained the yogi is beyond limitations of mindbody and gains mastery over Mind, Breath and Life Force.

The goal of the greatest yogis is therefore a full 24-hour cycle without changing posture because it is said to guarantee liberation from all past karma. Such a confrontation puts aside all concerns for the welfare of the mind and physical body and will expel the yogi from the dreams of Maya, both past and present. For this reason it is said that it is harder to subdue oneself than subdue any external adversary.

> "Greater than to conquer 1000 men in 1000 battles is the victory of that person who conquers himself."
>
> Dhammapada 103

In every 24-hour cycle – providing immobility is held – the life-force energy (prana) will make a complete circuit twice through the network of nadis (as shown in the chart) – 'there-and-back' – in every density of element. That is to say it will travel through every single channel of the entire nadi network unless interfered with by changing posture.

If during any moment of crisis the yogi succumbs to changing posture, this immediately aborts confrontation with the dukkha of that particular sankhara by diverting the flow of prana to another (open) pathway. This is how we reinforce what lies within our *comfort zone*, and how we avoid confrontation with its opposite – our *discomfort zone* (Jung's unconscious).

Because so few people are capable of taking on and completing such an ordeal, out of compassion for the world Siddhartha Gautama discovered an ancient and direct path – ekayano maggo – trod by Awakened Ones of former times leading to liberation of the Mind from all codes (sabbe sankhara).

This method has been described in Chapter 8, Satipatthana, and does not require the physical, mental and emotional ordeal of sitting unmoving for a full 24 hours or even for 12 hours. Experienced satipatthana practitioners assure us that three 3-hour sittings a day (3x3) should be enough to do the job within six months. This is the sadhu's equivalent to a day at the office! The Buddha himself declared that 'for those with little dust in their eyes' even seven days satipatthana practice can do the job.

Only in the realm of the Codeless can direct knowledge and insight into the Real Nature of Existence be fully realized. The path requires perseverance and sustaining continuous Remembrance of the Real in the Real. Sooner or later this sustained application of discernment will accomplish the task of *"doing what has to be done"*.

Whatever the chosen path or method, recollection of breathing plays the vital role.

Chapter 11: Tapas

> There is no greater tapas than the austerity of physical immobility while remaining aware and watchful of what happens to mindbody.

This has been discussed in Chapter 5, Asana, where a yogi develops and perfects a single asana of her or his choice in order to be able to maintain it for prolonged periods. Savasana is excluded because lying down sooner or later induces drowsiness and sleep. The asana of choice must hold the spinal column in a vertical position between sky and earth. The goal of great yogis is a full 24-hour cycle.

Background

It is common knowledge among yogis and sadhus in India that the ancient path of yoga – the most direct path – inevitably involves TAPAS, which requires steadfast maintenance of equanimity while enduring confrontation with six pairs of *impostor*s whenever these make their appearance in our life:

- **Pleasure & Pain**
- **Heat & Cold**
- **Gain & Loss**
- **Praise & Blame (criticism)**
- **Honour & Dishonour**
- **Name & Fame**

Gain & Loss | Praise & Blame | Honour & Dishonour | Name & Fame

Each of these four pairs can and do arise during the course of everyday life! Each one presents a different opportunity for tapas and for applying recollection of the Real in the Real with equanimity. But unlike the next two pairs of impostors, these four cannot be deliberately staged.

Pleasure & Pain | Heat & Cold

All four of these situations can be arranged (staged) as well as arise during the course of natural circumstances.

Pain

The Sramana movement in India at the time of Mahavir and the Buddha went to great pains – no pun intended! – to practice equanimity in the face of pain and discomfort. Many of these extreme practices persist even to this day among contemporary sadhus.

The Jains were among those advocating extreme forms of penance. It is interesting to note that Jains at that time considered the followers of the Buddha's Middle Path – that of avoiding indulgence in either extremes of pain or pleasure – to be "softies"!

Yet compared to our modern pampered comfort-obsessed consumer lifestyle, the *middle path* of the Buddha during his lifetime looks extremely austere. The keenest monks at that time were encouraged to:

- never lie down and instead sit up throughout the night in asana
- wear robes only from sewed up remnants of discarded cloth
- eat one meal a day at one sitting
- live full-time outdoors in the forest, in the Nature
- be unrelenting in their practice of satipatthana until the final goal was attained

This gives us an idea of what at that time was considered a *middle path* compared to more extreme forms of asceticism and self-torture where yogis ran the risk of damaging themselves mentally, emotionally or physically or of becoming addicted to the pursuit of *siddhis* – superhuman powers that can arise as a result of the 'fire of tapas'.

Modern extreme endurance sports can certainly be considered a form of tapas, and no doubt their practitioners experience the beneficial effects. The important point is not to get hooked into playing the game of the sensations as SN Goenka warned as otherwise it only replaces one form of addiction with another form of addiction (albeit a healthier one) instead of fulfilling the highest goal of yoga which is to free oneself from all addictions (asava) and end compulsive behaviour (bhava).

The fire of tapas stoked by such ascetic practices is humorously said in ancient Indian texts to cause the throne-seat of Brahma to become so uncomfortably hot, that it forces the first born Trimurti to grant the boon of a 'siddhi' to the yogi in order to distract him or her from further tapas!

'Desist and be entertained by siddhis!'

Unwelcome as this may sound to our modern ears and eyes, all forms of entertainment in those ancient days were discouraged among the sramana communities because they considered them distractions and diversions from the path of yoga.

Pleasure

Many centuries later – after the pitfalls of painful forms of asceticism had been thoroughly experienced, and its downsides had become evident – tantra arose as a reaction to the extreme asceticism of pain, and thus pleasure began to be systematically investigated in various tantric schools among Hindus, Jains and Buddhists.

Tantra is a huge subject in itself – a much later development which generated a new attitude towards the body and led to the development of hatha yoga as a branch of yoga in itself.

Calmly facing any of these six pairs of impostors – the 12 situations – with a correct attitude and correct focus on body, sensations and mental reactions provides an opportunity to 'wipe out the tapes', a wonderful opportunity to de-condition, de-program, de-code and clean out the sankharas from the plumbing of the nadis thereby freeing the mindbody from limitations and blockages self-imposed in ignorance either by our ancestors or by ourselves in this lifetime. Thus, the life-force intelligence can again flow freely, unimpeded, with the full power Nature intends.

Heat

The yoga of heat has been practiced in India for millennia and also by other cultures notably Polynesians (fire walking) and North American Indians (heat lodge, sweat lodge) with proven benefits. In Scandinavia and Türkiye the sauna and Turkish bath has long been a part of wellness regimes.

In hot countries such as India, by lighting fires during the midday sun at four cardinal points around the yogi, this form of tapas is relatively easy to arrange and mostly avoids doing the permanent kind of damage to the body that fakirs, nagas and aghori ascetics are susceptible to. However, a sudden change of wind can cause havoc with the set-up!

Cold

> "The cold is genius! Implacable and relentless but just!"
>
> Wim Hof

Exposure to intense cold provides a perfect scenario and opportunity for a few precious minutes in which to experience the mind focused fully on the here and now of body, sensations, states of mind and mental reactions.

Exposure to cold is a valuable short cut to *stopping the thinking mind – citta vritti nirodha –* allowing the deeper mind to do what it is capable of doing to restore homeostasis. Unlike most other forms of tapasya, it is safe when managed correctly and also beneficial for overall health and wellbeing.

I asked my friend and *'cold yoga'* mentor Wim Hof, the iceman himself, to contribute to this chapter but literary commitments with his publisher prevent this. So from my own experience of soon-to-be three years of *daily* cold exposure – sometimes twice daily – and that of close friends and colleagues, I have added this section on its benefits in order to encourage those of you yoginis and yogis who have not yet given it a try to become acquainted with the yoga and tapas of cold and see for yourselves.

Ehi passigó
Numerous valuable health benefits – both preventative and curative – of cold exposure have been clinically verified and documented, with further promising research still ongoing. Here we look at the value of *cold exposure* from the standpoint of tapas, yoga and satipatthana practice.

Firstly, I know of no other safe tapas or yoga practice which shuts down the thinking mind faster than cold exposure! It is both an *asana* in the sense of setting up a scenario for confrontation as described in Chapter 5, as well as a safe form of *tapasya* (austerity) if handled with care and attention.

A 10 to 15-minute cold exposure in water with a yogic mindset can catapult the bodymind into a state of awareness, perception and insight equivalent to the 6th or 7th day of a 10-day vipassana course. That's how fast and easy it is!! But it depends on the attitude of mind. No two cold exposure sessions are identical. As Heraclitus famously remarked, 'One does not dip twice in the same river'.

Heraclitus could also have pointed out that the mindbody that goes into the river is also never exactly the same. The mindbody is also a stream of energy and particles in constant renewal although its repetitive patterns give rise to the illusion of sameness and permanence. Yet similarity is not the same as sameness. Repetition of similarity conceals subtle changes and differences.

***

To be effective, water temperature should be below 17C/63F, with more noticeable effects from temperatures in the 13C to 17C range (55/63F), with deepest effects in the 3C to 11C range (37/52F).

An ice bath could be defined as water temperature between 3C and 8C regardless of the visible presence of floating ice. The colder the water, the more caution needs to be exercised in the duration.

> Note: Cold water removes body heat around 35 times faster than equivalent temperature of air on bare skin in windless conditions.

Cold water produces an *immediate confrontation – it's a lightning fast track to insight into Real Nature.* There is no gradual build-up of discomfort such as can occur during a hathayoga asana, or during prolonged sitting asana. At the instant of immersion in cold water below 17C there is no transition from comfort to discomfort. It's sudden and immediate! It brings the entire body and mind straight and fully into a present moment of NOW, eclipsing past and future, stilling the thinking mind.

The confrontation with cold sets up an emergency face-off between real forces of Nature and existing artificial parameters of the thinking mind. The sudden, immediate impact jolts the body into a state of survival-response in which the thinking mind at most can only play a limited subsidiary role. Mostly it shuts up after two to three minutes.

After about two to three minutes of primary reaction to the impact, the thinking mind – unable to escape and no longer having the wherewithal to deal with the situation – is eclipsed by the deep mind.

At this point the deep bodymind – what I call the 'heartmind' – takes over and that particular Dim tendency dealing with body temperature and bodily survival does what millions of years of evolutionary wisdom with the raw elements knows how to do. It survives by switching into a deeper gear of power and awareness.

> To what extent the cold stops the thinking mind is something to be explored carefully by each one of us. At the beginning, the exploration of cold should be done under supervision of an experienced instructor.

Each day each one of us naturally has a different mental, energetic and bodily state so the experience varies from cold exposure to cold exposure. No two cold exposures are completely alike. Different effects and fresh insights emerge as layers of coding get peeled off. It depends on the degree of cold, the duration of exposure, on our attitude of mind at that moment, how carefully we observe the process, how we are feeling on that particular day combined with many other internal and external factors.

The Tapas of Cold

To practice yoga in the cold was formerly only accessible to those living in cold climates, such as Scandinavia or Russia, or to specific locations high up in the Himalayas (Nepal and Tibet) or Andes. The yoga of cold is an ancient practice but in India far less widespread than other forms of tapas.

Currently cold exposure is enjoying a huge surge of interest and uptake thanks to the extraordinary feats of endurance of athletes like Wim Hof and open cold-water swimmers like Stephen Redmond and Adam Walker. Redmond was the first swimmer to complete the seven oceans marathon swim challenge. Since then, more than a dozen endurance swimmers including Walker have repeated the amazing feat. The Oceans Seven challenge consists of seven open water long-distance channel swims in different part of the world. It was created in 2008 as an equivalent feat to the Seven Summits mountaineering challenge which also involves enduring extreme cold exposure at high altitudes as well as oxygen deprivation.

Some of these open-water swims, depending on currents and conditions, can take up to 15 hours or more to complete, and temperatures of the water can be as low as 9C which is well below what normal people and conventional science would consider possible for such prolonged swims. No wet suits are allowed!

Wim Hof has set 26 records for extreme cold endurance, and by offering himself and groups of trained students for testing at laboratories and universities has provided incontrovertible evidence that the human being is capable of far more than was formerly thought possible in science.

The method consists of a specific breathing technique reverse engineered from confrontation with the cold and gradual progressive exposure to cold, both undertaken with a yogic mindset.

A yogic mindset means adopting the ancient attitude of awareness and equanimity in the face of whatever discomfort arises at any of the three levels: physical, emotional or mental. As such it is a fast track to directly accessing deep levels of awareness and perception beyond the thinking mind.

Cold exposure is of three kinds:

- *Cold showering* daily throughout the year. A 'cold' shower is considered cold when water is at or below 17C/63F. According to Chaitanyananda – applying the yogic rule for any asana – minimum exposure should be three minutes, three minutes being the minimum time it takes for a full bodymind reaction to yoga asana. Shorter times may abort the reaction.

- *Cold swimming or immersion in open water* (lakes, oceans, rivers, outdoor pools). Here the variables of water temperature, duration of swim, sea conditions, current and your own experience have to be carefully evaluated. Always swim accompanied, err on the side of caution and watch for signs of hypothermia such as trembling in the water and/or loss of ability to close fingers (known as claw hand) both of which are signs to *get out* as soon as possible.
- *Ice bath*. This means immersion up to the neck in a standing body of water containing enough ice to bring the water temperature down to close to arctic water temperatures above freezing. Anywhere between 3C/37F and 7C/45F is extremely cold. Initial supervised exposures of three minutes are safe for people in good health. If in any doubt, consult a sports doctor.

In all the above three forms of cold exposure, the effects can vary considerably. And will tend to vary at every exposure. This makes the yoga of cold challenging and interesting each time.

In my own experience, winter open water swimming produces the most intense connectedness to wild Nature. The heightened sensations and awareness are maybe due to swimming crawl and keeping the head constantly in contact with the cold water. In a cold shower – if the water is cold enough – it can be painful to maintain a continuous flow directly onto the head. And in an icebath the head for obvious reasons is out of the water. Therefore, each of these modalities of cold exposure bring their own challenges and different effects.

The thinking mind and the body as a whole never get used to the impact of intense cold. Experience of having confronted the cold before is of course gained along with the knowledge of coming through it successfully without harm but each exposure of cold is equally implacable and relentless, going deep into the mindbody.

It is a form of yoga which does not allow for subtle distractions or subtle forms of escapism unlike other traditional forms of yoga such as hathayoga, pranayama, dhyana – not to mention tantra – all of which can, to a certain extent, be made easier or even faked. The only exception to this is immobility in asana discussed in Chapter 5 and Chapter 10, Kriya yoga, both of which take up far more time but can go deeper if sufficiently prolonged.

> By 'made easier' or 'faked' is meant not only to other people but especially to oneself, which slows down progress in 'wiping out the tapes'.

Chapter 5, Asana, already discusses in detail how *changing the posture* is a typical way a yogi avoids confrontation with what has to be confronted. And thereby delays her or his progress in the decoding process.

Nothing is harder than changing habits, especially if we don't try. *And even if we do try, we need to beware of getting caught up in the trying and still not changing!* Drastic problems require drastic solutions. Cold exposure is drastic.

The thinking mind is the thief of most of the things that are of real value in life. How is the instigator of the theft going to compensate the victim of the theft?

By more theft of course. How else? How can the instigator of a shipwreck be expected to organize the rescue operation? How can the solution come from the perpetrator of the problem? Ten thousand years of recorded history have shown this never happens, despite all the fancy rhetoric.

A jolt from another level is needed!

Whatever unpleasant sensation arises on the framework of the body during a cold exposure can be contemplated in exactly the same way as any other sensation arising in the course of satipatthana practice (Chapter 9). Getting out of the mindbody's normal comfort zone actually enables it to get comfortable in the Real World of Nature. The yoga of cold directly teaches us how to do this.

> During some summer weeks in the Mediterranean I would regularly spend nights sleeping outdoors under pine trees near the sea in only a sleeping bag on a mat. It was rarely comfortable, and even in summer could become cold if the north wind came up. Even after a lousy night's sleep, it was always a surprise to feel so great the next morning! So filled with energy! And the first swim at dawn is always priceless. On first plunge it washes away all cares, stiffness and wrinkles of the night.
>
> More recently in two winters of winter swimming in Cadaqués (north Spain's Costa Brava), I found that after a 12 to 17 minute swim in 11C to 12C water, I was able to comfortably stay without putting dry clothes back on for up to one hour – even 90 minutes – providing the sun was shining and providing I kept moving and power breathing from time to time when the body demanded it. Even if it was windy in January or February I could stay at least the same time as the swim or more before drying off and dressing.
>
> During the course of experimenting with continued exposure *after* the winter swims or *after outdoor* cold winter showers on the balcony – or even after outdoor ice-baths – I have come to the understanding that clothing, which acts as a preventor of elements coming in and touching the body, also acts as a preventor of cosmic rays and natural elements which can and do energize the body. Only humans wear clothing and this prevents us absorbing the freely available energy from wild Nature. Clothing has resulted in the atrophy of our natural ability to regulate our body temperature like animals do.

Real comfort is activated through the natural elements. When breath gets to flow naturally in the central channel – the Sushumna (Saraswati) – comfort is assured!

It certainly helps to know and keep in mind that throughout any uncomfortable situation the Dim tendency is present silently, invisibly at work, assisting.

Breathe through any intense physical, emotional or mental difficulties that may arise – just watch them arise and pass away remembering to discern which reactions are Real from interaction with Nature and which are mind-made by way of habit-reaction patterns. A mind-made reaction means a reaction triggered by embedded coding. Watch the connection/s between the physical, the emotional, the feeling and the thinking and realize the omnipresence of code as well as the omnipresence of DIM.

By repeated practice the plumbing can be cleaned out steadily, naturally – the DIM operating throughout every level of mindbody will do the job by itself.

No need to interfere, no need to 'push the river' – the river by itself quite naturally goes down to the sea (see) driven by the force of gravity. And just as a strong river will flow over and around obstacles and eventually even push them aside, so too the Dim tendency activated by cold exposure, and aided by spontaneous power breathing – like natural forms of *ujjayi* pranayama – will blast away difficulties and impediments. No need for forcing. Just let Nature do its thing. The DIM knows what needs to be done to restore harmony, power and balance.

Imagination & hands

A few observations about hands and the close connection of hands to imagination.

Nearly half the people who begin to do intense cold exposure have a problem with their hands, and to a lesser extent with their feet. Some people experience such excruciating agony in the hands during an ice-bath that they remove them from the water and hold them together outside the ice water.

I used to experience excruciating pain in the finger bones. Sometimes in the first minute or two of immersion, the sensation reaches such an intense aching that the temptation to take them out is almost overwhelming. This pain is often so strong that it eclipses any other pain felt in the rest of the body, which in comparison seems to be suffering far less at that moment.

However, I encourage all cold *tapasyins* to resist the *siren call* of the thinking mind and ignore the impulse to take the hands out! Just breathe more deeply and evenly, focus intently on whatever is manifesting by way of changing sensations, and steadfastly focus on becoming one with the pain because it is a fantastic opportunity for decoding, deprogramming and deconditioning.

> Because of the close connection between hands and imagination, if the hands are removed from the cold water, the opportunity to explore this connection is lost.

Remember the Chinese hieroglyph for *'crisis'* is made up of two symbols, standing for *challenge* and *opportunity*. Remember also the test in Frank Herbert's *Dune* where the young duke Paul Atreides has to hold his hand inside a black box experiencing the agony of simulated fire carbonizing flesh and bones, all the while with the deadly gom jabbar at his throat in case he withdraw his hand and fail the test.

Encounters with acute physical pain can arise at any time in an ice-bath. Or the suffering can be mental or emotional. Whatever the feeling that goes beyond the bare sensation is caused by accumulated coding. The participating part of ourselves experiences bare sensations but the observing, thinking part of ourselves reacts to triggered coding. That confrontation between the thinking mind and the participating deep mind or heartmind is precisely a confrontation of the artificial world of **ab**stract codes, images and concepts with the Real World of Nature described in Chapter 3.

If the confrontation is sustained, the Real will prevail over the false and artificial. It has to, and will prevail. The Dim tendency of Nature is the constant ally of the yogi bent upon regaining full coherence with the Real. It is the ally of the real body, the real you. It is an irresistible force which sooner or later will push aside any artificial constructs blocking the free flow of life-force intelligence.

This is why a yogic mindset is so vital in such confrontations. Awareness and equanimity, remembering the Real in the Real, will undo all knots causing restriction, limitation and blockage in the nervous system and brain.

A warrior mindset – commendable as this is – is perhaps less productive of beneficial results than a yogic mindset. A warrior's mindset tends to be a forceful, forcing mindset which may induce shouting, singing or larking about. Effective as this kind of behaviour can be to "*get through an ordeal*", it almost certainly reduces the benefits, because to a certain extent it defeats the profounder purpose. It may go less deep than an attitude of intense, silent concentration on the face-off between the irresistible force (DIM) and the immovable object (a-dim).

A day will come when we can and will shout out, and it will be the victory shout of the Arahant, the Jina:

"Done is what had to be done!
in this state, there is no more of this or that!
Freed is Mind from all differentiation!"

***

Chapter 12: Consciousness | Ether

If the existence of two of my four grandparents is denied by a rigorous process and peer review of thousands upon thousands of able men and women, I nonetheless have good reason to believe otherwise. Do not forget that whatever knowledge a human being claims to be valid, he or she is always adding their belief in that knowledge to the knowledge. Beliefs evaporate in the face of direct experience.

At the beginning of this book we saw that the yearning for yoga arises in the human psyche because of *viyoga*. If viyoga did not exist – if there were no division/no separation/no fissures/no rifts deep in the human heart – yoga would already be present and flourishing. For after all, yoga is the supremely natural state.

> Viyoga is any hint of disharmony, unsatisfactoriness, unhappiness, listlessness, restlessness, bad mood, frustration, whereas yoga is a heartmind free from everything which prevents *satchitananda*: existence, awareness, joy of life.

Although it may not appear so to our biased way of looking at things, the Natural World is in an ongoing state of perfection. Nature may look implacably harsh and merciless but she is always just. And she is always in the best state she can be collectively and individually given prevailing circumstances.

Nature's 'order' is not the order we Imagine or believe or hope

Nature's order is not the order of our images of how things *should* be in the mental cinema of our thinking minds

The thinking human mind, by interfering intentionally with the Natural Order of Cause and Effect through **ab**use and misuse of the freedom to make (new) connections, has usurped Nature's Code/coding and superimposed our own code/coding upon Nature's own pathways in the human body thereby depositing these as extra layers of sediment hampering the flow of life-force intelligence. Undoing this entanglement is the sole purpose of yoga *sadhana*.

Language/thinking – the making of new **arb**itrary connections – first arises inside the human body in the brain and nervous system then propagates outside the human body in the form of actions/ deeds which disturb the harmony and balance of the rest of the Natural World with which we are in contact. Nevertheless, the Dim tendency of Nature is fortunately ever present, never absent always doing its best to correct imbalances and disturbances – both inside our mindbody as well as outside in Nature – as best it can within the circumstances.

Language, thinking and coding have generated and firmly establis-hed in the human mind an Artificial World – an internal cinema – which to a certain extent eclipses and hides the Real World of Nature with all its intelligence, power, beauty and magnificence. Thus, the human being has unwittingly cast himself/herself out of the Garden of Eden, ever to strive and labour to find the way back to Paradise Lost, to Immortality, to Eternal Life.

Yoga recognizes the origin of the problem is internal, not external.
The external is innocent!

The many systems of Yoga – whatever their names, origins, traditions, or labels – are all ways to dissolve the shadows of the artificial, false, phoney, make-believe human 'mind-made world' and return to Brahma Vihara, the abode of the gods, there to abide in *advaita* (non-separateness).

Yoga prescribes three main routes:

- stopping the thinking mind through one-pointed concentration: jhana I dhyana I samadhi
- controlling the vital force through pranayama: keval kumbhaka I effortless suspension of in and out breathing
- sublimating the sexual energy through asana I tapas I kriya yoga I transforming passion into compassion

Each of these three paths involves dedication and *surrender* known in yoga as *bhakti*. Bhakti is not a separate path in yoga. **Bhakti is integral to all paths.** The supreme path Tilopa called '*mahamudra*' – the great gesture in which all impurities are burned away.

By gradually rubbing out the *tapes* of coding deposited along the nadi pathways, by controlling the thinking mind, by going beyond mental constructs, the yogi plunges into the wild, pristine ocean of Nature, ultimately becoming one with heartmind.

Tantra arises from the understanding that **nothing artificial needs to be done to remove the artificial.** How could it be otherwise?

In fact even the word 'remove' carries the wrong connotation because Siva takes up everything around us, good as well as bad, with **absolutely** no discrimination whatsoever, knowing full well – as Mahavir put it – that "truth goes into all language (code) but truth does not come out of it".

Therefore, profound respect for all living beings – for everything in Life – is the quintessence of right attitude and right behavior. There is nothing we cannot learn from; nothing that if viewed correctly will fail to yield fresh insight. It all depends on attitude and perspective.

So, when tantra says "transform, not eliminate" what this means is that we take on every opportunity to carefully, conscientiously and steadfastly disentangle the muddle we have ourselves unwittingly created by applying the counter-habit of proper connectoring (satipatthana) to every process that causes negativity and disharmony.

Just as the quality of breath/prana at the entrance to the nostrils is the perfect barometer of our internal energy/emotional state, so too the perceived presence of un**sati**sfactoriness/dukkha is the unfailing indicator of mental state. If we learn not just to look, not just to see, but to look-and-see together with understanding – then this is *sampajañña*.

So again, it's a three-things-in-one like Siva's trident ψ (lll). Then every situation causing aggravation is revealed as a signpost that points to what needs to be revised in our attitude.

Satipatthana – 'proper connectoring' – as the Buddha declared, is the **only way** to do this systematically by remembering/recognizing/acknowledging the misconnectoring of the past and undoing its present effects. Transforming thereby the vicious movement of ignorance into the virtuous movement of wisdom, understanding and full alignment with DIM.

***

"Did you ever look behind your mind
To see a mirror from behind?"

From Chapter 13, The Song of Kalki

CONSCIOUSNESS mirrors all transformations of Mind–Matter. Like a mirror it does not participate in these transformations, nor cause them, neither is it affected by any transformation (vritti).

Furthermore, existence knows existence exists – it does not require the human being to come along and verify it.

We have seen how the thinking mind, by making connections in the way of equations of identity among ordinary mechanical pushes and patterns, creates knots and leaves traces as consequences of misdirected intentions and actions. And that these get registered and recorded on the framework of the body as strains/patterns/traces capable of triggering the original stresses/intentions/volitions.

This has occurred because what the coding does is transform *some* impressions of events into something other than mere mechanical events – into something we can call *psychemechanical* due the involvement of thinking, thought and memory.

So thinking is fundamentally making connections in our thinking mind about this or that which, depending on the intensity, can have actual physical repercussions on the arrangement of certain particles in the nadis or – if you prefer a more physiological picture – in our brain and nervous system.

Thus did Saraha declare:

"The fool in his mind thinks
That his thoughts are only thoughts."

Consciousness is not a product of mindbody.

You may have noticed that throughout all the previous chapters, use of the word Consciousness for any mental faculty or mental activity relating to mindbody has been carefully avoided. I have chosen instead to use words such as awareness, mind, thought, thinking, feeling, sensation, perception, memory in relation to the mindbody's faculties and mental properties.

The reason for this is to make order in semantics by reserving the word and concept CONSCIOUSNESS to stand for what it is and what it does.

And that is MIRROR-MIRRORING.

Samkhya's understanding on Consciousness and Ether

According to Samkhya – the ancient philosophical basis of yoga – *existence* has two fundamentally distinct primordial aspects:

- a **passive** | fixed | unaltering | unalterable | non-material mirror-like aspect called PURUSHA (translated as CONSCIOUSNESS)
- an **active** | creative | material aspect called PRAKRITI (translated as ETHER) equally fixed and stationary yet flexible | elastic | transformable | adaptable | malleable | ductile | impressionable | moldable which acts as the Producer/Carrier/Recorder of all Disturbances.

In tantra these two aspects are called Siva I Shakti. In Jainism jiva I ajiva could be the equivalents.

The mystery resides in the "*something third*" – the primordial thrust/force/impulse – that induces disturbance/s. Without Prakriti's Shakti being 'disturbed', the Cosmos would not oscillate in endless cycles of expansion from seed-form into manifestation, and contraction back again into seed-form.

***

To begin to understand the Enigma of Consciousness, it is helpful to realize that each one of us and every thing in Nature, in the Cosmos, stands, co-exists and lives individually and collectively inside a colossal omnipresent dimensionless *mirror* of immeasurable scope and properties.

This mirror is what Samkhya along with other ancient *darshanas* point to as Consciousness. **And it has nothing to do with mindbody, nor is it produced by any mind nor any body.** Yet it pervades mindbody because there is no Time or Place from when or where it is absent.

According to Samkhya, Consciousness is not of the domain of Prakriti – that is to say not of the domain of mind or matter. The properties of the Mirror of Consciousness can be understood such that it:

- takes up and reflects back to mind the forms of everything that mind-matter is capable of concocting, both Real and imaginary;
- unlike the mirror in our bathroom, it is self-effulgent. It is the light behind all lights without which no thing nor process can be perceived or known;
- the Mirror of Consciousness reflects everything with absolutely no discrimination whatsoever – it reflects absences as well as presences;
- just like any ordinary reflector it is totally unaffected by any reflection arising in it, retaining nothing except its own luminosity and its continuing potential to reflect;

- just like the mirror in our bathroom, it remains stationary, reflecting whatever is there then from all angles, regardless of what or who is present;
- it takes on the form and reflects all that is perceived passively by the five senses of sight, sound, taste, touch and smell as well as reflecting all **active** creative fabrications of the thinking mind;
- <u>like</u> ETHER the Mirror of Consciousness is unborn I unfounded I uncreated I uncompounded I simply existing I beginningless I timeless I eternal I the backdrop and substrata of everything, both existential and non-existential (potential);
- <u>unlike</u> ETHER the Mirror of Consciousness itself undergoes no modifications I no changes I no transformations I no expansion I no contraction I no oscillation I it merely momentarily takes on the shapes I shades I sounds I appearances I characteristics that it reflects.

"The entirety of manifest existence is like shadows passing through a flood of Light."

Ramana Maharshi

As yogis with some understanding of Samkhya we must therefore abandon the notion that Consciousness has anything to do with the mindbody of humans or the mindbodies of similar lifeforms with brains and nervous systems. Samkhya and yoga understand Consciousness as not something produced by anything else. It is not able to be produced – it simply is. It is always, in all ways here and present. It exists as the never absent Mirror that reflects back every disturbance and concoction Prakriti comes up with, regardless of whether we humans are awake, dreaming, sleeping, present or absent.

- The fact that existence exists and that we as humans are able to be aware of existence existing (at least to the extent it affects us) and discuss it, is an astonishing irrefutable fact.
- But we take existence along with us co-existing for granted because we have never known anything else other than

existence existing and hence we mostly don't appreciate the miracle of it.

- CONSCIOUSNESS is the enabler of all knowing.
- ETHER is the enabler of all structure I form I shape I all that exists materially in the Cosmos including mindbody.

If we accept Consciousness (Purusha) as the unchanging, permanent, self-effulgent Mirror, always present never absent, we can see that what we call our awareness borrows light from it the way a second mirror borrows light from a first mirror. Then we can view Prakriti as the sole source of mind-matter.

And once we understand that **both the mental aspects and the bodily aspects of mindbody are mechanical in Nature** we can delve into the *psychemechanics* of their interaction. Consciousness, the Mirror belongs to an **ab**solutely other domain of Reality.

If the above is accepted – *even if only provisionally as a working hypothesis/assumption* – we can then see the way to end the myth that Mind and Matter are somehow separate, different 'things'—a misconception which has caused and is still causing so much confusion.

The Main Division of Everything

The mistaken notion of Mind and Matter as the *main division of everything* has become so deeply etched into the human thinking mind as a basic tenet of its picture of Reality that it presents a formidable barrier to correct understanding of the actual Structure and Nature of Reality.

Push-pattern, or if you prefer the words *stress-strain,* are two fundamental aspects of Reality whose important differences have already been pointed out in earlier chapters. The inseparability of 'push' from 'carrier of push' is common knowledge to scientists and engineers yet perhaps not applied sufficiently widely.

In addition, over the last 150 years or so science has sussed out another fundamental *division of everything* – the *particle* and the *wave*. But mainstream science has yet to apply the implications of the particle-wave duality to the riddle of mindbody.

This is most likely because science has not yet spotted the difference between the *thing* and the *semi-thing*, nor understood the fundamental role the Code plays in the interaction between stresses and strains inside our brain and nervous system.

The Difference between Semi-thing and Thing

"Understanding the difference between **thing** and **semi-thing** enables far more precise connectoring, analysis and synthesis in every aspect of Life.

"Knowledge is not acquired by hard; it is acquired by soft, by elastic things...and the moment it's elastic, it's a semi-thing."

N. Dimovic, "Semithing Theory and Proper Connectoring"

So, let's consider **thing** and **semi-thing** as the main division of everything arising on the Ether *(arising in Prakriti)*, and see how this helps us to understand mindbody.

To understand the significance and usefulness of what Dimovic called '*semi-thing*', we first need a clear definition of what the concept and word 'thing' stands for.

The concept *thing* has existed in human culture since antiquity and probably every language in the world has an equivalent word for 'thing'. Everyone knows more or less what it means. But the precise meaning of *thing* was always a problem for philosophers. Scientists too are uncomfortable with it, probably because they feel it is too vague, too imprecise. But the word *thing* stands for **a most useful important general concept** and in the context of psychemechanics – what in Chapter 8 the Buddha 2500 years ago was already teaching as *satipatthana* – can be defined as:

- a concept and word pointing to such parts of the total reality as are provisionally integrated into a whole aggregate and which for the duration of this integration is then able to travel and move around in a same direction and at a same speed, whichever these may be, with its parts maintaining a similar configuration and relationship to each other.

• So long as such an aggregate* exists and persists, whether in the Real World of Nature or only in our thinking mind's imagination, such integrations or aggregations* can be described as *things*.

*khanda in Pali Buddhism equivalent to the Sanskrit *skandha*

Things can be either hard, soft or elastic or a combination of all three aspects like the human body.

Things have a beginning and an ending. They arise dependent upon conditions and cease when conditions no longer support the repetition of their integration. They do not last forever. They exist for a time. Their duration is a provisional state of affairs. As they disintegrate, other things are formed from them or from bits of them. Or they themselves become parts of other things by being absorbed by other things and integrated into them.

Whenever one thing attaches to another thing, for as long as this attachment lasts, these two joined-together things become a 'provisional new thing'. And this applies to any conflict or contact as long as that lasts.

Just as a persons who gets into a motor vehicle becomes assembled to it for a while, for the time they are joined together they are no longer two separate things, and have for the duration of the drive become one single thing. They are two things before they come into contact with each other but once they get into contact, even for a short time, they are then one single thing. This is extra-ordinarily important to see and appreciate because it leads to the kind of insight which dispels delusion and ignorance regarding the real Nature of Reality including mindbody.

For example, if we were to wrestle with somebody for 10 hours then the 'provisional new thing' would last 10 hours. Just because it lasts 10 hours or 10 seconds or 10 nanoseconds, or some other time period, it does not cross our minds that this is a **new thing** because people have not yet realized the simple yet subtle difference between the thing and the semi-thing.

> "The concept of semi-thing is a new one. Perhaps an important discovery. No language contains the word semi-thing because the concept until now has remained undiscovered."
>
> N. Dimovic, London 1987

Dimovic proposed its introduction because he saw the need to point to what can be defined as:

> "...such parts of a thing, as can move or seem to move for a limited time away from their normal or resting position on the thing but only up to a point before returning back to their normal position.

> "Semi-things have a beginning and an ending but only as *disturbances* (movements, oscillations, vibrations) of some part(s) of things. So they make what we can call semi-movements and have a semi-existence."

This temporary existence or 'semi-existence' is necessarily always of shorter duration than the duration of the thing of which they are only a disturbance/oscillation.

When a thing moves as a whole, the semithings have to move with it otherwise they break off and start a fresh new existence either as things or as semithings, depending.

But when they as part of a thing move, the remaining parts of the thing need not be moving, because their movement is only a local disturbance or semi-movement on the whole thing.

Examples abound. A door is a semithing on a doorframe. The doorframe stays still and the door oscillates: it can move open and move closed without any spatial displacement of the doorframe. Or the door plus doorframe can remain still if unused/undisturbed. Likewise, the door-handle on the door can behave as a semi-thing on the door which itself is a semi-thing.

> Wherever a thing goes, the semithings go with it. But a thing can stay where it is when a semithing moves so that after the semithing movement stops, nothing has changed.

Whenever we talk, our tongue and lips behave as semithings making just such semi-movements. When we stop talking, both lips and tongue return to their resting or normal position.

What counts above all else when considering a part of Reality either as a thing or as a semi-thing is where we stand when we are looking at them. It **depends on the connectoring** – precisely what Mahavir pointed out in his teaching on *anekantavada,* and what Einstein pointed out in Relativity.

The same part of Reality can be either a thing or a semi-thing but not seen from the same viewpoint. For example, a wave in physics, seen as a thing, has particles as semithings. A door seen as a thing has hinges and handles as semithings. A person seen as a thing has lips and fingers as semithings. But from the viewpoint of a satellite, the Earth is a thing, and waves and people and doors and hinges are all semithings. Looking at the solar system from outside the solar system, it would be seen as a thing and the planet Earth and the other planets as semithings.

Dividing Reality into these two fundamental aspects, not only follows Reality but results into much more precise observation. It is extremely useful in analysis and synthesis. And can prevent us from confusing specifics and getting lost into the labyrinths of language.

The proposed science of psychemechanics – combining semi-thing theory with the code's omnipresent role in mechanics – could not have been made without it.

We are certain it is a useful method and a new tool. Dimovic believed it might be an important discovery*.

* Safari on the Fundamentals of Reality – manuscript copyright 1997

Understanding Mindbody as Semi-things & Things

Once we have realized that the main division of everything is not what people have been guessing for millennia – namely mind and matter or body and spirit or some such similar mistaken notion – and once we realize the main division of everything is the thing and the semi-thing, we can begin to become much more precise and clear in our connectoring about what mindbody actually is and does. Through this we can gain insight into the process of conditioning – of cause and effect – and spot where it has been interfered with by our own codes (*satipatthana/anekantavada*).

> It also enables us in our conceptual thinking to keep more closely in touch with the actual events and processes going on in the Real World of Nature.

As pointed out in Chapter 8, Satipatthana, in viewing any aspect of Reality we must constantly remind ourselves (remember) that nothing is static, everything changes.

Everything is moving, vibrating, trembling, oscillating, spinning even if it appears to our senses to be still and stationary.

- *repetition of the similar disguises change*
- *compactness disguises emptiness*
- *similarities conceal differences*
- *differences conceal similarities*

So, there are certain things which, when we stand in a particular position and distance with respect to them, we can call *things* and see that some of them have on them or inside them certain other things which we can consider as *semithings*.

For example, a guitar or a piano, when it is not being played, is a thing. The moment we play it, then certain parts of it get disturbed and oscillate, and therefore exhibit the characteristic behavior of semi-things.

Without the piano's combination of fixed parts and movable parts, of 'thingness' and 'semi-thingness', piano music would be impossible.

Likewise for the guitar. Likewise for awareness, thinking, feeling and perception.

> Without the immutable Mirror of Consciousness and the mutable repetitive disturbances of Prakriti, Existence – Life as we know it would not/could not come into being, be perceived or known.

What we call *knowledge* is derived and acquired through the nervous system's capacity to 'oscillate' by virtue of its <u>elastic structures and properties</u>. The interaction between the non-traveling elastic oscillating parts of our nervous system and the bits of it that do move around and 'travel' can be likened to an orchestra of players with their instruments. Both are needed for a symphony but not all the musicians nor their instruments have to be active at the same moment nor stay in the same position/location. What we call melody or music is impossible without the combination of notes and gaps, of fixed parts and moving parts, of thing and semi-thing.

> "Knowledge is not acquired by hard. It is acquired by soft, by elastic. And the moment something is elastic – it's a semithing."
>
> Dimovic

The property of elasticity in any structure provides the potential for disturbance, for oscillation, and thus for semi-thing behavior.

Knowledge is acquired by our nervous system by virtue of its elastic properties. This elasticity enables it to be disturbed (oscillate) in countless different ways and also be in contact with (interact with) other disturbances, other oscillations. By virtue of repetitive contacts/collisions/conflicts, it is able to get feedback and gradually acquire knowledge about what is going on inside, outside as well as at the inside-outside interface.

> For example, our fingers and feet coming into conflict with a piano's movable parts when playing it, act at those moments as colliding semi-things.

The majority of the structures and systems making up the human organism – in particular the nervous system, the main participant in perception and cognition – are elastic*.

Flexibility and elasticity seem to be inextricably linked to how life arises. Life as we know it would be impossible without elasticity because without this quality, impulses could not travel along structures or mediums, which themselves do not have to change location. Through elasticity, disturbances (impulses) can travel to and from things which do not themselves travel nor need to travel.

> Without semi-things there could not arise the kind of repetitive interaction between colliding things and semi-things on which the acquisition of all knowledge and all information seems to be based.

The nervous system itself is an elastic structure, a thing on which awareness, sensation, feeling and perception are different kinds of melodies or vibrations.

A pattern or a strain could not be generated by a push or a stress without elasticity.

Without stresses there would be no patterns for us to recognize and give meaning to.

> What above all else counts when considering a part of Reality, either a thing or a semi-thing, is where we stand when we are looking at them. And how we look at what we are looking at.

It all depends on the six-field connectoring.

The concept of semi-thing is very important because it can help us to connector properly, to spot much more easily and quickly where and when and how we are making wrong connections, faulty deductions, wrong assumptions, confusing ourselves and confusing others.

*"It takes two to tango/two to tangle "plus" something **third** – a desire/willingness/intent to do it."*

The importance of getting a clear picture into one's head of the fundamental structure of the Natural World – what scientists nowadays call the Cosmos — cannot be underestimated because without this insight-knowledge, a human being is bound to remain hostage to beliefs, hopes and doubts instead of replacing all these with relative certainty.

> Both Mahavir and Gautama Buddha are recorded as stating that the knowledge of the path to Awakening to the True Nature of Reality is not their discovery and has been made known by Tirthankaras and Buddhas countless times before in former eras and other world periods.
> Yet, for one reason or another, it keeps on getting lost!

(relative) Certainty concerning the fundamental structure of the Real World of Nature as:

PURUSHA – PRAKRITI | SIVA – SAKTI | CONSCIOUSNESS – ETHER

Whatever pair of names you wish to give it. Having a clear picture about these two fundamental aspects of Reality does not by any means signify completeness of knowledge of details but it does at least provide the *big picture's framework*.

For those who incline towards a nondual vedantic view like Shankara's or Ramana's, then the Mirror of Consciousness can be considered an integral property of Prakriti or vice versa. It doesn't matter. Either way you are inclined to view it, Reality can be symbolized by **IZ** – namely co-existence of both a fixed unmoving aspect and an elastic moving aspect.

Given that '**sam**' points to three it is more than likely Samkhya has come down to us without its 'third fundamental' which somehow got lost or went unrecorded in the later texts that make references to earlier Samkhya texts which did not survive.

My own research inclines towards a tri-vial view because there has to be something *third*, something which induces Prakriti into action, even if that force is imagination only. Something somehow *disturbs* Prakriti for her to unfold the Cosmos.

Either way, with this big picture in mind, the extra-ordinary mystery of our own Natural World can be explored in full recognition and acknowledgment that *there is no such thing possible as absolute knowledge or absolute certainty*.

Such a notion as *absolute knowledge* is delusional even from the viewpoint of higher mental faculties developed in dhyana, samadhi and samyama.

On the other hand there is no need to get lost in many details either. Once the fundamental Ether | Consciousness interaction is seen and understood *as it is* (*sati* is), all else flows coherently from such knowledge and understanding.

> As Mahavir pointed out in his teaching on Anekantavada, '*all intellectual knowledge is relative*', relative to other intellectual knowledge. The knowledge pointed to by the great siddhas is not intellectual knowledge, not representational knowledge but Life itself as it expresses itself through each of us from moment to moment. Going further is just having fun making guesses.

The point to appreciate is that CONSCIOUSNESS acts as a passive MIRROR which at all times and in all places/spaces and in all ways, reflects whatever Prakriti's Nature happens to be orchestrating at that moment.

Consciousness as a reflecting mirror is present whether the thinking, imagining mind is awake or asleep. Whether the thinking, imagining mind is in the dreaming state, in the deep sleep state or in the waking state makes no difference to Consciousness because Consciousness does not belong to the realm of mindbody.

During the switched-off state of thinking mind in deep sleep, the mirror of Consciousness reflects absence of mental activity. During dreaming it reflects the thinking mind shuffling the symbols of dream. During waking state when the mindbody is fully into interaction with the inside-outside World of Nature, the mirror of Consciousness reflects everything Prakriti is capable of creating and manifesting.

From the fundamental 12 numbers – three **absolute** and nine **ordi-nary** – the Mind of Nature, of Prakriti, is *somehow* able to conjure up any structure or combination of structures out of the darkness of Pandora's box.

Seemingly mimicking this capacity, the thinking mind is bent on concocting anything potentially concoctable by means of connecting and encoding.

All done by the simple trick of connecting similar with non-similar. Amazing.

***

Na tatra suryo bhati na chandra tarakam
nema vidyato bhanti kuto-yam agni
tameva bhantam anubhati sarvam
tasya bhasa sarvamidam vibhati

Not there the sun shines, nor the moon nor stars
There the lightning shines not,
How then this fire?
Verily, it is after *That* shining,   (Consciousness)
that all things do shine.

Katha Upanishad

The immeasurable, unfathomable ocean of Ether (Prakriti) is thus the playing field where every ongoing creation, manifestation and trans-formation takes place.

The daily moment-to-moment challenge we are faced with as humans is distinguishing within ourselves Nature's Mind from our own thinking mind. The Mind of Nature within us is that part of our nature that knows but does not speak – it just gets on with the orchestration of the best symphony it can produce. That part of us which instead plays mental tennis and generates internal cinema is the thinking mind.

To put the thinking mind in its place, what needs to be done is to Remember the Real, recollect what is Real and Authentic, recognize it, acknowledge it, embrace it, flow with it – all else is just mind-disturbing, heart-fragmenting fabrication.

By adhering to the Real, what is inherently false, make believe and pretence is bound sooner or later to fade into the background and get relegated to junk status.

Outside the thinking mind of the human being everything is perfect. Even now.

***

Chapter 13: The Song Of Kalki

Cadaqués, July 1978

"All that changes is purposive and changes for a reason.
That which exists behind the change is purposeless, void.

The change is Lila, the music of a magic flute.
The changeless is the instrument upon which the events in Time are played,
Krishna's invisible flute.

The ego-bound are fulfilled through manifold unfolding purposes.
The egoless wander through life without self-purpose.

Things are going on because there is no one to impede the movement of energy.
Onwards roll these waves of empty phenomena, since beginingless Time they roll
on to the unknown shores of eternity.

When the human mind becomes anxious It creates questions, then supplies the answers.
The questions are meaningless. The answers are more meaningless.

Truth is beyond all questioning and answering.
It resides where all questions and answers have ceased.
For all individual things are like waves and eddies on the surface of an invisible ocean.

There are times when the ocean is still, then only the Changeless exists.
There are times when the ocean moves, then only the changes are
obvious.
The Changeless underlying the changeful is not easily perceived.

I am the Eye of the Ocean and I laugh at myself.
I laugh both at my opaqueness and at my transparency, but there
have been times when there is too much sorrow for a smile, too much
foolishness for a tear.

When I finally stop talking to myself I merely hum. And from this sound
come forth
humour, humbleness, harmlessness and harmony.
humour is the highest expression of intelligence;
humbleness is the highest expression of understanding;
harmlessness is the highest expression of behaviour;
harmony is the highest expression of aesthetics.

The whole existence is an ongoing process of miracle; only the inter-
pretation is faulty lacking the perfect perspective.

The correct view is to have no views at all only then is the vision bright
and clear like a cloudless sky.

Birth is a miracle, life is a miracle, death is a miracle.
Ignorance and Knowledge,
Light and Dark,
Shape, Shade and Sound,
all these too, and more, are miracles.
Look at the keys—they stare you in the face.
But you know not the language of Siddhas.

There are no entities, only processes.
There is no flower, only sprouting
no flower, only flowering
no flower, only fading.

But the Seed is always otherwise all that exists would be impossible.
Because of moisture a seed germinates in darkness and grows towards
the light.
Without moisture a seed remains unborn.

Sex is the Seed, moisture the desire.
Once you know you are not the master you become the master of
nothing.

Of all things nothing is the hardest to master. Rel-ease yourself from
its dis-ease and remain at-ease. Non arising is bliss. Remain in the
unborn state.

Misery and anguish are only for those who believe they are born. For
He who knows he is not born there is neither bondage nor freedom.

Whenever you act, you are bound by the laws of action. It is natural,
for only nothing is without laws. Whenever you just allow being to be,
there are no laws.
But this does not mean you become lawless.

In due course you will come to realize that greatness resides where self
no longer exists.

The more effort is made, the more frustration, tension is created. This
is excellent and should be so. For under intense heat, by the power of
fire, a thousand elements are melted into one.

There is no drug like Durga for Durga cures the ill effects of all drugs.
Once you have suffered her ultimate death, you are transformed through
the Hole of her Womb into the Deathless.

I am happy because now I know there is no parting of lips. Wherever
you go in this life or in lives to come I shall be with you.
Of That have no doubt

And do not fear,
For in Truth there is nothing to worry about.
I say there is nothing to worry about,
So be careful of this 'no-thing'
Lest it lead you astray.

Intelligence holds the key to Time.
The denser gravity, the slower the time;
the lighter gravity, the faster time
until beyond the speed of thought
relative time is transcended.
Then you can move forwards or backwards
through this deepening ocean of Time and Events.
It makes no difference.
It is like circus horses.
But much more fundamental – a game of the mind.

Intelligence is waiting.
How long the wait takes makes no impact
upon the Timeless.
All things came from intelligence,
even foolishness
and all things will return to That which waits.
All things come to the Buddha, the Awakened

What does it matter from which point
the Calm begins to re-extend itself
across the unfathomable ocean spread?

The Awakened are reliable friends. No one is excluded, not even the
lowest of the low.
In the end all things will be taken up, good as well as bad.

Most beings and things will be reborn in the realms of radiance as sons
and daughters of the Earth.
Some will go beyond this sun system to a higher hierarchy.

*But a few will go beyond this Galaxy, leaving the dance of the suns
behind.
Like butterflies freed from the chrysalis they will go on to a destiny
neither Gods nor men can know, for that is the limit of their perception.*

*I have heard the song the stars sing along the shores of eternity. And I
have seen the emerald glow from afar. How near and clear it all seems
now the dreaming is over.*

*The self is a dream, a mirage, bubbles of dew. The self exists only until
the gate. The moment you enter the gateway to the heart, the self is no
more. It becomes reversed as six becomes the nine.*

No-self-realization is the goal.

*Only the Buddha dares to say it. Others prefer sugar to salt in their tea.
Oneness can only exist in the absence of self.
All characteristics are in fact not characteristics.
All characteristics are in fact relationships,
there are really no qualities as such,
they are simply the play of colours within the Diamond's purity*

*Each diamond is unique.
The colour, clarity, carat and cut – the four c's
are really something.
But its real nature remains behind the mind.
Did you ever look behind your Mind
To see a Mirror from Behind?*

*A diamond is so hard
it can cut into anything known.
Even itself. That is why it is so precious.
How else could a diamond be penetrated, how else cut?
In fact a diamond can even probe the Unknown.*

This game of hide and seek,
of laughter and tears,
only when it becomes too painful
will we finally stop playing
and take a rest.

When your whole life has become a meditation, even your dreams and
sleep, then you are close to the death of self, close but not closed to
the Real Eyes.
While this flowing of energy has been going on and on
the eternal has been waiting
even for you.

Meditation means dying to me and mineness.
Until this death is suffered,
meditation, samadhi, the process, is necessary.

A man who has died does not bury himself. Others will do it for him.
That is why the Sage who does not meditate
goes on recommending meditation.

It is far harder to realize you are dreaming, than to dream you are
realizing.
So beware of false sleep and false awakening.
Take care that your wakefulness is not impaired by sleep.
And that your sleep is not impaired by wakefulness.
Both are fitful, second best.

Once the not-self is known
there is no alternative.
Choiceless, the arrow flies to the target
released from the hunter's clasp.
Where the arrow falls,
there will I be buried.

The mind is unable to resolve
The fundamental problem of suffering.
Suffering is a creation of the mind, just accumulated ignorance,
Dust of Ages lying thick upon the Eye of Truth.
Dissolve the mind and all problems are solved. The sun is seen.
When seen, it reveals that really there has never been a problem, just
a game, a play.

It is not possible for the thinking mind to understand this or that. It
always misunderstands. It is itself the departure from Suchness. Mind
is born of the idea of self. Self-idea is the error, The Thief of Peace.

The real meaning of understanding is to stand under, bow the head,
silence the mind.
Only then can the non-dual be realized.
Only then is the Heart experienced directly.
The Heart encompasses everything. Its real meaning is He Art.
Just a little gap is needed to see what you see.

I am an Eye, but if 'I think'...I have already gone astray. And if 'I think
I'...then duality has arisen. This is how the split occurs.

Lao Tzu says:

"That which speaks, does not know; that which knows, does not speak."

Kalki says:

"Put your sex in your heart, not your heart in your sex"

" What can be said has been said,

What cannot be said is left unsaid."

***

APPENDICES

Acknowledgements
Glossary
References/ recommended reading
2 Yoga tables
Goenka letter

Acknowledgements & Thanks

In its unique expression through each of us, life can be likened to an immensely rich tapestry, countless threads dyed with all manner of influences, woven into a synthesis, every singular thread, remembered and unremembered, playing a part in the whole. I have been most fortunate to share time with many wonderful people and learn from outstanding teachers, some during many years, others for brief flashes of insight but of value nonetheless. All of them, including many not mentioned here, have enabled the weaving of this magic carpet.

Heartfelt thanks

- To Nina, my beloved wife and companion of 36 years, mother of our two amazing sons Jetsun and Harrison, who jointly showed me the way of the householder. Nina has become an accomplished hathayoga teacher, and in so doing, given great satisfaction.
- to my two sons Jet and Harry who continuously show me that the youngest people on the planet are often the oldest and wisest because they carry the previous generation's knowledge plus a new perspective on Life.
- to my dear, free-spirited parents Rodney and Phryne; to my equally free-thinking brothers & sisters Carlos, Charis, Sandra and Ivan; to Rosa, Mallory and beloved aunts, cousins and family members for all the camaraderie, support and good times.
- to my incomparable godfather Dr Nebosja Dimovic – 'Dimmy' of the Sphinx-like smile and penetrating insight – without whose decades-long patient guidance I might still be engaged in a never-ending game of mental tennis ... to Duska Milewski, his daughter, for assisting in the transliteration of recorded conversations with Dimmy on the Safari on the Fundamentals of Reality, and generously entrusting his library, notes and charts to my safe-keeping.

- to Ramiro Calle, my first guide on the path of yoga; for the foreword to this book and unforgettable moments shared; to his brothers Miguel Angel and Peter I am indebted for beginning Karate-do at about the same time as Yoga.
- to Yosuke Yamashita Sensei for 17 years of authentic Karate-Do Goju Ryu imparting something of the warrior spirit of the samurai; to my dojo brothers and sisters.
- to Nacho, my great friend and unconditional life-ally, comrade–at–arms, a rare example of generosity, strength, wisdom and composure; fellow advaita vedanta traveller and tai chi/chi kung adept, not to mention nutrition adviser!
- to knights in shining armour Leopold, Jonathan, Rafael, Rohan and Ricky, each in his own way a grand ally of many virtues and talents; for many great times spent together!
- to Ingeborg Zänder of Sa Riera – egyptologist–hermeticist–astrologer supreme – for decades of enjoyable exchanges on symbolism, numbers and archetypes.
- to Swami Chaitanyananda Saraswati, yoga vedanta adept, siddha and hatha yogi, for imparting the genuine yoga of sadhus and the 'seemingly lost' kriya yoga technique of Shankaracharya.
- to Grandmaster Lung Kai Ming, my kungfu father in Hong Kong studying tai chi, sword and Northern Shaolin since 1978; fond memories of his visits to Spain to enjoy our passion for swimming!
- to Carlos Moreira sifu for taking up the gauntlet from Yamashita Sensei and Lung Sifu after travel commitments prevented me maintaining classes and students of my own; for generously welcoming me into the Barcelona Wushu family more than two decades ago; for completing the missing Northern Shaolin forms. Among his many virtues Carlos has shown the side to martial arts where kungfu family spirit is more important than punching and kicking.
- to my publishers Agustín and Ana Pániker for their faith in what is written here and role in bringing it to light
- to Jiddu Krishnamurti whose silent transmission was one of the deepest exchanges with any human being before or since.

- to SN Goenka, who selflessly taught me Satipatthana from 1984 to 1994 at numerous Vipassana retreats in India and Europe, and who never asked for nor expected anything in return.
- to John Coleman with whom Nina and I sat 4 memorable vipassana retreats in Italy in the same tradition of U-Ba Khin.
- to Buddhadhasa Bhikkhu for 2 memorable weeks in Suan Mok in 1978; for his outspokenness in questioning traditional interpretations of the ancient words.
- to Oscar Pujol for sharing his insights into Patanjali's Yogasutra and the extent to which it draws on the legacy of Mahavir and Buddha.
- to Dr Michele Salmeri of Catania, Sicily, whose research and insights into the nature of the structure of language shed additional light on the discoveries of N. Dimovic. Not knowing anything of tantra, Michele taught the essence of tantra *'transformare non eliminare'* and pointed out that Aristotle had already spotted how the encoding inherent in language deforms the natural order of Real Things.
- to Robert Venosa and Martina Hoffman, Peter Staples and other dear Cadaqués friends for their inspiration and friendship.
- to my oldest friends Carles Riera (Barcelona) and Bill & Peter Ja'afar (KL)
- to Kalu Kempo Rimpoche (Darjeeling); Venerable Saddhatissa (London); John Blofeld (Bangkok); Chueng Chun Wa (Hong Kong); Jackie Hitchcock; Wilf Proudfoot; Dilip Kumar, for their invaluable time and input.
- to Dr Alex Santos, NLP–alchemy—living proof the Heroine and Hero are alive and kicking in each one of us, even when we take time off to regather strength for the next leg-up on the Quest.
- to Wim Hof, my cold yoga mentor and newest great friend, for introducing me to the 'way of the cold'– a throwback to the yoga and tapas of the ancients adapted to modern times ... and to all the great WH Summer 21 family.

This little book is very close to the heart of things, and if it is able to convey the messages intended, then I hope it will become close to your heart too. As the great Wittgenstein wrote in his Tractatus

Logico-Philosophicus – any writing can only be as free of imperfection as language is, and in turn language can only be as free of imperfection as the author is.

Therefore let's work everything out for ourselves and go beyond language!

***

Glossary

(p = Pali; skt = Sanskrit)

adharma (skt) disharmony (in the sense of going against the law of Nature)

adinava (p) danger; misery as in 'satisfaction, misery and escape'

advaita (skt) nonduality

ahimsa (p) harmlessness; unconditional respect for all life

ana (p) inbreath; inhalation

apana (p) outbreath; exhalation

aparigraha (jainism) non-acquisitiveness; contentedness with whatever Life/Nature offers in the way of sustenance/support; attitude of non-attachment to worldly possessions; not owning anything

anicca non-eternal; something that does not last indefinitely; transitory

anatta (p) *anatman* (skt) lit. not-the-thing-itself; not-self; not-Real

anupassana (p) contemplation

appamada (p) diligence; steadfast effort

attention the direction of the connectoring; focus of connectoring

arahant (arihant in jainism) he or she who has removed all obstructions to the free flow of life force intelligence by complete realignment with true Nature; he or she who thereby knows existence 'as it is' in its expression in them

asteya (jainism) refraining from taking anything that is not freely available or that has not been given/granted; in the narrower sense to refrain from stealing

atman (skt) *atta* (p) equivalent concept to *jiva* in jainism; purusha *in samkhya; Consciousness* in English as defined in chapter 12

asana (skt) attitude/posture in the face of any physical, mental or emotional stress or discomfort (or combination of these)

asava (p) asrava (skt; jainism) lit. 'influxes'; impurities; in jainism a literal 'accrual *of particles'*

ayatana (p) any one of the 6 sense-fields of connectoring

awareness that part of the mind or aspect of mental faculties we have identified as "I", "me" and "mine" and which is able to get the feedback from all the other parts or aspects; the 'master code'

bhava (p & skt) habits and tendencies which manifest in specific patterns of *beha*viour, and thus lead to particular ways of life that result into specific outcomes

bodhi (skt & p) from the root *budh* meaning to 'awaken', to blossom in understanding hence *buddha* means a human being who has awakened fully to Reality 'as it is' free from the thinking mind's fabrications (codes, images and concepts)

brahmavihara (p) the highest states of mind – loving kindness (*metta*); compassion (*karuna*); joy at the good fortune of others (*mudita*); equanimity (*upekkha*)

cit, citta (skt & p) mind; mind as the 6th sense that participates in the 5 other sense fields making connections between them and the previously built up internal cinema

connectoring is the three dimensional process of connecting together different connectors *within* similar classes (apples and pears) as well as *across* different classes of mental objects (apples and democracy)

chandra (p) moon; 'power of thought & imagination'

darshana (skt) Sanskrit term used to designate one of the philosophical standpoints/views of ancient India, of which there are 9 principal ones

dhyana (skt) one pointed concentration of mind leading to full concentration as in chapter 7

dhamma lit. that which carries; the 'bearer'; Reality; truth; nature; mental construct (as in chapter 2) *dhatu* (skt & p) element; *mahadhatu* include the 4 derived great elements earth, water, fire and air and also the underived great element ether

duhkha (skt) dukkha (p) is a key concept in *samkhya*, yoga, jainism and buddhism that –depending on context – can refer to any aspect of unsatisfactoriness and degree of suffering

domanassa (p) discontent; depression of spirits (the opposite of gladness)

ehi passikó (p) 'see for yourself!' – the recommendation to cross-check the truth of something for yourself

ekagrata (skt) one-pointed concentration of mind on a single object and focus of attention

hrid (skt) seat of awareness; heart-mind

intention (volition) determines if an action – of thought, speech or body– is karmically positive, neutral or negative

jhana (p) one pointed concentration of mind leading to full concentration (as in chapter 7)

jñana (skt) *ñana* (p) knowledge; knowledge of Life

jiva (jainism) equivalent to *purusha* in *samkhya*; *atman* in vedanta; *consciousness* (as specifically defined in chapter 12 by the author)

karma (skt) law of cause and effect

karmavipaka (skt) lit. the maturing/ripening of the fruit/s of action; present consequence/s of past action/s

kaya (p) physical body; bodily structure (any material bodily structure large size or small)

karuna (skt & p) compassion

keval (skt) pure; absolute

kumbhaka (skt) the pause in between inhalation and exhalation – brief or prolonged – up to spontaneous and effortless suspension of in-and-out-breathing

kilesa (p) another of several terms for 'impurities', 'defilements' which obstruct the *nadi* network

loka (p) world; realm; can refer to a physical or mental location

lokiya (p) world of representations; 'world' as perceived by the mind; mental cinema

lokuttara (p) supramundane realm; Real World beyond codes, images and concepts (thus unconditioned by coding)

marga (skt) *magga* (p) path in the context of yoga specifically the path to what is Real and True; *'ekayano maggo'* referred to by the Buddha is the path trodden by enlightened men and women of former times

metta (p) maitri (skt) unconditional loving kindness founded on the unshakeable knowledge of the oneness and indivisibility of all Life

manas (skt) *mano* (p) mind; another word for mind along with *citta* and *viññana*

majjhima patipada (p) middle path; temperance; balance

moha (p) bewilderment; delusion; confusion

mudita (p) boundless joy at the success of others; especially at the awakening of others to truth

nadi (p) channel; pipe; tube; conductor; network of subtle plumbing through which the 'life force knowledge/intelligence' (*viññana*) flows back and forth throughout the mindbody to every part

nivarana (p) obstacles; hindrances such as greed, covetousness, ill will, delusion, laziness, restlessness, sceptical doubt and such like –all of which are perceived as barriers to progress on the path of yoga

nirodha (skt) lit. 'no further rolling on'; standstill; bringing the thinking mind's disturbances to a standstill; often used as a synonym for *nirvana*

nirvana (skt) *nibbana* (p) lit. 'cooled down'; blown out; no more vanity; no more inflation; the complete ending of internal cinema

paccaya (p) cause; causation; condition; influence direct, mutual, reciprocal or indirect. In the Pali texts 24 modalities of conditionality or conditioning factors are enumerated

prajña (skt) *pañña* (p) wisdom; knowledge; that quality of understanding which springs from direct insight into the true nature of Reality; insight from higher mental faculties as developed in *jhana* and *samadhi*.

paticcasamuppada (p) 'dependent origination'; the Buddha's unique formulation of connected propositions showing the conditional and causal origination of *dukkha* and its cessation in reverse

patisambhida (p) a little understood teaching of the Buddha pointing to 4 different 'orders' or 'levels' of Reality which co-exist but are not to be confused. Discernment of the conjoint fourfold nature of Reality ie. (1) the realm of Nature and natural things (2) the DIM/ Dim tendency as fundamental law of Nature (3) and (4) the code and the image. Knowledge of how these four different aspects or levels of Reality function together, interpenetrate, overlap and interact with each other.

phassa (p) sense-impression; sensory disturbance; contact-impact giving rise to sensory impression

piti (p) bliss; rapture felt whenever there is a free flow of energy throughout the mindbody

prana (skt) life force; equivalent to ch'i (Chinese); ki (Japanese)

pranayama (skt) regulation of the life force through modes of breathing with the aim to reach stoppage of in-and-out breathing *keval kumbhaka*

prapañca (skt) 'proliferation of mental cinema' along with the internal and external consequences of interference with the natural order of things in the Natural World

purusha (skt) Consciousness as described in chapter 12

raga (skt and p) passion (related to English word 'rage' and Spanish word 'rabia')

rishi (skt) ancient Indian sage; accomplished yogi who is a teacher

rupa (p) form, pattern, image (can be real or imaginary; gross or subtle)

samadhi (skt & p) full concentration of mind; equivalent to 4th *jhana*. *Samadhi* can occur in *yoga* when the sun-breath and moon-breath

are merged/joined in *sushumna*; not to be confused with *samatha* (p)
which means calmness/tranquillity

samskara (skt) *sankhara* (p) code; coding—extensively explained
throughout the book. There is no more important term and concept
to fully understand than this one.

sampajañña (p) thorough understanding—repeatedly found in the Pali
phrase *atapi sampajanno satima* translated by the author as 'ardent,
thoroughly comprehending, remembering the Real in the Real'

satipatthana (p) applications of remembering the Real in the Real in
regard to 4 main aspects (as in chapter 8); remembering the identification of coding; hence *samma sati* means *proper connectoring*

satya (skt) truthfulness to oneself and to others; adherence to truth, to
what is Real

siddha (skt) term used in yoga and jainism to indicate a yogi whose
accomplishments include *siddhis*

siddhi (skt) various 'mental powers' conferring the ability to interact
in various superhuman ways with, manipulate and control the four
great elements

sila (p) morality; ethical conduct

skanda (skt) *khandha* (p) aggregate/s ('aggregates' exist as aggregations
of mental constructs as well as aggregates of material, physical
constructs)

sukha (p) happiness; pleasure; satisfaction (opposite of *dukkha*)

suññata (p) *sunyata* (skt) no-thing; nothingness; voidness; emptiness—
a later development and preoccupation of Mahayana Buddhism
attempting to reconcile the inconsistencies of earlier teachings
on the three characteristics of existence. According to *samkhya*
'nothingness' is an impossibility because of the omnipresence of both
Consciousness and Ether. Even science in the last 50 years has come
to the realization and admission that so-called 'empty space' is not
empty at all. And that's not even taking into account the indispensable presence of Consciousness for any such statement to be made!

surya (p) sun; life energy; 'will power'

tanha (p) lit. 'thirst'; compulsion; compulsiveness; threefold craving/raving (greed, hate and delusion)

tattwa/tattva (skt) from the Sanskrit word *tatha/tathata* meaning 'that-ness' or 'suchness', which refers to the primary 'attribute' of the basic things that make up our fundamental experience of existence. Thus the primary attributes of the 4 great elements are solidity (earth); liquidity/fluidity (water); temperature (fire); motion (air). Different systems have different lists of *tattwas* ranging from 24 to 36.

tool is precisely defined as
-- something we add to ourselves or us to it whenever required
-- something that therefore must stay sufficiently the same to be able to be used again and again in a similar manner
-- something that alters our power or capacity in some way
-- something used for some form of real or imaginary advantage or improvement
-- may involve learning and habit

upadana (p) identification; to make this insufficiently understood Pali word even clearer the author has rewritten it showing its Latin root *idem*-tification. The making of equations of identity that cause nonsimilar things to be considered the same when they are not the same. Idem-tification is at the heart of coding (*sankhara*), and the root-cause of *dukkha*

upekkha (p) detachment; equanimity; impartiality; preferencelessness — the master attitude enabling *decoding* (*sankhara upekkha*)

vasana (skt and p) imprints of memory, which please note are not of the actual events as they happened but the imprint of how the actual events were interpreted (how these affected the mind and nervous system) — thus closely related to encoding

vedana (p) sensations; feelings; sentiments

vijñana (skt) *viññana* (p) lit. 'knowledge of life'; life force intelligence; awareness of existence — also often translated as 'mind' and also confusingly as 'consciousness' *vipassana* (p) insight; insight into the real nature of something; seeing it correctly 'as it is'; in Pali Buddhism often used in conjunction with *samadhi*

viraga (p) vairaga (skt) dispassion; detachment; opposite of *raga* (passion, rage, raving)

visuddhi (p) purification; cleaning out of impediments and obstructions; cleansing

viyoga the opposite of yoga; separateness from Real Nature; disharmony; disconnect

vritti (skt) oscillations of mind; disturbances of mind; perturbations of mind. *Yoga* is defined by Patanjali in *sutra* 1.2 as *citta vritti nirodha*—the bringing to a standstill of the mind's oscillations

***

Recommended Reading / References

NYANATILOKA (author); NYANAPONIKA (compiler). *Buddhist Dictionary: Manual of Buddhist Terms and Doctrines*. Colombo, Sri Lanka: Frewin & Co, 1972

BUDDHAGHOSA, BHADANTACARIYA (author); ÑANAMOLI, BHIKKHU (compiler). *Visuddhimagga: The Path of Purification* (2 vols.) California, EEUU, Shambala Publications Inc. Originally published in Sri Lanka, 1956 & 1964.

BENGALI, Baba. *Patanjala Yogasutra*. Poona, India. Published by N.R. Bhargawa, 1943.

PUJOL, Oscar. *Patanjali Yogasutra, Translation, Introduction and Commentary*. Barcelona, Spain. Kairós, 2016.

SHANKARACHARYA. *Viveka Chudamani, Jewell-Crest of Wisdom*. Chennai, India: The Theosophical House, 1932.

PÁNIKER, Agustín. *Jainism – History, Society, Philosophy and Practice*. Delhi, India. Motilal Banarsidass, *2009*

JAIDEVA, Singh. *Shiva Sutras – the Yoga of Supreme Identity: Translation and Commentary*. Delhi, India: Motilal Banarsidass, 1979

JAIDEVA, Singh. *Vijñana Bhairava Tantra: Translation and Commentary*. Delhi, India: Motilal Banarsidass, 1979

WILHELM, Richard. *The Secret of the Golden Flower, with Foreword and Commentary* by JUNG, Carl Gustav. London, Routledge & Kegan Paul, first edition 1931.

MALLINSON, James and SINGLETON, Mark. *Roots of Yoga: translated and edited with an introduction.* UK: Penguin Random House, 2017.

BERNARD, Theos. *Hatha Yoga.* Victoria NSW, Australia: Hutchinson Publishing Group, 1950.

BUDDHADASA, Bhikkhu. *Mindfulness with Breathing.* Somerville, MA.USA: Wisdom Publications, 1988

HART, William. *'The Art of Living' — Vipassana Meditation as taught by S.N. Goenka.* Amazon Books.

KORZYBSKI, Alfred. *Science and Sanity.* Pennsylvania, USA. International Non-Aristotelian Library Publishers. Second Edition, 1941

CALLE, Ramiro and MUNDY, Simon. *The Diamond Sutra and Synthesis of Buddhism.* Madrid: Altalena, 1981

CALLE, Ramiro. *The Fakir.* Madrid, Spain. Mandala, Amazon books in English, 2016.

SERRANO, Miguel. Foreword by JUNG, Carl Gustav. *The Visits of the Queen of Sheba.* UK, Routledge & Kegan Paul, 1972

DEAKIN, Roger. *Waterlog.* UK, Chatto & Windus, 1999; Penguin Books, 2008.

DEAKIN, Roger. *Wildwood, A Journey Through Trees.* UK, Hamish Hamilton, 2007; Penguin Books, 2008.

***

2 Yoga Tables, J. Mallinson & Colleagues

YOGA

Yoga physiology		Three bodies · Five sheaths · Chakra · Nadi (Sushumna) · Prana
Hinduism	**Four Yogas**	Karma yoga · Bhakti yoga · Jnana yoga · Rāja yoga
	Classical yoga	Yoga (philosophy) · *Bhagavad Gita* · *Yoga Vasistha*
	Concepts	*Yoga Sutras of Patanjali*: Eight Limbs (Yama · Niyama · Asana · Pranayama · Pratyahara · Dhāranā · Dhyana · Samadhi) · Kriyas · Mudras (Mula Bandha · Mahamudra · Viparita Karani · Khechari mudra · Vajroli mudra) · Shatkarmas (Neti · Dhauti · Nauli · Basti · Kapalabhati · Trataka)
	Mantra Yoga	Pranava yoga · Nada yoga
	Tantra	Yogi · Yogini · Siddhi · Shaiva Siddhanta · Kundalini · Chakra · Subtle body
	Hatha yoga	*Amritasiddhi* · *Bahr al-Hayat* · *Hathabhyasapaddhati* · *Hatha Ratnavali* · *Hatha Yoga Pradipika* · *Hatha Yoga: The Report of A Personal Experience* · *Gheranda Samhita* · *Joga Pradipika* · *Shiva Samhita* · *Sritattvanidhi* · **Vasishtha Samhita** · *Vimanarcanakalpa* · *Yogasopana Purvacatuska*
	Related	Lotus position · *Roots of Yoga* · Shinshin-toitsu-do
Buddhism	**Theravada**	Samatha · Samadhi (Buddhism) · Vipassana · Anapanasati · *Visuddhimagga*
	Mahayana	Yogachara · Zazen
	Vajrayana	Indian Buddhist Tantra (Anuttarayoga Tantra) · Tibetan Buddhism (Trul khor · Six Yogas of Naropa · Tummo · Dream yoga · Luminous mind) · China (Tangmi)
	Japan	Shingon Buddhism · Tendai
Yoga as exercise		Asana (Downward dog · List) · International Day of Yoga · *Light on Yoga* · Surya Namaskar · Vinyasa · Yoga for therapeutic purposes (Trauma-sensitive yoga) · Yoga for women · Yoga mat · Yoga pants · *Asana Journal* · *Yoga Journal* · List of Indian asana yoga gurus · List of yoga schools · Yoga scholars (template)

Compiled by Prof. James Mallinson & colleagues

HATHA YOGA

Yoga physiology	Three bodies · Five sheaths · Chakra · Nadi (Sushumna) · Prana
Asanas	Ancient meditation seats *Darshana Upanishad, Pātañjalayogaśāstravivaraṇa, Goraksha Satake* (Gomukhasana · Muktasana · Padmasana · Siddhasana · Simhasana · Sukhasana · Svastikasana · Virasana) Ancient non-meditation *Ahirbudhnya Samhitā, Pātañjalayogaśāstravivaraṇa* (Dandasana · Kurmasana) 10th C. *Vimanarcanakalpa, Goraksha Sataka, Amritasiddhi* (Mayurasana · Muktasana) 11th C. *Yogashastra* (Shirshasana) 13th C. ***Vasishtha Samhita*** (Kukkutasana) 14th C. *Shiva Samhita, Sharngadhara-paddhati* (Gorakshasana · Viparita Karani) 15th C. *Hatha Yoga Pradipika* (Baddha Konasana · Dhanurasana · Matsyendrasana · Paschimottanasana · Utkatasana) 17th C. *Gheranda Samhita, Hatha Ratnavali, Bahr al-Hayāt* (Bakasana · Bhujangasana · Kakasana · Kraunchasana · Makarasana · Mandukasana · Matsyasana · Vajrasana · Vrikshasana) 18th C. *Hathabhyasa-paddhati, Joga Pradipika* (Adho Mukha Vrikshasana) 19th C. *Sritattvanidhi* (Akarna Dhanurasana · Bhairavasana · Durvasasana · Garudasana · Halasana · Navasana · Pashasana · Setu Bandha Sarvangasana · Tittibhasana · Urdhva Dhanurasana) Late (1905 *Yogasopana Purvacatuska* · 1943 *Hatha Yoga: The Report of A Personal Experience*)
Mudras	Maha Bandha (Jalandhara Bandha · Mula Bandha · Uddiyana Bandha) · Viparita Karani · Khechari mudra · Vajroli mudra
Shatkarmas	Dhauti · Basti · Kapalabhati · Nauli · Neti · Trataka
Pranayama	Anuloma · Bhastrika · Bhramari · Kumbhaka · Ujjayi
Related	Modern yoga · Yoga · Yoga as exercise · Category:Medieval Hatha Yoga asanas

Compiled by Prof. James Mallinson & colleagues

Letter from S.N GOENKA, 20ᵗʰ May 1991

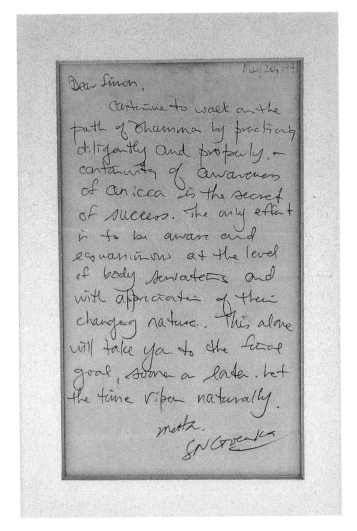

Letter from S. N. Goenka 20th May, 1991
following an exchange on the proper method of practice

Printed in the USA
CPSIA information can be obtained
at www.ICGtesting.com
LVHW070945171023
761168LV00022B/418